Philip, Prince of Greece

Philip, Prince of Greece

The Duke of Edinburgh's Early Life and the Greek Succession

Constantinos Lagos and John Carr

PEN & SWORD
HISTORY

First published in Great Britain in 2021 by
Pen & Sword History
An imprint of
Pen & Sword Books Ltd
Yorkshire – Philadelphia

ISBN 978 1 52679 082 8

Printed and bound in the UK by CPI Group (UK) Ltd,
Croydon, CR0 4YY

Pen & Sword Books Limited incorporates the imprints of Atlas,
Archaeology, Aviation, Discovery, Family History, Fiction, History,
Maritime, Military, Military Classics, Politics, Select, Transport,
True Crime, Air World, Frontline Publishing, Leo Cooper, Remember
When, Seaforth Publishing, The Praetorian Press, Wharncliffe
Local History, Wharncliffe Transport, Wharncliffe True Crime
and White Owl.

For a complete list of Pen & Sword titles please contact

PEN & SWORD BOOKS LIMITED
47 Church Street, Barnsley, South Yorkshire, S70 2AS, England
E-mail: enquiries@pen-and-sword.co.uk
Website: www.pen-and-sword.co.uk

Or

PEN AND SWORD BOOKS
1950 Lawrence Rd, Havertown, PA 19083, USA
E-mail: Uspen-and-sword@casematepublishers.com
Website: www.penandswordbooks.com

Contents

Acknowledgements

We would like to thank the following who made this book possible:

Mat Blurton
Evaggelia Charemi
Matt Jones
Nikolaos Kalogeropoulos
Fotis Karyanos
Konstantinos Kotsonis
Alexandra Loliaki
Marlena Savva
Philip Sidnell
Alexandros Tzamarelos
Pantelis Vatakis
Paul Wilkinson

List of Illustrations

1. The first known photograph of Andrew (1886); he is four years old and clutches a toy gun that the photographer, Petros Moraitis, gave him to hold. (*Published in A. Ξανθάκης, Ιστορία της Ελληνικής Φωτογραφίας 1839/1970*, 67)
2. Photograph by Carl Boehringer made into a postcard showing second lieutenant Prince Andrew (right) with his fellow officer and future ADC Menelaos Metaxas in 1902-1903. (*ΕΛΙΑ Archive. Reference no. 1E40.001*)
3. Group photograph by Carl Merlin of Andrew (back row, second from the right) and some of his fellow cadets at the Greek Military Academy (*Schole Evelpidon*) in Athens in 1898. (*ΕΛΙΑ Archive. Reference no. KOU 1.087*)
4. Andrew and Alice photographed on the Royal yacht *Amphitrite* on the day of their arrival at Piraeus, Christmas 1903. (*ΕΛΙΑ Archive. Reference no. 04.16.3.038*)
5. Alice photographed on the Royal yacht *Amphitrite* on 24 April 1904, dressed up in Andrew's cavalry officer uniform and wearing his spectacles as well. (*ΕΛΙΑ Archive. Reference no. 04.16.3.046*)
6. A group photograph from 1910 depicting the families of Andrew (standing, right) and his brother Nicholas. Nicholas and Ellen had three daughters while Andrew and Alice at the time two, as Cecile and Sophia had not yet been born. Andrew and Nicholas had been dismissed from the Greek army in the previous year and are photographed in civilian clothes. (Tatler, *30 March 1910*)
7. A photograph taken by Italian photographer Luca Comerio in 1907 showing the car driven by Andrew arriving outside the palace at Tatoi with Vittorio Emanuele III and George I in the back seat. Next to Andrew sits Vittorio Emanuele's bodyguard. (*Private collection*)
8. Photograph of Andrew and Alice which appeared on the cover of *Tatler* during the First World War, 12 January 1916.

9. The front page of *Daily Mirror* of 10 May 1917 attacking Prince Andrew and accusing him of being a Germanophile and ungrateful to the British people.

10. Andrew (centre), with his siblings Maria and Christopher photographed on the deck of the Greek warship *Ierax* in November 1920 while returning to Greece from their exile. The Naval offi cer next to them is Perikles Ioannides commander of Ierax and future husband of Maria. (Pinterest: https://gr.pinterest.com/ pin/417286721719744646/?nic_ v2=1a4geF3GG)

11. Andrew (centre) photographed in 1921 in Asia Minor with other Greek commanders. (*ΕΛΙΑ Archive. Reference no. 2643*)

12. Andrew on the Asia Minor front in July 1921 photographed outside his tent next to a pelican. (*France. Agence Rol*)

13. Andrew as a lieutenant General in Athens in 1921 after he had returned from Asia Minor. (*France. Agence Meurisse*)

14. Andrew with his baby son, Philip.

15. Photograph of the judges at Andrew's court-martial in 1922 as its president is about to announce the verdict. Andrew and his attorney, Damaskinos, are seated opposite the judges' bench. (*France. Agence Rol*)

16. The cover of *Tatler* of 12 July 1921 with Philip's four sisters who were photographed in London where they attended Dickie Mountbatten's wedding as bridesmaids.

17. Andrew playing around with Philip's tricycle at Saint-Cloud.

18. Andrew, Alice and their two eldest daughters, Theodora and Margarita, are photographed in London in December 1922. (*France. Agence Rol*)

19. A photograph of Alice (far right), her eldest daughter, Margarita (forefront), and three unidentified Greek ladies in the shop 'Hellas' which Alice ran in Paris, selling silks, perfumes and other luxury products from Greece. (The Graphic, *3 December 1927*)

20. Andrew (centre under the banner) photographed at Halandri, Athens, on 21 May 1936 during his visit there to a gathering of monarchists. (Ellinikon Mellon, *22 May 1936*)

21. Alice's tomb in Jerusalem. Pinterest. (*https://i.pinimg.com/1200x/2c/ 41/1d/ 2c411d2430ff83fd6b87b3d75b31b099.jpg*)

Prologue

Throughout the entire story of the dynasty there seemed to flow a theme of fluctuating extremes of good and ill fortune that had about it something of the inevitability of a Greek tragedy.

Air Vice-Marshal Arthur Gould Lee

In early September 2020 the news broke that Prince Philippos, the youngest son of ex-King Constantine II of Greece, had become engaged to Nina Flohr, a Danish businesswoman. Like his elder brothers, Paul and Nicholas, Philippos had avoided the society spotlight and was holding down a job as a hedge fund analyst in New York City. The announcement of their engagement must have triggered a sense of *déjà vu* among older members of the Greek and British (not to mention the Danish) royal families, as less than a hundred years ago another 'Prince Philippos' of Greece was creating society headlines.

This was none other than Prince Philip, the Duke of Edinburgh, who began life as a scion of the Greek royal family and grew up to be an officer in Britain's Royal Navy and later, of course, Queen Elizabeth II's consort. Along the way he morphed through several identities, largely caused by the turbulent circumstances his family went through. But the history of Greece in the 1930s and 1940s is replete with references to 'Prince Philippos', whose early backstory we will attempt to present here.

As European monarchies go, that of modern Greece was not one of the longer-lasting ones. From the accession of King Otho in 1832, when the Greek state was a mere two years into independence, to the de-throning of King Constantine II by a military-backed government and his replacement by a republic in 1973, the one hundred and forty years of Greek kings remain a controversial contribution to the nation's modern history.

And Prince Philip, the Duke of Edinburgh, was born bang in the middle of it. What is more, he played a hitherto little-known role in the troubled Greek monarchy of the 1930s and in World War Two – and was an ace away from being handed the Greek crown itself. These experiences definitely affected the way he saw and subsequently handled himself. It may be no mere flight of fancy to think that Prince Philippos's Greek years were instrumental in enabling him to completely and comfortably adjust to British royal life after and since the war. Whether a Greek royal until 1947, or the Queen's consort since, Philip has been one of the more remarkable European personalities of the age, drawing together two noble traditions.

The modern Greek kingdom began with Otho, an idealistic young Bavarian princeling aged just seventeen, placed on the Greek throne by the Treaty of London of 1832, when Great Britain in particular wished to stabilize what had been an unruly corner of the Ottoman Empire. That corner had just been devastated by the eight-year Greek War of Independence and was by no means stable. Britain, along with the other major European powers, had to pacify the infant Greek state so that it could hopefully be a rock of stability in the vital eastern Mediterranean. Europe's statesmen at the time visualized a strong man at the Greek helm in the form of a king who would be the country's active sovereign and political master, the fount of all authority.

The march of events, of course, belied many of those hopes. It was partly because of the sweeping powers given to Otho (who himself was mild-mannered and quite flattered to be the monarch of the land of Homer and Plato and entered into Greek life enthusiastically) that a revolt deposed him in 1862. He was replaced by another German prince of the Glücksburg house – of course with the great powers' approval – who became King George I, founding the present dynasty.

For historians Greek and foreign, the Greek royal house has been a subject of the bitterest controversy. The left-wing Marxist-orientated school has seen no redeeming value at all in the modern Greek (or any) monarchy, investing the institution with every political evil and blaming it for decades of political ills. Ideologically driven, this extreme view lacks common sense. On the other side, nationalist and conservative writers have largely admitted that, although the monarchy was a potential force for unity throughout the late nineteenth and early twentieth centuries, individual kings and their advisers made many mistakes in a country that by nature is politically volatile and unforgiving of royal errors, and that they essentially undermined their own throne by handing propaganda ammunition to the institution's enemies. The fault was not so much the acts of the kings themselves but the institutional nature of the Greek monarchy which, unlike other European royal houses, was built on a flimsy social and political foundation.

It was at the height of one of those periods of instability when the Greek throne was shaking badly in a time of political earthquakes that Prince Philip was born – in a hasty delivery on the dining room table – in an ornate palace on the Greek island of Corfu on 10 June 1921.

Several excellent biographies of the Duke of Edinburgh have been written over the years. But we believe that few, if any, have taken advantage of the fresh research material that has been lying in Greek archives and reports hitherto unavailable to the English-speaking public. We sincerely hope that this work will bring a new dimension to the historical image of a royal personage who in a long life has helped embody the heart of the British polity – albeit with a Greek twist.

Chapter 1

1921

June in Greece is one of the most glorious of months. The post-Easter spring has got into its stride and the Greek sun is out for good. The beaches fill with bathers, limbs and faces become bronzed, and the Greek countryside erupts in a riot of green and varicoloured wild flowers. This is especially true on the island of Corfu, where on such a morning – 10 June 1921 – Prince Philip was born. He came into the world in the elegantly neoclassical Mon Repos Palace, already for decades a favourite haunt of Greek and European royalty, nestling in its lush gardens of bougainvillea and oleander, shaded by orange and plane trees. On the coast just a few kilometres south of Corfu town, Mon Repos, completed in 1831 for a British High Commissioner (who only enjoyed it for a couple of years), offers a superb view of the Greek and Albanian mainland opposite, with its majestic, almost Wagnerian, mountain skyline, as if protecting the placid island, and the European royalty that relaxed there, from the world's storms.

One of those storms was raging a few hundred miles to the east, across the Aegean Sea in Asia Minor, where the infant Philip's father, Prince Andrew, was commanding a corps in the Greek Army that aimed to secure old Greek lands while fending off nationalist Turkish resistance. Andrew's brother, King Constantine I, was at the front taking personal charge. Greece itself was on an enthusiastic war footing. The Greek royal family, however, had barely survived a major crisis during the First World War and high (some would say unrealistic) hopes were pinned on Constantine to keep the Turks, the traditional foe, away from Greek territory.

And as for Andrew, though he may not yet have known it, he was in deadlier danger from his own people rather than the enemy. As the child's mother, Princess Alice of Battenberg, nursed her son in the idyllic cocoon of Mon Repos, she had no way of knowing that she had brought him into a uniquely hazardous environment. In fact, the Greek royal family into which Philip was born seemed in danger of extinction any day.

Four months later, on 24 October, Philip was baptized at Corfu during a glittering ceremony attended by all the local dignitaries and military authorities. He had two godparents – the Municipality of Corfu (representing the people) and his grandmother Queen Olga, who was unable to attend and was represented by her namesake granddaughter, the daughter of Prince Nicholas.

Beyond the palace gates, however, Greece's political and dynastic problems were ever at risk of getting out of hand. There were royalists versus republicans, pro-Germans versus pro-British, an irresponsible and rabble-rousing press, and the pervasive poverty under which the great bulk of the country people lived. For some years the monarchy had been a lightning-rod for political discontent; however, in 1917 Constantine had been ejected from his throne, only to regain it four years later, just before the birth of Philip. It was anybody's guess how long he would be allowed to sit on it this time.

Constantine I was the second member of the Glücksburg dynasty that had been reigning since 1863, having originated in North Germany and Denmark. Constantine, King since 1913, had initially been popular with his people as a successful Crown Prince-cum-commander-in-chief who had helped Greece win back territory from the crumbling Ottoman Empire in the Balkan Wars of 1912–13. Yet when the First World War drenched Europe in blood, Constantine had felt drawn by kinship ties to Germany's Kaiser Wilhelm II, his brother-in-law. This family bond kept Greece neutral through most of that war, to the great chagrin of Britain and France, but pro-royal and anti-royal factions had battled it out in a brief civil war in Athens in 1916, when British and French forces had to intervene to suppress the Greek royalists.

In 1916 a breakaway pro-Entente Greek government set up shop in the northern port city of Thessaloniki and was promptly recognized by the Allies. Greece contributed troops that acquitted themselves well on the Macedonian front in the last two years of the war. All of which did not redound to King Constantine's credit at all. In early June 1917 the Entente High Commissioner to the northern Greek government, French General Charles Jonnart, lost patience and ordered the Kaiser's Greek brother-in-law to step down and renounce his throne. As Constantine's second son Alexander succeeded to the throne, Constantine and his family went off to exile in Switzerland.

The year 1921 was not an optimistic one for Europe's royal houses. The recent war had swept away two of the most powerful, the German Hohenzollerns and the Russian Romanovs. Memories were still painfully fresh of the massacre by the Bolsheviks of Tsar Nicholas II and his family, to which Constantine I and his brothers were related on their mother's side. A new German republic was trying to find its feet, but hopelessly hobbled by insane reparations imposed on it by the vengeful French. In Britain, King George V reigned over a country trying to recover from the bloodletting in conditions of economic crisis and rising unemployment. The savagery of the Irish rebellion and British reprisals were in full spate. To Greece's east another royal house, the Ottoman Sultanate, was staggering through its last days and would soon be history.

What all this would mean for Greece's royal house was far from clear as Prince Philip was nursed in the safe cocoon of Mon Repos, yet facing a very uncertain future as a European royal. The family was fully familiar with its 'portmanteau occasions' when, in the words of Arthur Gould Lee, it 'waited with bags packed, ready to leave the country in a British warship.'[1] When would the next such occasion arise?

Chapter 2

The Making of the Greek Dynasty

The founder of modern Greece's royal dynasty had an impressive pedigree. Prince William George, the second son of King Christian IX of Denmark, belonged to the house of Schleswig-Holstein-Sonderburg-Glücksburg. In 1863 he was just eighteen and good-looking in a sensitive way. Britain, casting about for a replacement for Greece's previous king, the deposed Otho, wished to maintain a foreign-blood monarch to keep Greece tied to the great European royal houses in the interests of general European stability. On 18 March 1863 the Greek National Assembly approved the choice by a vote, on condition that all successors of George I (as he now became) would follow the Greek Orthodox faith. He had no problem with that, so on 25 May a Greek delegation travelled to Copenhagen with the formal offer of the kingdom. The young Danish prince was truly dazzled by the honour. 'My sole duty is to live and die as a good Greek,' he wrote to the Assembly. On 12 October he disembarked at Piraeus for the ride to the palace in central Athens.

Forty-two years before, on 25 March 1821 (since then celebrated as Greece's Independence Day), the Greeks first raised the standard of revolt against their Ottoman overlords. The resulting eight-year war was fierce and bloody; more than once the rebels appeared to be on the verge of destruction (as much from internal dissentions as from the Ottoman Sultan's levies), and were saved only by the intervention of Britain and France, and to a lesser degree Russia.

Not that those particular powers had any great liking for the Greeks, whom they considered degenerate descendants of the luminous classical Greeks of old. The name, the temples and the language were there, but not much else. When an independent Greece was formed in 1830 – the initiator, it turned out, of a series of Balkan revolts that would shatter the European portion of the Ottoman Empire within a century – the

European powers turned their thoughts to how they could make that dirt-poor mountainous peninsula into a rock of stability. The solution, natural for its time, was to give Greece a monarch. Greece's ancient and mediaeval history, of course, was replete with kings: the Mycenaean house of Atreus, glorified in Homer's epics; the earliest rulers of Athens (one of whom is supposed to have had a serpent's tail); the celebrated kings of Sparta, the Macedonians who spawned Alexander the Great, and the ninety-eight emperors and four empresses of the thousand-year Byzantine Empire. But no-one remained from those distant lines to be recruited as a genuinely Greek monarch.

The powers had to act fast. The Greek mainland was already sinking into widespread violence; a European king, it was universally agreed, would pull the infant nation together and in effect be the state. And besides the fact that it would have been manifestly impossible to convincingly find any blood descendant of, say, the ancient Spartan kings and pluck him out of the sheepfolds of the Peloponnese to set him on a throne, like Saul was made king of the Israelites, a foreign king would presumably be above party and personal faction and be a neutral broker in the inevitable power struggles to come. It was a noble ideal, representing a compromise between tradition and the ideas of the Enlightenment, as elegant as the neoclassical buildings going up in Athens, the new capital. But the classical era was long gone and in the rough surroundings of the nineteenth-century Balkans, the ideal would be proved utterly unrealistic.

It is the custom among almost all historians of modern Greece to treat its monarchy as an incongruity – an artificial dash of northern European courtly glitter grafted onto a dirt-poor nation of goatherders and fishermen with no tradition of organized statehood. That is at best a half-truth. At no time did the post-Ottoman Greeks as a majority actively disdain the idea of a king; indeed, many were proud that their new little country could display the trappings of a proper European nation. Besides, even the Greek rebels, or the most influential of them, believed a newly-reborn Greece had to have a king 'so that all division and rivalry for preference should cease among us.'[1] Moreover, a foreign king would actually be preferred, as it was felt that a native Greek would be too attached to a particular party or set of vested interests to act as a true impartial arbiter.

The aim of the great powers that underwrote Greek independence – mainly Great Britain, France and Russia – was above all to create a stable entity in a notoriously unstable part of Europe. Anarchy was the great bugbear, which is why the Protocol of 3 February 1830 and Treaty of London of 1832 insisted that the government of Greece be a hereditary monarchy and the monarch a sovereign in the maximum sense – the undisputed master of the state.[2] The powers' choice fell on Otto, the son of King Ludwig I of Bavaria. All of eighteen years old, Otto sailed to Greece in a British frigate to assume the Greek throne as King Otho. The newly established kingdom comprised only a small part of today's Greece, namely, the Peloponnese, Central Greece (Sterea Hellas) and the Cyclades islands. Even after 1832 most ethnic Greeks continued to live under Ottoman rule (and those of the Ionian islands under British control).

Though during the 1820s the Greek rebels had fought bravely against their Ottoman overlords with an admirable spirit of liberty, at no point in Otho's thirty-year reign (1832–1862) was Greece allowed to become a properly functioning parliamentary democracy as we would understand it today. The risk of 'anarchy' was too great. Otho himself was not the most astute of men. Though very fond of the Greeks and of his adopted country, he essentially failed to understand them; he imagined Greece could be governed like one of the orderly and boring principalities of Germany. Yet democratic reforms could not be indefinitely postponed, and in September 1843, ten years into his reign, a popular revolt forced Otho to grant his subjects a constitution. Otho himself unwisely meddled in Greek politics, attempting to exercise an independent foreign policy steering Greece away from Britain, which essentially had control of the country. In theory Great Britain, France and Russia were the guarantors of Greece's independence. In the case of France, the creation of the Greek state was the first time France emerged as an important international player after the end of the Napoleonic Wars – though second in importance to Britain. Russia had the advantage of being most Greeks' favourite foreign power as it shared the Greek Orthodox faith, but it could never hope to supplant Britain as the major influence on Greece.

During the Crimean War of 1853–56, Otho and the Greeks openly sympathized with Russia against the Ottoman Empire and its supporters

Britain and France. Otho's help to Russia consisted of instigating revolts against Ottoman rule in Thessaly in central Greece and Macedonia in the north. However, both he and Greece were humiliated as the British and French navies blockaded Piraeus (incidentally triggering a deadly cholera epidemic that was easy to blame on the foreigners). In 1862 the majority of Greeks, humiliated, expressed their discontent by forcing Otho to abdicate; his policy of running counter to Britain was just too risky. As the country sank into chaos, consumed by civil strife and on the verge of disintegration, representatives of the two major political factions made desperate pleas to Britain to send a replacement king with better prospects than Otho had for remaining on the throne. Most Greeks seemed to favour Prince Albert, the Duke of Edinburgh and son of Queen Victoria, who in a plebiscite of 241,202 citizens gained exactly ninety-nine per cent of the vote. (The number of votes against was precisely one! And a mere ninety-three Greeks voted for a republic.) But there was no chance a British prince could become a king of Greece, as Britain, France and Russia had already vetoed the candidacy of their own royal houses. None of the three powers wished to give any one of them such leverage in Greece. What the vote did do, however, was to raise Britain's profile as the most trustworthy procurer of a new king.[3] By that time Otho was history, though he never accepted his dethronement and lived for five more years bewailing the absence of Greece in his life.

Britain's choice fell on Prince William George of Glücksburg, the second son of Prince Christian (later Christian IX of Denmark). The Prince's British connection was that he was the brother of Alexandra, who would shortly wed Edward, the Prince of Wales (and future Edward VII). His accession as King George I of Greece was a signal diplomatic victory for Britain, which agreed to cede the western Greek Ionian Islands (including Corfu) to Greek sovereignty; the unspoken corollary, however, was that Greece in return should abandon expansionist moves that would upset the European equilibrium.[4] There was also a Russian connection: George's sister Dagmar in 1866 married the Tsarevich Alexander of Russia who eventually would become Alexander III. Those dynastic mooring ropes, it was hoped, would keep the Greek ship of state steady.

George I realized very early that he had to make himself popular with his new people. At the same time, however, he had to avoid displeasing his British suzerains. George consciously adopted the Glücksburg motto, 'my strength is the love of my people', as that of the Greek crown (a motto that remains to this day). Before leaving Copenhagen he wrote to the Greek National Assembly that his 'sole duty [was] to live and die as a true Greek.'[5] Could this have been sincere from a Danish prince barely out of his teens, whose knowledge of Greece must have been confined to classical studies? After all, opportunities to be a king didn't come around every day. It's easy to be cynical, but when we consider the historical fact that all the Glücksburgs, from George I to the present ex-King Constantine II, publicly and emphatically never ceased to think of themselves as anything but Greek, George's enthusiastic promise has the ring of youthful sincerity. George may well have been aware of the dictum of the ancient philosopher Isocrates that 'a Greek is anyone who partakes of Greek education and culture.' Whatever you feel yourself to be, you are.

The dominant powers of Europe, Britain and France, were approaching the apogee of their power. The failure of the European revolutions of 1848 had given new impetus to the monarchies. Britain was rapidly industrializing and building an empire under the august reign of Queen Victoria. France was a major (and none too trustworthy) player under the Second Empire of Napoleon III, who could never keep his hands off European affairs and tangled them more often than not. Italy had been united in 1861, adding its weight to the European family of nations. In Germany Otto von Bismarck was busy forging a patchwork of petty states that would in a few years unify that country as well. Russia's Tsar Alexander II had just emancipated the serfs but was seriously rattled by a Polish revolt, which turned him into a reactionary. Across the Atlantic, the United States was consumed in the Civil War. Little Greece didn't loom too large in anyone's calculations except Britain's.

Early in his reign George realized that he had to prove his words in practice. Domestically, this meant backing Greek popular enthusiasm for what was known as the Great Idea (*Megali Idea*), which was an irredentist drive to claw back Ottoman territories that in ancient and mediaeval times were Greek – not only in Europe but also in Asia Minor, including Constantinople. Many of these territories still possessed a large percentage of Greek inhabitants. Throughout the late nineteenth century and well into the twentieth the Great Idea was to become the Holy Grail of Greek foreign policy, and the source of innumerable woes into the bargain. But here George I would come into conflict with his great protector Britain, which wished to preserve intact what remained of the Ottoman Empire in order to safeguard the all-important route to India. It was a dilemma which he never quite resolved.

The British ties were very strong. George's sister, Alexandra, as we have seen, was married to Edward, the Prince of Wales and future Edward VII. To curry Greek favour, Britain ceded the Ionian Islands to Greece in 1864. All of this made George very reluctant during his long reign to run counter to British interests in the eastern Mediterranean. Four years into his reign, in 1867, George made a clever move by marrying Grand Duchess Olga Konstantinovna, a niece of Russian Tsar Alexander II; in one stroke the King reinforced his Orthodox credentials as his people applauded – after all, Russia was seen as the great protector of Orthodoxy. The British sniffed, but could do little about it. In just a few years George, instead of becoming an officer in the Danish Navy as his father, Christian IX of Denmark, had planned, had morphed into the crowned head of a country far away from his own. Greece may not have been an important country but neither was Denmark; in 1866 the latter suffered a humiliating defeat by Otto von Bismarck's Prussia. So George might well have considered himself lucky.

Though when he was eighteen George may have devoutly promised to be a Greek in all but blood, as his reign progressed he appears to have had second thoughts. He spent long periods of time outside Greece, in the courts of his royal relations (his sisters had married European monarchs; his father Christian was well nicknamed 'the matchmaker of Europe'). This close association with the powerful European royal houses actually impressed the Greeks and at the same time enabled him to keep some distance between himself and his subjects. The result was as he wished – to appear to be above their never-ending political quarrels. During his half-century reign, George's throne was more or less secure. In the few cases when it appeared to be under threat he knew how to preserve it by working in the background, not becoming involved in the Greek political scene – a tactic that earned him popular respect.

To be sure, there were mistakes – how could there not be in a reign of that length? – but never on such a scale as that which got Otho thrown out on his ear. At times he had no choice but to accede to the demands of the Great Powers, for example in 1869 when Bismarck forced Greece to drop its claim to Crete. George's most serious misstep came in 1897 when he went along with the overwhelming popular demand to make war on the Ottoman Empire in the hope of gaining territory – a key part of the Great Idea described earlier. He could have helped Greece avoid getting embroiled in a war which he knew it could not win, but dared not go against the strong tide of jingoist public opinion. (In fact he was making the same mistake as Otho had made four decades earlier in the case of the Crimean War.) Greece was heavily defeated by the Ottomans in 1897 (see below); as a result George's popularity with the Greeks suffered its greatest blow. One year later, two Greeks tried to exact revenge for the defeat and shot at George while he and his daughter Maria were riding in a carriage on the main road to the coast; the shots missed, but wounded the driver.[6]

On the domestic front George unfortunately stuck to the Othonian tradition of being entitled to appoint the prime minister without consulting the Parliament and lacking a majority of deputies. This angered liberal-minded politicians. One of them, Harilaos Trikoupis, in 1874 had penned an explosive newspaper article condemning George's 'absolute monarchy.' Trikoupis was jailed for his impertinence; a year later, however, he became the prime minister, and thanks also to the King's good sense was able to enshrine the principle that the candidate with the highest number of deputies in a national election was entitled to form a government whether the King liked it or not. (However, it was the Greek Parliament in the 1860s that had given this right to George without his even asking for it.) By this famous compromise of 1875 the prestige of the dynasty was preserved in the public eye.

George and his wife Olga had eight children. The eldest was Constantine (1868–1923 – destined to become Constantine I), who married Princess Sophia of Prussia. Following were Prince George (1869–1957), who married Princess Marie Bonaparte; Princess Alexandra (1870–1891), who married Grand Duke Paul Alexandrovich of Russia; Prince Nicholas (1872–1938), who married Grand Duchess

Elena Vladimirovna of Russia; Maria (1876–1940), who married the Grand Duke George Mikhailovich of Russia and later Admiral Perikles Ioannidis of the Royal Hellenic Navy; Princess Olga (1880), who died aged seven months; Prince Andrew (1882–1944 – Philip's father), who married Princess Alice of Battenberg; and Prince Christopher (1888–1940), who married an American widow, Nancy Stewart Worthington Leeds, and later Princess Françoise of Orléans. All five of George's sons were trained as professional military men.

Olga Konstantinovna was a hugely stabilizing influence on the Greek monarchy, thanks partly to her solid Russian Orthodox background and membership in the Romanov family. In terms of religious beliefs, her marriage to the firmly Protestant George I was strikingly successful. Differences in doctrine and practice, as far as is known, never clouded it. Maturity and a sense of grand responsibility on both sides played their part. As Olga made sure that all her children were strictly brought up in the Orthodox faith and regularly attended church services, George never demurred; in fact, he was there on all the ceremonial religious occasions such as royal baptisms, never wavering in his respect for the creed of his subjects.

The Russian connection was strong. George's Danish sister, Princess Dagmar, had converted to Orthodoxy in 1866 after her boyfriend the Tsarevich Nicholas of Russia died as the result of a fall. That year Dagmar – now renamed Maria Feodorovna – married Nicholas' brother, the Tsarevich Alexander, who on his father Alexander II's assassination in 1881 had become Tsar Alexander III. (Dagmar would live through the whole of the Russian tragedy as, fifty-three years later, her son Nicholas II and his family would be butchered by the Bolsheviks and she would leave Russia in a British warship.)

On 15 October 1867 George and Grand Duchess Olga, the Tsar's niece and sister of Grand Duke Konstantin Konstantinovich (we see here the Orthodox predilection for the name of the first and last emperors of Byzantium) were married. Olga was just sixteen at the time and, not surprisingly, brought her collection of dolls to her new home. Prince Christopher's memoirs record that she arrived in Athens in a pretty dress of blue and white, the Greek national colours, captivating the enthusiastic crowds.[7] Fair-haired and well-built, with penetrating blue eyes, Olga would come to be a well-liked figure, and be a rock of common sense for her husband among the treacherous shoals of Greek politics over the next fifty years.

In the final decades of the nineteenth century unrest simmered in the ranks of the Greek military. Many officers fretted at not being able to measure swords with the traditional foe, the decaying Ottoman Empire. In 1893 a severe Greek debt crisis slashed the defence budget, which only increased their frustration. The following year a secret society, the National Society (*Ethniki Etairia*), sprang up, consisting of ambitious junior officers and militant writers and journalists from civilian life, all of whom shared the aim of clawing back parts of the ancient and mediaeval Greek world from the Turks whenever possible. Among the chattering classes the romantic Great Idea was in full spate. Greek governments, however (not to mention their creditors), knew that such a policy would be financial and political suicide and did their best to hinder the National Society's schemes. But such was the society's strength that on 27 March 1897 it sent 3,000 men into Ottoman-held Macedonia to attack Turkish garrisons.[8]

A week before, Britain had virtually ordered Greece and the Ottoman Empire to withdraw their forces fifty miles from the frontier to reduce the chances of a clash. If Greece did not comply, warned British Prime Minister Lord Salisbury, then a blockade of Greece might be in order. King George bridled at this, whereupon London tried to win him over with a plan to give Crete autonomy and make the King's second son, Prince George, governor of the island. Meanwhile, Crown Prince Constantine had already been placed in command of the Army in case of war. Moreover, the Great Powers were by no means in agreement over whether Crete should be autonomous or not. Kaiser Wilhelm had sent military advisers to train the Ottoman Army, and hoped to see results; at the same time he sought ways of tripping up the pro-British Greek king. The incursion of 27 March handed a *casus belli* to the Turks on a platter.

At the helm in Athens was a sabre-rattling prime minister, Theodoros Diliyannis, who had long been whipping up war fever. Crown Prince Constantine set off for the frontier to command the 42,000-man Army of Thessaly. Before any real clashes could begin, Constantine abruptly changed the planned deployments, which threw transport services into chaos right at the beginning. Facing him was General Etem Pasha with 62,000 men based at Elassona and more than double the number of artillery pieces that the Greeks had. Five days after the fighting started on 6 April, the Army of Thessaly had been driven from all the main passes leading southwards from Macedonia and was in jumbled retreat towards Larisa. Etem Pasha occupied the key port of Volos but in order to defeat the Greeks he needed to attack them at the elevated strongpoint of Domokos. This he did, successfully, and on 7 May both sides signed a cease-fire. The war had lasted barely a month and had badly stained the reputation of Crown Prince Constantine, discredited the Army leadership and brought back Greece's creditors with a vengeance.[9] King George considered abdicating, but was mollified by Britain, which backed Greece in the peace negotiations.[10]

Despite Constantine's tarnished military record during the War of 1897, in the first decade of the twentieth century George was confident of the abilities of his Crown Prince to reign when the time should come. But an influential clique in the military didn't quite agree; they had little use for the governments of the time, which they viewed as weak and corrupt, and on 15 August 1909 staged a successful coup. One of the soldiers' main complaints was that the promotion of able officers was being held up by royal favouritism; they demanded for a start that the King's sons be debarred from senior military positions. For a time the throne was in danger. George wrote of feeling 'deeply affronted and hurt by such treatment after forty-six years of hard work… I have been forced to make many sacrifices and swallow much bitterness so that the peace and order in this country should not be disturbed.'[11]

Fortunately, the King found an ally in a Cretan revolutionary named Eleftherios Venizelos, who had played a key part in freeing that island from Ottoman rule. The junta running Athens invited him to sort out the mess, which he did. In a letter to Venizelos, George pledged 'help with all my strength.'[12] There was a definite meeting of minds. And just in time, as Greece and Serbia joined forces to launch the First Balkan War in 1912 with the intention of freeing the 'unredeemed Greeks' of the Balkan peninsula from Ottoman rule. The war was successful, as was the brief Second Balkan War of 1913, this time against Bulgaria, a former ally in the first war. Crown Prince Constantine, as commander-in-chief of the Greek Army, had cleared northwestern Greece of the Turks by the start of 1913. Above all, the great Greek port of Thessaloniki was back in national hands after some 500 years of alien rule. George I could be justly proud of his heir, but the personal triumph did not last long.

The Crown Prince fretted over his father's new habit of strolling around Thessaloniki without adequate security.

'You can't do this, Father,' the Crown Prince would say often. 'This town was under the Turkish yoke for so long. There must be plenty of people around who want to harm you.'

'Mind your own business,' was the King's gruff reply. On 18 March 1913 George decided to walk to the waterfront, accompanied only by a major from his personal guard, to visit the German battle-cruiser *Goeben*, which was in port. On the way he passed a café, where three men sitting at an outdoor table rose and doffed their hats in respect; moments later one of the men drew a pistol and shot the King in the back, fatally. The perpetrator was a mentally unstable man who shortly afterwards committed suicide. (George's bloodstained neck-chain and cross pendant are still in the royal family's possession.)[13] For years the young Prince Philip would be haunted by accounts of the murder.

The half-century reign of George I was most remarkably stable for a poor and chronically unstable country such as Greece. Yet the assassination, coming at the moment of his greatest triumph at the age of sixty-eight, demonstrated that a Greek king could never really feel secure on his throne. George (and his successors) had to constantly keep looking figuratively over their shoulder. He had striven mightily to keep the state on an even keel under extremely adverse domestic and European circumstances. According to Air Vice-Marshal Arthur Gould Lee, RAF, who in the mid-twentieth century had close ties to the Greek royals, George was 'a trusted sovereign, wise and enlightened, whose moderating influence had helped his fractious subjects to work in harmony, and whose insight into foreign politics had steered his Ministers round many an awkward corner.'[14] His act would be a hard one to follow.

One of the peculiarities of modern monarchy is that members of a royal family diffused through several countries are likely to find themselves on opposite sides in time of war or international crisis. In the twenty-first century this is a negligible risk. But in the late nineteenth and early twentieth centuries it happened often. The predicament of King Constantine I in the First World War was a concentrated textbook case. Related to both Kaiser Wilhelm II and King George V, he had a supremely hard tightrope act to conduct, an act that would ultimately prove too much for him.

The Crown Prince, who became Constantine I (Philip's uncle), was a man of a different stamp, in some ways a more complex character than his father. Born in 1868, he was the first Greek royal to come into the world in Greece. Like all George's children, while an infant he was baptized Orthodox. Thus in the eyes of many when he acceded to the throne, Constantine was in some sense the country's first 'real' king, in a spiritual as well as a national sense. Even his name had been deliberately chosen, as it had echoes of the eleven Emperor Constantines of the Byzantine Empire; many, in fact, would refer to him as 'Constantine XII' to stress the supposed continuity. His name also reinforced the popular legend that as Constantinople was lost to the Turks by a Constantine (XI, in 1453), another ruler of the same name would in time recapture the great city. In the public mind, then, Constantine quickly became the living embodiment of the Great Idea, to his eventual downfall.

The result was that the young Crown Prince (known also as the Diadoch, or Successor) did not and probably could not follow his father's footsteps and avoid getting involved in the political affairs of Greece. Even in his youth he was partial to certain politicians who were his friends, and even though he studied in the Greek Military Academy and entered the Army, he managed to become a divisive figure, such as the time in 1895 when Constantine ordered the troops under his command to violently disperse an anti-government protest in Athens. This led directly to the resignation of the country's government at the time. Whereas the Danish-born George I had made a conscious effort to be as Greek as his subjects, lacking nothing in patriotism, Constantine somehow overdid that ideal. Moreover, his marriage to Princess Sophia Dorothea of Hohenzollern, the sister of Kaiser Wilhelm II, though perfectly allowable in the dynastic politics of the time, inevitably came to work against him.

Since his youth Constantine had been an ardent admirer of Germany, whose unification he was old enough to have observed. His father, moreover, in keeping with royal tradition down to our own day, decided that all his sons should have military careers; therefore Constantine was sent for staff studies in Germany. The Kaiser, either out of admiration for the Greek Crown Prince's abilities or figuring that he could cultivate a potential ally, made Constantine an honorary marshal of the German army, an honour that flattered the Diadoch no end. Constantine's glittering marriage to Princess Sophia in Athens in October 1889 added a reinforcement to this cement. In attendance was Wilhelm himself, who marched out onto the palace balcony to greet the crowds and turned towards the Acropolis about a mile away, snapping to attention and saluting it. For a moment, German and Greek nationalism became soul mates.[15]

Constantine's marriage to the sister of the most powerful man in Europe raised his global status overnight. The British were not worried – this was before the days of the Kaiser's sabre-rattling that would help trigger the First World War. To them it was just one more move in the complex chess-game of European power relationships which did not threaten British interests in Greece – and was not Wilhelm himself Queen Victoria's grandson? Germany was busy building new prestige in the eastern Mediterranean and the Middle East through connections with the Ottoman Empire, which Britain wished to preserve as a bulwark against Russia. For Greece to associate itself with the rising power of Germany was seen as prestigious, a sign of national maturity. And there was an understandable feeling in many quarters in Greece that vassalage to Great Britain had gone on for too long anyway. Not until much later would Constantine's German connection bring him more trouble than he could imagine.

Much has been made of Sophia's Germanic mentality and stern upbringing of her children which was supposed to reflect that. There was no doubt an element of that in her character, but it has generally been exaggerated. She wished to raise her children with a minimum of fuss and in scrupulous cleanliness. And she had much to be concerned about. The royal palace in Athens scarcely had a working bathroom, so most of the family's time was spent in the country palace at Tatoi. Sophia kept a close eye on the princes' tutors, replacing anyone who was not seen as strict enough. One tutor, a Pomeranian named Herr Honig, would fix his pupils with a grim stare if anyone dared step out of line; any prince rash enough to try to flee the room would be halted by a sharp *'da bleiben!'* ('stay where you are!'). Sophia's control extended to religious observances. She would insist that her children scrupulously observe Orthodox church services in the Tatoi palace chapel, where they would take communion under the guidance of Queen Olga. Prince George, the eldest, loved to play with toy soldiers, especially during holidays at the Hesse palace in Germany.[16]

Yet for all that, Sophia was very much attracted to the English way of life. The children's tutors and governesses were not only Germans but also Britons, and holidays were spent not only at Hesse but also at Eastbourne on England's south coast. Teachers such as Herr Honig might bark in German, but it was English that was preferred at court. Compared to the general run of European royal courts, that of Greece was extraordinarily simple and uncluttered, largely free of the stifling coruscations of excessive ceremony that would weigh down other courts and contribute to their noisy fall.

Constantine's military training and talents naturally gained him much support in the Greek Army officer corps. He had in fact been designated the Duke of Sparta (though that appellation never quite caught on). That popularity, however, took an abrupt dip after the fiasco of the 1897 mini-war with the Ottoman Empire (see above), for which the Crown Prince, fairly or not, was widely blamed. Perhaps it was not so much his fault as that of the impossibility of the task that feverish public opinion demanded that he carry out. The Turkish forces were far more numerous than his, and moreover, the Prince had been appointed to overall command a mere few days before the outbreak of hostilities and had no time to work out a proper strategy.

Agitation for the Diadoch to leave the Army became louder; national humiliation is generally a most effective lever of political change. As we have seen, the 1909 military coup at last forced him to resign his Army commission. Coming to his rescue, ironically, was Prime Minister

Venizelos, the former Cretan revolutionary leader. In a display of wise statesmanship, and deftly sidelining the military men, Venizelos reinstated Constantine in the Army, giving him the post of inspector-general. Venizelos himself wanted to severely clip the powers of the Greek throne, but at this stage overly alienating the palace would have been foolhardy. The Balkans were already roiling with the tensions that would soon erupt into the Balkan Wars. Yet he made sure that capable officers were there to keep an eye on Constantine all the time in case the Diadoch made any misstep – memories of 1897 were still fresh.

The policy appeared to work. When the First Balkan War, with Greece, Serbia, Montenegro and Bulgaria lined up against their Ottoman overlords, erupted in October 1912, Venizelos had enough confidence in Constantine to give him back his old job of commander-in-chief of the Army. Here he admirably restored his reputation by seizing Thessaloniki in October 1912 and clearing the Ottomans out of Epiros in northwest Greece. A grateful public proclaimed him a *stratilatis,* or grand military leader, a term borrowed from the Byzantine era, carrying overtones of legendary glory. Now, surely, was the time for the predicted Constantine of legend to reconquer Constantinople from the despised Turk! It was not to be. It was hushed up at the time, but the Diadoch had made a serious strategic error during the First Balkan War in planning to attack the Turks who were retreating before the advancing Serbs, instead of leading his army eastwards towards Thessaloniki which was being evacuated by the Ottomans. Bulgarian forces were approaching this key city, and even though at the time Greece and Bulgaria were allies, they were vying for the same portions of the Ottoman empire. Constantine appeared more interested in winning a battle with the disorganized Ottoman army than securing Thessaloniki. From then on the relations between the two strong-minded men, Constantine and Venizelos, could only worsen.

Chapter 3

Andrew and Alice

Prince Andrew was born in Athens on 2 February 1882, the fourth son of George I. Like his eldest brother, Crown Prince Constantine, Andrew made a conscious effort to be identified as Greek, quite distinct from the German/Danish and Russian antecedents of his parents. The palace, naturally, was a fairly polyglot place; but from the outset, we are told, Andrew insisted on speaking only Greek to his parents, even though he could get by quite well in German, English, French and Russian. He wanted them to address him by the Greek form of his name, Andreas.

When Andrew was about four years old he was photographed with the rest of the family. He is seen holding the hand of his sister Maria, the next youngest sibling. Another photograph taken in the same year is of Andrew on his own clutching a toy rifle. In these photographs Andrew resembles very much his son Philip when he was the same age. The idea of Andrew's holding a toy rifle was the photographer's, and may have been prophetic, as Andrew, like all his brothers, ended up as a professional soldier. When Queen Olga brought Andrew to the fashionable Moraitis studio to be photographed, as she had done with her previous children, the photographer mistook the child's clothes as an imitation of an evzone palace guard's skirted uniform. Moraitis asked the child if he was an evzone, received an affirmative reply, and said an evzone should have a rifle. As little Andrew didn't have one, Moraitis sent out to the nearest toy shop for the necessary prop.[1]

In 1898, aged sixteen, Andrew was enrolled in the Military Academy (*Scholi Evelpidon*) which his elder brothers Constantine and Nicholas had attended.[2] Like them, Andrew trained to become a professional officer in the Greek military; however, as we will see, this proved to be something of a trap, as it got the young princes embroiled in political issues, as the military at the time had arrogated to itself an important role in politics.

One of Andrew's classmates in the Military Academy was an intense young cadet named Theodoros Pangalos, the consistent top of the class. In the following year the commandant of the Academy, Colonel Zorbas, made Pangalos a Sergeant First Class of Cadets, the highest ranking a cadet could attain.[3] Zorbas, however, was pressured by royal circles to promote Andrew to the same rank as Pangalos, but Zorbas refused. In fact, the commandant ignored a rule that a prince in a military academy could not have a lower rank than any fellow-cadet. He promoted purely on merit and Andrew, admittedly, was not quite the best of the cadet corps.[4] This episode marked the beginning of a rivalry between Prince Andrew and Theodoros Pangalos, whose paths were destined to cross in later tumultuous years.

There exist two group photographs of Andrew with some of his fellow cadets (among them Pangalos) taken at roughly the same time. They were dated 1899 but since the photographer, Carl Merlin, died in 1898 the latter year is more accurate.[5] Therefore the photographs must have been taken shortly after Andrew had enrolled in the Academy. The five other cadets pictured with Andrew include Alexandros Apostolou, Basileios Kourousopoulos, Eustathios Margaritis, Theodoros Pangalos and Alexandros Othonaios. At first glance Andrew seems no different from his fellow cadets; however, there is evidence that Carl Merlin wanted to draw attention to Andrew, and almost certainly arranged where the students should sit. The cadets form a pyramid with their bodies and Andrew is at the top. Another interesting detail is that Theodoros Pangalos and Alexandros Othonaios show that even in this early stage of their careers they were friends. In the second photograph, Apostolou has changed positions with Othonaios, who is shown lying on Pangalos' stomach. Pangalos appears to be the most relaxed of all the cadets. This may be attributed to the fact that he was top of his class. Pangalos and Othonaios may have been photographed at the bottom of the 'pyramid' in 1898 but many years later both would control the fate of Greece, the former becoming Greece's first dictator (1925–6).[6] One of the photographs bears the coat of arms of Greece and the name of the photographer, indicating that copies were sold to the public.

In November 1899 the King decided that Andrew needed extra help by private tutors in order to finish his studies and become an officer, preferably within two years and before his twentieth birthday. He arranged private tuition for the Prince from Major (later General) Panagiotis Danglis, an artillery officer who was an expert on various military topics and who had taught at the Military Academy. As Danglis was not one of the favourites of the royal family, the request came to him as a surprise, but he was considered as one of the best experts on military subjects in which Andrew was lagging, and was also known for hard work and an ability to enforce discipline. Danglis taught Andrew over a period of a year and a half, even during holidays.

Danglis came to know Andrew well and gives many details about the Prince's personality in his diary.[7] He found Andrew highly intelligent, in line with the general belief that Andrew was the smartest of the King's sons, but negligent in his lessons and a bit lazy at the beginning of tutorials. The Prince had alarming gaps in knowledge of subjects he was supposed to have been taught in the Military Academy the previous year; it would appear that Andrew, though keen on becoming an officer, did not do the hard work that was demanded and may have expected that he could achieve his goal by simply being a prince. This may have been the case in earlier years with his brothers Constantine and Nicholas, but as was made clear to him, the Military Academy under commandant Zorbas no longer gave a prince a free ride. King George must have known that Andrew was not doing as well as expected, and for that reason summoned Danglis to help him. Danglis concentrated on the toughest subjects in the curriculum, such as topography and artillery tactics. Andrew had tutors for other subjects as well. Press reports said that besides military subjects, Andrew also had tutors in mathematics, Greek literature, and English.[8] However, the most important tutor was Major Danglis and under his tuition and guidance Prince Andrew found the self-discipline he required in order to study well and eventually become a good cadet.

On 14 and 15 May 1901, in a room on the ground floor of the palace, Andrew sat the final exams to become commissioned.[9] The examination board consisted of the King as chairman; its members were Crown Prince Constantine, Prince Nicholas, Prime Minister Theotokis, the Minister of War, the Military Academy commandant Zorbas, and the prince's tutors including Major Danglis. The Greek newspapers published official brief announcements about the progress of the exams. The highest-circulation newspaper, *Akropolis*, had a scoop with details about the first day of Andrew's exams.[10] The members of the board were seated opposite a table where Andrew sat. An empty chair was placed next to Andrew for the tutor-examiner of each subject taken. All the questions were oral and Andrew answered the same way – in the case of mathematics, writing on a blackboard beside him. Before the examination a bishop who had been invited by King George conducted a blessing. George observed his son's examination anxiously. When the mathematics exam was to begin he was overheard telling the prime minister: 'Let's see now how he is going to do with the difficult subjects!' Every time Andrew correctly answered a difficult question the King gave a cry of satisfaction. Of all the examiners, Danglis asked the most questions and spent a full hour on them. When it was clear that Andrew had passed all his subjects on the first day, the overjoyed King kissed and congratulated him.

The next day Andrew was examined in modern Greek and English (this by an Englishman called Elliot, possibly the British ambassador Sir Francis Elliot), and in military subjects by Danglis, but Andrew successfully negotiated all of them. Danglis later claimed that no favours were shown Andrew. This may well be true, and Danglis was known for his integrity and honesty; but just to be on the safe side, King George had brought with him several medals and awards which he distributed to the tutors as thank-you gifts for passing Andrew. Danglis himself was pleasantly surprised to receive the nation's highest award, the prestigious Saviour's Gold Medal of Merit.[11] There followed a lavish banquet in the palace attended by members of the examination board during which Prime Minister Theotokis toasted the young prince and his 'excellent' studies.

The problem with Andrew had been how to pass the exams to become an officer in the first place, and not which branch of the Army he would serve in, as some British writers claim, probably in error.[12] It was well known that his dream had been to become a cavalry officer and Danglis took that for granted when he started tutoring the prince. On the same day that Andrew passed his exams King George signed his commission as a cavalry officer.[13] But this presented a problem for Andrew as he was short-sighted, something that would ordinarily have kept him out of the cavalry arm. That, however, was not an issue that the board had any power to decide on. Nevertheless, the fact remained that Andrew's sight deficiency meant that he could be in serious danger if he were ever to lead men in front-line combat. As soon as Andrew was commissioned he attempted to disguise this problem by publicly wearing a monocle (though in private he wore spectacles). At the time monocles were quite rare in Greece, worn only by a few upper-class older men. The monocle became a bit of a joke among many Greeks, who saw something snobbish and artificial in it, certainly nothing that would befit a man of the people.

On 21 May 1901, at an official ceremony in the palace attended by King George, the royal family, the prime minister and his cabinet, dignitaries and foreign diplomats, the Archbishop of Athens administered to Andrew his oath as an officer in the Greek Army.[14] Second Lieutenant Prince Andrew's first posting was to 1 Cavalry Regiment and a year later, in 1902, to 2 Cavalry Regiment based at Goudi, a suburb of Athens. He became good friends with another second lieutenant named Menelaos Metaxas, six years his senior. Metaxas was one of the best cavalry officers in Greece at the time, a graduate of the famous Belgian Army Cavalry School at Ypres. It is likely that the King chose Metaxas as his son's mentor on merit. Sometime between 1902 and 1904 the German photographer Carl Boehringer (who after the death of Carl Merlin became the official photographer of the Greek royal family), photographed Andrew and Menelaos Metaxas in the uniforms of second lieutenants.[15] In the photo they are seated facing each other, Andrew smoking a cigarette while lighting another in Metaxas' hand. As was usual for royal photographs at the time, this one was reproduced and sold as a postcard. In later years, when Andrew was promoted over Metaxas, the latter became his aide-de-camp, continuing to be a close friend and confidant even after both had left the Army.[16]

In 1901 Britain's Queen Victoria died, to be succeeded by King Edward VII. The following year, Prince Andrew travelled to London for the coronation and was there smitten by a young pretty woman who was introduced to him as Princess Alice of Battenberg, with English and German connections. Alice was born on 25 February 1885, the first great-grandchild of Victoria from her namesake granddaughter, Victoria of Hesse (later Marchioness of Milford Haven), and the German Prince Louis of Battenberg. Queen Victoria anticipated the birth of her first great-grandchild, a special occasion in her life, and insisted that Alice be born in Windsor Palace so that she could witness the joyous event personally.[17]

Alice was also smitten by Andrew.[18] This was one of the rare instances where a genuine romance blossomed between members of royal families and the tie was not politically arranged. Though Alice was a princess from a lower-tier European royal house and Andrew came from a higher-tier kingdom, Alice more than compensated for her 'lower' status by the fact that her family had strong ties with the British monarchy and establishment.

People who knew Andrew and Alice were certain that they would make a fine couple as they matched emotionally and both had genial, easy-going and humorous characters. However, what seems to have attracted the couple to each other, oddly enough, were also what might be considered serious defects in a blue-blood family. Alice suffered from a severe hearing problem which made her practically deaf, though she was fluent in several languages and an efficient lip-reader. Andrew's short-sightedness was his own unique burden, and both worked together to conceal the defects from the public. They got engaged in London in May 1903. That same year Andrew travelled to Germany to complete his military studies; marriage followed in Darmstadt, the ancestral home of the Battenbergs, in October. The couple initially lived in Darmstadt before moving to Greece. Though Princess Alice looked forward to the idea of living in sunny Greece, she declined to convert from her native Lutheranism to Orthodoxy. Hence the couple had two religious wedding ceremonies, a Protestant and an Orthodox one, plus the civil ceremony obligatory in Germany.

On Christmas Day 1903 (old calendar) Andrew and Alice arrived at the port of Piraeus on board the royal yacht *Amphitrite* which had brought them from Brindisi. [19] They had planned to arrive on 23 December so that they could celebrate their first Christmas in Athens with the royal family, but bad weather kept the yacht immobile for two days at Loutraki near Corinth. Andrew and Alice intended to settle permanently in Athens. Their official welcome took the form of a Te Deum in Athens Cathedral attended by the members of the royal family and local dignitaries. After that Andrew took Alice to the Acropolis and showed her around the monuments. Even though it was Christmas Day, thousands of Athenians lined the streets to greet Andrew and Alice as their carriage was driven to the Cathedral. All main streets had been decorated for the occasion. The event was marked on postcards printed with a large Greek flag over the couple's heads.[20] Alice was photographed on the *Amphitrite* wearing a heavy white fur coat shortly before disembarking. Her face has a serious expression befitting royals in their public photographs.[21] However as the voyage from Italy had been rough, Alice could well have been seasick and besides, it was very cold that day in Piraeus. One newspaper quoted a bystander who saw Alice waving at him through the carriage window and noticed that 'she is a pretty blonde girl but her face looks too pale!'[22]

King George took an immediate liking to Alice (unlike his attitude to some of his other daughters-in-law); when she and Andrew arrived in Athens on the train from Piraeus, the King actually took Alice by the hand and personally introduced her to the various dignitaries who were waiting at the station. As George had a close-knit family, he kept a tight rein on them to make sure that all members made Alice feel welcome.[23] The King was careful to keep the awareness of Alice's deafness strictly within the family, and as she could lip-read very well, the secret was not difficult to keep. In Greek newspapers at the time there is not even a hint of Alice's problem which was, however, occasionally mentioned in the foreign press.

Under Andrew's influence Alice became a loyal Greek and for the next sixty-three years until her death would call Greece her home.[24] In her new home she concentrated on meaningful social work, thanks partly to her upbringing in Britain where volunteer work for the underprivileged was expected of royals, in contrast to the institutionalized snobbery of most European royal houses, including that of Greece. Alice began working at the School of Embroidery helping poor Greek girls learn a trade to support their families. There Alice acquired skills in weaving and sewing women's clothes and in her turn taught many girls. She used every opportunity to advertise the school's products, as attested by extant photographs showing Alice and her mother and sisters-in-law wearing traditional dress made by the girls of the school. On 12 December 1907, during a visit to Athens by the King's daughter Maria (Grand Duchess Georgievna) of Russia and her family, her husband Grand Duke George Mikhailovich, and her brothers Constantine, George, Nicholas and

Andrew, they were all photographed outside the palace wearing their uniforms. Their wives and Queen Olga wore traditional Greek costumes made by the girls in the School of Embroidery where Alice worked.

Alice possessed a cheerful character, loved jokes, and smiled a lot. She and Andrew frequently used the *Amphitrite* to cruise the Mediterranean. There are several known photographs of them relaxing on this vessel. In one of these, taken in April 1904, just three months after Alice arrived in Greece, she is shown laughing and dressed in Andrew's cavalry officer uniform, wearing his spectacles as well.[25] It was one of Alice's practical jokes, but the photo was never published as it would have presumably embarrassed the royal family. The picture stayed in the private collection of the officer who took the photo and was most likely a close friend of the couple.

Alice's smiles could have been a way of concealing her hearing problem. Already multilingual, she learned Greek quickly and could even lip-read in Greek. The people who met Alice when she first came to Greece were impressed by her friendly demeanour and the fact that she had little difficulty in learning their language. Alice had begun learning Greek before her marriage and by the time she arrived in the country she already had a command of it. The Greek-Cypriot newspaper *Alitheia* on 16 January 1904 reported on Alice's Greek:

> In Athens the talk of the town is how perfectly Princess Alice speaks Greek. The ladies who were introduced to her had already been informed that the princess was learning the language. They would never have hoped, however, that they would find that she possessed almost perfect command of it. The princess converses freely and with ease...sometimes she stops in an attempt to find words and often her phrasing has a German syntax...with the verb at the end.

Ordinary Greeks considered Alice much more approachable than the other foreign princesses who had married the sons of George I. She worked alongside the working-class girls at the Embroidery School. A contrary example was Ellen, Prince Nicholas' wife, who as the daughter of a Russian grand duke considered her station as far above that of the other foreign princesses in Greece and expected to be treated accordingly.[26] (Ellen was also strikingly beautiful.) Alice's own pretty and girlish features endeared her to the people. The royal family's physician, Konstantinos Louros, who was invited to the wedding of Andrew and Alice in Germany in 1903 described her as 'a little bud that has barely opened its petals'.[27] Ironically, of all her sisters-in-law it would be Ellen with whom Alice would associate most closely in later years. In her simple ways Alice was an asset for Andrew and though she was a foreigner most Greeks took a liking to her, which was not the case with the other princesses and especially the wife of Constantine.

It is no coincidence that the name Alice, which was foreign to the Greeks, from the early twentieth century onwards became a popular girls' name in Greece (and remains so today). Top secret reports of the Austrian ambassador in Athens to his foreign minister dating from 1910, and published half a century later, reveal that Alice was the most liked by the Greeks of all the foreign princesses.[28] These reports also reveal that Alice was also very active in promoting Andrew's position vis-à-vis his brothers and especially Crown Prince Constantine. In one of the reports, the Austrian ambassador records that Alice's sister-in-law, Princess Sophia, wife of the heir, was extremely jealous and openly hostile to her. What made things worse, according to the ambassador, was the fact that Sophia hated Greece and the Greeks, both of which Alice loved. As we shall see, in 1912 during the First Balkan War Alice's popularity with the Greeks would reach its zenith.

The happiness of the young couple was enhanced by the birth of their first child, Margarita, on 18 April 1905, followed a year later (30 May 1906) by a second daughter, Theodora.

In 1905 and 1906 Andrew served in the 1 Regiment at Larisa training recruits. Alice moved to Larisa with him during this period. But life in this provincial town, at the time on the Greek-Turkish frontier, was rather more spartan than they had been accustomed to in the palace in Athens. Besides his military duties, Andrew in Larisa also exercised the prerogatives of a prince. According to reports in the local press, his aide-de-camp, Menelaos Metaxas, distributed titles of 'Suppliers to HRH Prince Andrew' to various local businessmen, a confectioner, a goldsmith and a bookseller.[29] Though Andrew loved horse riding and was an excellent horseman, Alice's efforts in that direction were futile. At one point she was riding so badly that Andrew told his ADC to help her sit properly so 'she wouldn't fall and break her neck'.[30] In the autumn of 1906 Andrew and Alice were back in Athens with their two small daughters.

The first years of Andrew's and Alice's marriage were the happiest, not only for them but also for the Greek royal family. For almost half a century during the reign of George I, the royals had the respect of the majority of Greeks. The 1897 defeat at the hands of the still-kicking Ottoman Empire had thrown a shadow over this relationship, but the royals continued to live as before. However, the Goudi military revolt of 1909 would end this carefree period. Then, beginning in 1912 and for the next forty years, Greece would be embroiled in foreign and civil wars (including participation in both world wars), national rifts, revolutions, military coups, dictatorships and almost unceasing civil unrest. The royal family would be exiled three times, and the monarchy would even be replaced by a republic for eleven years. Yet in March 1907 Andrew's popularity among the Greeks took an unexpected dive by an event which to this day remains unknown outside Greece, as it was not reported in the foreign press. It was a result of the enthusiasm Andrew had for the newly-invented automobile.

Andrew's visual deficiencies did not hinder him from making frequent use of a car to travel. He even ventured to use it outside Athens where all roads were still dirt tracks. For example, in October 1904 the Prince's car broke down at Thebes and he returned to Athens by a special train sent to pick him up.[31] Andrew's car broke down again in the following month; it took four months to repair as the engine had to be sent to England.[32] By the spring of 1905 Andrew was back at the wheel; on 29 April the newspapers reported that Andrew drove British officers to Eleusis to visit the archaeological site there; reportedly there was also a second car in this excursion.[33] It is uncertain when and how Andrew got his first car. It is not even clear if he possessed one before 1903, when we know that he acquired one from Tsar Nicholas II as a wedding gift to Alice.[34] The car was a Wolseley which Andrew brought with him to Athens when he returned from Germany with Alice.[35] At the time there were just four cars in Greece. Two of these belonged to members of the royal family (one to King George and the other to Crown Prince Constantine). The third belonged to a shipping magnate named Embirikos and the fourth to another wealthy Greek. Constantine's car, it turned out, was the very first to be involved in a road accident in Greece. During a drive to the summer palace at Tatoi on 21 September 1902, his German-trained chauffeur wrenched the wheel the wrong way. Constantine had been sitting next to the driver in the open vehicle and working the horn to warn any pedestrians and horse carts in the way. Perhaps trying to avoid an obstacle, the car toppled over and was fortuitously stopped from tumbling down a precipice by three stout pine trees. All three passengers, who included a doctor for use in any emergency, were thrown clear and lightly injured. Andrew and Princess Sophia were riding in a carriage following behind. The accident, in fact, happened just hours after the car had arrived at the port of Piraeus and was being tested for speed.[36] The following day the newspapers reporting the accident quoted Andrew to the effect that 'cars are dangerous'. Little did he know then that within a few years he would again prove that very point.

Between 1903 and 1907 the number of cars in Greece had jumped from three to seven.[37] In the latter year Andrew was involved in the country's first road fatality. On 4 March 1907 Andrew was driving his car from Athens to Piraeus with Alice and Menelaos Metaxas as passengers. The car was speeding down Syngrou Avenue, the first road in Athens comparable to those in other European cities. The avenue was, and is, an arrow-straight thoroughfare running from central Athens to the coast, and ever since has been a favourite for speeders.[38] As he raced down the road, another car drew up alongside at high speed. It was driven by his friend Nikolaos Simopoulos, a wealthy parliamentary deputy whose father was the finance minister at the time. Simopoulos was the first businessman to import and sell cars in Greece and he liked to show them off by roaring through the empty streets of the capital. On that day he may have wanted to demonstrate a new car to Andrew and interest him as a potential buyer.[39]

Hurtling at high speed down Syngrou Avenue with Andrew driving alongside, Simopoulos hit a young woman named Euphrosyne Vamvaka (or Kalogeras) who was crossing the road. It was too late for Andrew to stop, and he, too, ran over the unfortunate woman, who was killed. One of Vamvaka's children narrowly escaped with its life. At the inquest Simopoulos claimed that he did not actually hit the victim, who instead had been pushed in front of the Prince's car by the wind of passage from his own. According to the coroner's report Vamvaka may have still been alive before being hit by Andrew's car, which seems to have done the greatest damage. Alice received the shock of her life; eyewitnesses reported her as breaking down in hysterics at the sight of the victim's mangled body. Simopoulos fled from the scene in panic while Andrew kept his cool and transported the body to the hospital.[40] Andrew was questioned by a prosecutor for two hours in the palace about the accident but no charges were brought against him. Andrew's short-sightedness may well have been a factor but was delicately left unmentioned by prosecutor and press, as it had not been common knowledge. Most newspapers, however, tended to blame the Prince for Vamvaka's death anyway. Some reports gave credence to local gossip to the effect that the Prince's car may have been the only one involved in the accident and that Simopoulos was purposely framed as a scapegoat to enable the royal family to escape scandal. But the available evidence does not bear out this theory.

Andrew paid all the expenses of Vamvaka's funeral. Alice sent a wreath with a touching message she had personally written. King George sent a wreath of flowers in the shape of a cross. There is no record of Alice mentioning this event in later years, but it may well have affected her psychologically. Interestingly, though Alice and Andrew were often mentioned in the foreign press, at the time Vamvaka's death went unrecorded outside Greece, hence its non-appearance in biographies written in other countries. The inquest put most of the blame on Simopoulos but also on the victim. Its main recommendation was that car owners 'should be careful not to run over pedestrians since there is the possibility of killing them.' The incident was shelved and quickly forgotten.[41] No-one was punished for Vamvaka's death and even though charges of involuntary manslaughter were brought against Simopoulos, he was never brought to trial, as he had parliamentary immunity, and by the time his immunity lapsed he was protected by the statute of limitations. Nearly fifteen years after the accident, in 1921, Simopoulos' daughter Virginia was one of Alice's ladies-in-waiting who attended the baptism of her son Philip at Corfu. (In fact Virginia Simopoulos would remain a close friend and lady-in-waiting to Alice until the former's death in January 1955.)

The death of Euphrosyne Vamvaka represented a low point of popularity for the Greek royal family. The decline had started a few years before, in 1897, following the military defeat by Turkey when some newspapers began attributing all the nation's problems to the royals and their 'extravagant' lifestyle in a poor country. At the time Greece was also battling a severe economic crisis. The press made great hay out of the Syngrou Avenue accident as showing how arrogant and out of touch with the common people the royals were, when their young princes and their expensive toys could kill poor people – and get away with it.[42] There are records that in the few days after the accident, people threw stones at any car they saw in Athens. But Andrew was far from dissuaded from driving around.[43]

On 28 March 1907, three weeks after the tragic fate of Vamvaka, when King Vittorio Emanuele III of Italy was on a state visit to Athens, Andrew drove his father and Vittorio Emanuele to the summer palace at Tatoi in George's car. Almost all the cars then in Athens were used to transport the two royal entourages. Even the vehicle owned by Simopoulos, who was involved in the Vamkaka accident, brought up the rear (presumably for security reasons); in his car rode the chief security men, including the Director of the Athens Police, Damilatis, and a high-ranking Italian secret police official.[44] Damilatis had been among the first at the scene of the Vamvaka accident and put in charge of the investigation. He had told the newspapers that 'not all the blame should be attached to Mr. Simopoulos, for one can argue that the deceased actually committed suicide. Because if she had remained on the pavement, as her young son did, the automobiles would have passed her by and nothing would have happened. But by the look of things, the boy had more brains in his head than his mother'[45] – an amazingly callous statement by any standards. A photograph taken by Italian photographer Luca Comerio shows the car driven by Andrew arriving outside the palace at Tatoi with the two kings in the back seat. Next to Andrew sits Vittorio Emanuele's bodyguard. (We can assume that the bodyguard also kept a close eye on Andrew while he was driving.)

Thankfully this drive went off without incident. But in 1910 Andrew was involved in yet another serious car accident, this time without fatalities but with the King as his passenger. In September of that year the car collided with a peasant's cart and overturned it. Luckily both occupants of the cart were thrown clear and not injured.[46] Andrew and George stopped to check out the condition of the stunned peasants. One of them, named Fafoutis, physically assaulted the King and Andrew and threatened to kill both. Andrew tried to calm him down and Fafoutis raged that if he had his gun with him he would have shot him on the spot as responsible for his accident. Having escaped an assassination attempt a decade before, the King, shocked in his turn, pressed charges against Fafoutis for threatening his life. (This is probably the only case when George took legal action against an individual of the lower classes in Greece during his fifty-year reign.) Fafoutis fled into hiding and on 21 December 1910 was sentenced in absentia to a year's imprisonment.[47] The court's sentence appears to be rather lenient and probably was due to Andrew's testimony that Fafoutis was drunk and he was certain that he did not recognize the people whom he was threatening.

(But Andrew's automotive mishaps were not over. In 1926 he and Alice would be involved in a car crash in Roskilde, Denmark, having just visited the Glücksburg Chapel at Roskilde Cathedral where members of the Danish Royal family are buried. As Andrew and Alice were leaving the cathedral their car collided with that driven by a mechanic. Both cars were wrecked but no one was hurt.[48] Four years later Andrew would be involved in another automobile accident which was not his fault. A car in which he was a passenger collided with another one in the centre of Paris at the Avenue Foch. Both cars were badly damaged but again no one was hurt.[49] It is worth pointing out that even though Andrew was involved in four serious car accidents in just two decades, with the exception of the Vamvaka fatality, no-one was injured in these.)

In 1908 Andrew and Alice decided to live permanently in the summer palace at Tatoi. It is likely that as the family by now included two young daughters aged three and two respectively, Alice would have preferred the family to be somewhat away from Athens. But this move did not shield them from politics, as it was at Tatoi that they were confronted with the first big political upheaval since Alice came to Greece.

The fifteenth day of August is a sacred one in the Greek Orthodox calendar, and coming at the height of summer it's always a time for complete inaction. Perhaps that is why on that date in 1909 dissatisfied elements of the Greek Army staged a coup d'etat while the royal family was relaxing at Tatoi. The insurrectionists had a rather large bone to pick with Crown Prince Constantine and demanded reforms not only in the Army but also in society and the economy. The dissident officers, mainly of the rank of captain and below, complained that the princes in the Army enjoyed unfair privileges and tended to promote personal friends, not always on merit. To combat this they formed a clandestine organization known as the Military League (Stratiotikos Syndesmos) to push their aims. A prominent figure in this organization was Andrew's old fellow student and rival at the Military Academy, Theodoros Pangalos, in whose home the League was founded and where most of its meetings took place. Colonel Zorbas, the commandant of the Military Academy when Pangalos and Andrew were cadets there, was one of the few high-ranking officers to join the League and hence became the one who ordered and mobilized the 15 August coup.

The prime minister, Dimitrios Rallis, rang the palace that day to inform the king about the coup. The call was taken by a senior naval officer, Pavlos Koundouriotis, the King's ADC. Though Rallis requested urgently to speak to the King, Andrew came to the phone.[50] The Prince heard dumbstruck that among the insurrectionists was his own cavalry unit stationed at Goudi – in fact, his equerry was one of the ringleaders. This was 2 Regiment, which had been considered one of the most loyal to the King; nevertheless, its commander had been confined to barracks and the insurrectionists had taken even his horse.[51] King George hastened back to Athens that same day to accept the resignation of Rallis and his government and swear in a new government more to the Army's liking. A seriously embarrassed George toyed with the idea of abdicating and leaving the country with his family, but decided to stay on. One of the top secret reports of the Austrian ambassador in Athens in 1910 records that Andrew refused to leave Greece in 1909, and was planning to stay behind; as all his brothers would have left with George, Andrew would most probably have been chosen by the military as regent in his father's place. According to this report, Alice was the real power behind Andrew, having concocted plans for his 'regency'; Alice's ultimate intention was to eventually make her husband King of Greece instead of his elder brother, Crown Prince Constantine.[52] Though George eventually did not abdicate and leave the country, this reference by the Austrian diplomat shows that Andrew and Alice were the most attached to Greece. As we shall see, in 1917 and 1922 when the Greek royal family was forced to leave the country, Andrew and Alice with their own family tried to stay as long as possible; in fact, they were the last royals to leave Greece on both occasions.

One of the first moves of the new administration put in place by the military was to force Andrew and his royal brothers to resign from the Army. In Andrew's case he was merely suffering the fallout from politics, being made to share guilt for the abortive 1897 war with Turkey, though he had been a mere fifteen years old at the time. Alice believed that Andrew might have remained in the Army after the resignation of his two older brothers, Constantine and Nicholas, but he did not, and thus the issue is academic.[53]

As Andrew no longer had a commission in the Greek Army he decided to use the free time available to him to further his military training in Germany, as his brother Constantine had done, strengthening the link between the Greek royals and Berlin. As the Diadoch had married Kaiser Wilhelm's sister Sophia, so Andrew had married the daughter of another German, Prince Louis of Battenberg. (Yet by a curious twist of events Louis had settled permanently in Britain and was an officer in the Royal Navy.) For high-born European royalty, Germany was the place *par excellence* for military training. But his absence from the Greek Army did not last long. In 1910 Eleftherios Venizelos, the capable Cretan politician whom we have seen before, accepted an invitation by the Military League to govern Greece and implement the League's programme. After Venizelos and his Liberal Party won an impressive victory in the 1910 general election, the Military League was disbanded. But Venizelos tried a more comprehensive approach to leadership and suggested to the King that the princes' commissions in the Army be restored. Andrew was only too happy to return to the Army. A few months later, on 22 June 1911, Alice gave birth to another girl, Cecile.

Chapter 4

Troubles in Paradise: Balkan and World War

The 'Great Idea', as we have seen, was a pervasive populist policy aimed at clawing back old Greek lands from the Ottoman Empire. Strongly whipped up by a jingoist press, it was also a mantra of any politician who had even slight hopes of being elected to any position of power. Therefore, at the turn of the twentieth century armed conflict appeared inevitable. As professional soldiers, Andrew and his brothers were expected to be on the front line for the next round of battle; the debacle of 1897 was a humiliation that the Greeks yearned to avenge. However, this was not mere revanchism, such as the French dreamed of applying against the Germans after 1870, but aimed at the 'completion' of the kingdom of Greece through the incorporation of all territories of the Ottoman Empire where the majority of the population were ethnically Greek.

The outbreak of the First Balkan War in 1912 found Andrew as a major on the General Staff; he was promoted to lieutenant colonel in 3 Cavalry Regiment and placed in command of a field hospital. Prime Minister Venizelos had cannily arranged that Andrew should be kept away from any real front-line danger. When the Greek Army was operating in Epiros, between December 1912 and March 1913, Andrew joined the staff of his brother Constantine, who had been appointed supreme commander. Alice volunteered as a nurse of the Greek Red Cross, a decision that marked the beginning of the philanthropic work that later would endear her to the mass of Greek people. She had been inspired by her aunt, the former Princess Elizabeth (Ella) of Hesse, later Grand Duchess Elizabeth Feodorovna of Russia, who had founded a religious order dedicated to philanthropy, in the end becoming a nun and giving all her possessions to her order, a true saint. As a nurse for the Greek Army, Alice felt obliged to actually do the messy job of tending the wounded soldiers rather than simply don the uniform of a nurse for public relations purposes. In the field she assisted at operations and helped set up hospitals.[1] These actions have been well-documented in the letters Alice sent to her mother Victoria, reports by her friends who accompanied her and extensive coverage in the Greek press.[2] Alice worked tirelessly in the military hospitals and in this respect differed from her mother-in law Queen Olga and other female royals whose role was limited to visiting wounded soldiers and handing out parcels to them. Alice's work impressed even her cousin, King George V of England, enough for him to award her the Royal Red Cross in 1913, even though she worked exclusively for the Greek Army. Alice was personally thanked by Venizelos for her work during the war.

Alice's contributions in the First Balkan War definitely endeared her to the Greeks. Wounded officers and soldiers in the military hospitals were surprised to find out that one of the nurses tending them tirelessly and doing the most menial tasks was Princess Alice. For example, a Greek officer recorded many years later that as long as he lived he would always treasure in his soul the memory of Alice washing with her own hands the wounded feet of soldiers in the hospital while two other nurses held them down. It is interesting that this statement was made by an anti-monarchist in 1930, at a time when the Greek monarchy had been replaced by a republic, and the royals were in exile with little hope of ever returning.[3] However, Alice's popularity was not so much the result of her actual activities, that directly benefited only a few hundred men and a limited number of medical and military personnel. Neither was it the publicity, as the newspaper reports mentioned all the princesses as nurses of the wounded; Alice's sisters-in-law, Princesses Ellen and Marie Bonaparte, for example, also had volunteered as nurses and financed field hospitals for the wounded soldiers, and Constantine's wife Sophia founded her own charitable establishment. Besides, many newspaper readers suspected a certain degree of exaggeration.

In fact Alice won the affection of the Greek people for an initiative she publicized on 6 October 1912, the same day that Greece entered the First Balkan War and a few days before she left for the front to start organizing hospitals. On that day she made a public appeal in the press requesting help for the conscripted soldiers and their families. Alice's initiative resonated throughout Greece and beyond its borders to the Greek communities abroad. This request eventually benefited not just the few hundred wounded but many thousands of soldiers and laid the groundwork for aid organizations for conscripts who would fight Greece's wars in the next forty years. Alice's appeal united all Greeks in a way no other person could do, by addressing everyone, rich and poor. Her words touched a chord with their sense of honour, addressing them as equals:

> I would like to supply as soon as possible garments to each conscript that our country has called to arms… I will accept the penny of the poor and the contribution of the wealthy… I am certain that no Greek, man or woman, will deny me the contribution that I ask for the sons of our beloved country.

Alice went on to ask Greek women to come to the palace and work with her sewing the soldiers' clothes.[4] The response was tremendous and instantaneous. Almost overnight Alice morphed from just another 'foreign' princess into a Greek household name. Hundreds of women went to the palace in response and filled its halls; the number of volunteers was so large that even Queen Olga had to help Alice oversee the work of sewing the clothes.[5] The day after the appeal was published, one of the most popular Greek poets, Ioannis Polemis, wrote a poem entitled *For Princess Alice* that appeared on the front page of the newspaper *Estia*. The poem bursts with lyric praise of Alice and was later set to music by the composer Samaras, famous for putting music to the Olympic Hymn which is still played at the Games' opening ceremonies. Alice's song became an instant hit. The newspapers published the names of donors to Princess Alice's Soldiers' Fund and the sums they donated. The donors vied among themselves for recognition of their generosity. Polemis went on to write a series of patriotic poems praising the conscripts fighting the war, while Samaras, put them, too, to music – all published in *Estia* in the form of a special supplement.[6] The supplement at once sold out its first print run of 2,000 copies, all proceeds going to Alice's fund. Schools and other organizations ran appeals to collect money which they turned over to the palace. It was the first time that Greeks gladly and voluntarily gave money to the royals!

Alice at the time, however, seems not to have realized how great an impact her campaign made, as she had left Athens a few days after the outbreak of war. There was little effort on the part of the state to provide the conscripts with items other than military equipment. Underwear, for example, was in short supply and most soldiers lacked woollen garments. There was almost no care for the families back home. Alice aimed to supply the armed forces with 125,000 vests corresponding to the number of conscripts in the Greek Army in 1912, a colossal task. She wrote to her mother that on her way to the front to organize military hospitals she saw soldiers wearing garments made by the girls at the Embroidery School.[7] Thousands of soldiers were adequately clad thanks to Alice.[8] (In fact, long after 1912, whenever there was a war and conscripts were called to arms, the organization that Alice created provided them with the necessary clothing, especially during the Greek-Italian War of 1940–41, when consignments of woollies saved the lives of countless Greek soldiers fighting in atrocious winter conditions in the mountains of Albania.) There was, of course, a downside: Crown Princess Sophia (and Queen from March 1913), who as we have seen was envious of Alice's popularity even before the Balkan wars, after 1912 could no longer hide in public her feelings about her sister-in-law and on one occasion lashed out at Andrew about her activities.[9] Inevitably, rivals at the palace would have seen Alice's efforts as publicity seeking and playing to the gallery, which they almost certainly were not.

As we have seen, the First Balkan War ended well for Greece but sadly also in the March 1913 assassination of George I in Thessaloniki. Prince Nicholas, the military commander of the city, cabled the tragic news to Andrew in Athens. It was Andrew who told his mother, Queen Olga.[10] He accompanied her to Thessaloniki with other members of the family on board a destroyer which brought George's body back to Athens for burial. From his father Prince Andrew inherited the palace of Mon Repos on Corfu, into which he and his young family moved on a permanent basis. The end of the Balkan Wars, it was hoped, would usher in a period of peace and stability for Greece. The country had to digest large chunks of territory wrested from the dying Ottoman Empire and Bulgaria and incorporate them into a functioning Greek state. In the space of less than a year Greece had almost doubled in size and population. Meanwhile, life at Mon Repos proceeded peacefully; on 26 June 1914, Alice gave birth there to a fourth daughter, Sophie. It seemed that she would be the final member of the family.

After the assassination of George I, Constantine found himself King at the mature and experienced age of forty-five. Tall and prematurely bald, he was described by one of his staff as 'honest and frank, very observant, persistent and courageous.' The same officer, however, listed the new King's weaknesses as a lack of initiative, an inclination to laziness and excessive readiness to be influenced by others out of a naïve faith in their frankness.[11] Constantine used his newly-restored popularity among the Greeks to directly interfere in politics. This tendency was a prime cause of what became known as the National Rift (*Ethnikos Dikhasmos*), which pitted royalist against republican for the next thirty years. Instead of scrupulously remaining above the fray as his title, King of the Hellenes, demanded, the impulsive Constantine set himself up essentially as a political leader heading the royalist faction, with Venizelos heading the anti-royalist party. And thus divided, Greece sat uneasily neutral while Europe in 1914 hurtled into the holocaust of world war.

It was a war that King Constantine was determined to stay out of. For all his marriage kinship with the Kaiser, for all his admiration of German strength and efficiency, he firmly resisted any attempt to join the German cause. Wilhelm, in fact, before the war had haughtily written to his brother-in-law: 'In case of war you must be at my side.' Otherwise, he warned, he would withdraw Constantine's honorary German Army marshal's baton.

The King's reply came swift and cutting – and in precise English: 'You can stuff it up your arse.'[12]

It was at home that Constantine had to fight his real war – against the adherents of Venizelos, who himself was not a fanatical republican but who found himself leading voters who were. Venizelos also was winning elections, which made him an opponent to be wary of. He also, crucially, from the beginning of the war backed the Entente and wanted to enlist Greece into the cause. Twice the King managed to manoeuvre Venizelos out of power, and twice was stymied by the latter's election victories. Constantine's judgement has been severely criticized here. It may be that poor health – he became seriously ill with pleuritis – affected his thinking. He was, rightly or wrongly, believed to be influenced by his wife Sophia and her German entourage. Even after the immediate illness passed – thanks, according to legend, to a miracle-working icon brought in specially from the island of Tinos – Constantine's health never really recovered.

In order to prod Greece into a more pro-Entente stance, British and French forces occupied parts of northern Greece in 1915 – the year of the ill-fated Gallipoli campaign. The move triggered a counter-move by German and Bulgarian troops, adding to the confusion. Greece was only just hanging on to neutrality. The following year Venizelos formed his breakaway National Defence (*Ethniki Amyna*) government which, based in Thessaloniki, declared war on the Central Powers. Greece was now split in two: the neutral southern part under the control of Constantine, and the pro-Entente north under Venizelos. At this point the British and French decided that overt force was required to remove the King. What followed was what one leading historian of modern Greece has called 'the most grotesque instance of foreign intervention that Greece had ever experienced.'[13]

Prince Andrew, as was to be expected, lent his full support to his brother and his neutrality policy. The position of Alice, however, was peculiar, since on the one hand she belonged to the German royal Battenberg family, but on the other, her mother was British. Her father Louis, an officer in the Royal Navy and First Sea Lord at the beginning of the war, sent a loud echo down through subsequent British history by changing his surname Battenberg into its nearest English equivalent, Mountbatten (as George V, also de-Germanizing, would take on the new name of Windsor in 1917). Yet Alice remained faithful to her Greek family by supporting Constantine's neutrality. This, of course, did not go down well with the Entente powers, but they couldn't do much about it – yet. Andrew spent most of the First World War as a colonel, first in 3 and then 1 Cavalry Regiment. In early 1916 Andrew was in Thessaloniki where he oversaw the evacuation of Greek troops as the city was being occupied by the Allies.[14] While he was there, the city was bombed for the first time by German aircraft that had taken off from Bulgaria; one of the bombs exploded close to where Andrew was riding his horse, nearly killing him.[15] Alice had accompanied him to Thessaloniki and also faced danger from the German air raid.

The year 1916 was a crucial one for Greece and Constantine. Britain and France were stuck in bloody stalemate with Germany on the Western

Front. Hardball was the name of the game, especially concerning piddling Balkan countries such as Greece that had to be wrenched into line. But the Foreign Office's policy on Greece was far from coherent; a British intelligence officer, Captain Compton Mackenzie, was sent to Athens to actively, and if necessary clandestinely, intervene in favour of Venizelos and his liberals. The issue became urgent after the Greek government surrendered the frontier fort of Rupel to the Bulgarians, allies of the Germans; this left the whole of eastern Macedonia open to enemy attack. The British and French, rightly or wrongly, attributed the move to German pressure – was not Constantine the Kaiser's brother-in-law? The Entente, though, chose to ignore the many signs that Constantine had not the slightest intention of becoming a German ally and in fact rather despised Wilhelm. All he wanted was to keep Greece out of the bloodletting. Even Mackenzie, committed as he was to the Allied cause and distrustful of the Greek royalists, was soon at the point of asking himself 'whether indeed there were stupider people than those selected to represent the brains of Great Britain in war.'[16]

Mackenzie was in a front-row seat to witness the sheer bullying of Greece that London and Paris now undertook – and of which he heartily approved. The country had a friend, however, in the British ambassador, Sir Francis Elliot, who vainly tried to explain matters to his boss, Foreign Secretary Sir Edward Grey. Lord Grey's only reaction was to wearily dismiss what he saw only as 'tiresome Greek complications', but he was soon out of office. It was the French, in fact, who decided to play bad cop by roughly trying to force the King out. France had long dreamed of building a sphere of influence in the East Mediterranean, to replace the Ottoman Empire and include Greece in it.

In the spring of 1916 King Constantine attended a glittering service in Athens Cathedral to mark Saint Constantine's day. As the priests chanted, Greeks were reading in their newspapers the badly-reported news of the battle of Jutland which gave the erroneous impression that it had been a British defeat. Then they would look up and see German and Austro-Hungarian diplomats in their most dazzling uniforms rolling up to the Cathedral. A small boy had the temerity to hit the carriage with the British representative in it, only to be hauled off by the police. Also there was a chagrined Venizelos, 'in unrelieved black.' He had not yet taken the momentous step of forming his breakaway government in Thessaloniki, and many were wondering whether he might be having second thoughts.

But the French were impatient. Without consulting the British diplomatic mission in Athens, they slapped a naval blockade on the port of Piraeus, Greece's main entry port for imported foodstuffs and other vital provisions. Lord Grey lamely went along with the move, but Elliot refused to accept the Foreign Office's excuse, namely, that it was being done at Venizelos' request. In the midst of this confusion royalist mobs in Athens began attacking the offices of liberal newspapers and moved threateningly on the British Legation. From his office there, Mackenzie listened to 'the sounds of riot and destruction that were to my ears as musical as the song of the nightingales.' The royalists were giving themselves a bad image. To Mackenzie, Venizelos 'was a devoted friend of the Entente' and deserved all the British help he could get. And when an Allied fleet was reported heading for Piraeus to enforce its will, he was there to watch.

On a blazing hot day in June 1916, Constantine's troops marched down to Piraeus to repel any attempt at a landing by the Allies. A battle seemed imminent until the evening, when a relieved Elliot was told that the King's government had caved in to French pressure and agreed to let Entente troops enter northern Greece. At this critical juncture in his relations with the Allies, Constantine decided to send Andrew as an intermediary to London and Paris to assure their respective governments that Greek neutrality was not aimed against the Entente and did not favour the Central Powers.[17] Constantine considered Andrew quite up to the task as intelligent and retaining close ties to Britain, as he often visited the country and Alice's relatives. Andrew thus gave the impression that, even though fiercely loyal to Constantine, he was the Greek royal most favourably disposed towards the Allies. The German military attache in Athens got wind of Andrew's mission and sent an urgent telegram to the German General Staff in Berlin. In it he recorded the exact date that he was leaving for his trip (10 July 1916) and that the official reason for it would be that Andrew was to visit relatives in Britain and France. The telegram ended with the observation that Andrew was capable for this mission as he knew well the military situation in Greece.[18] On 10 July 1916 Andrew left Greece on his undercover diplomatic mission, accompanied by his ADC Menelaos Metaxas who appears to have played an active role in the subsequent meetings.

They spent more than two months in England during which Andrew had meetings at the Foreign Office; nothing positive came out of these. In late September 1916 Constantine sent Andrew an urgent telegram to go immediately to Paris and await further instructions there.[19] Andrew's visit to Paris turned out to be very brief as the fanatically republican French were openly hostile towards King Constantine and bluntly told Andrew that they had nothing to discuss with him. Andrew and Metaxas left Paris for Naples where a Greek destroyer picked them up for their trip home.[20] It was Constantine's anxiety about what Andrew was told in London and Paris that made him send one of the fastest ships in the Greek Navy to bring Andrew back to Greece. The king is likely to have already suspected that his brother's diplomatic mission was a failure as by this time Constantine – or 'Tino', as the Allied press was mockingly calling him – was suspected of aiding Germany simply by his neutral stance.[21] But this suspicion was not limited just to Constantine. By the summer of 1916 many in France and Britain considered the whole Greek royal family, including Andrew, to be pro-German. In high quarters in England there was barely-veiled suspicion that Andrew might be a German agent who used the occasion to spy on Britain while travelling there.

While Andrew was still in London, in the afternoon of 1 September 1916 the Allied fleet under French Admiral Dartige du Fournet that was blockading Piraeus finally sailed into the port; it looked as if Entente troops would land there to march against Athens and force the Allies' will upon Constantine. When the British ambassador in Athens, Sir Francis Elliot, heard what happened, 'he picked up his top-hat and threw it on the floor' in his fury.[22] Elliot had just come back from conferring with the King and had come to a general agreement that Britain and Greece would maintain cordial relations; now this latest development would make him look like a liar. Elliot fired off a cable to the Foreign Office urging that the Allied naval expedition be cancelled at once. Of course, the Foreign Office had no intention of doing anything of the kind, content to meekly follow the Quai d'Orsay's lead.

Admiral du Fournet now took it upon himself to dictate the course of Greek affairs. 'The French design to establish a political and commercial supremacy over Greece was [being] taken a long step on the way to accomplishment.'²³ Soon afterwards, with French and British blessings, Venizelos left for northern Greece to set up his pro-Ally administration, accompanied by many liberal officers. Sir Francis Elliot's effort to heal the deadly rift between the King and Venizelos had come to nought. The Foreign Office now threw its weight behind the drive to get Greece into the war on the Entente side by fair means or foul, caring little for constitutional procedures or national rights.

Du Fournet demanded imperiously that the King's government hand over 32 batteries of artillery, 40,000 Mannlicher rifles and 140 machine guns. The government refused. Du Fournet then demanded that 10 batteries of mountain artillery be handed over by 1 December 1916, adding ominously that if he did not 'receive satisfaction' by that date, he would be 'obliged to take any measures which the situation may demand.' To counter du Fournet's threat, royalist reservists assembling in Athens were given 150 rounds of ammunition each. The European war itself was getting closer; the British ocean liner *Britannic*, a sister ship to the *Titanic*, had just been torpedoed and sunk off Kea, with the loss of thirty British soldiers and civilians. Britain's response was to use the Royal Navy to expel the German and Turkish consuls from nearby Syros, the chief island of the Cyclades. The presence of the royalist forces rattled Mackenzie, who feared for his safety and that of the other British in Athens.

Battle was joined on 1 December with the expiry of du Fournet's ultimatum. French and Greek royalist troops clashed around Philopappos Hill just south of the Acropolis. Du Fournet himself was so incautious as to have himself driven to the ornate Zappeion Mansion near the royal palace, believing that the mere sight of him would intimidate the Greeks; instead, he found himself surrounded by royalist machine-gunners. Some fifty French troops had been killed so far. Royalist sailors and several British Legation personnel exchanged fire until a frantic Elliot ordered his men to cease firing, rushing between the lines like 'an elderly gentleman waving his umbrella to stop a bus.'²⁴ Minutes later the legation was completely surrounded. Du Fournet had somehow escaped the trap at Zappeion and in revenge ordered two of his light cruisers to shell Athens; about sixty shells were fired, but caused little damage. One shell exploded near the Embroidery School, where Alice was at the time, and shattered one of the windows.[25]

To mollify the French, Constantine offered to surrender six mountain batteries. According to Mackenzie, a dud shell landing outside his window made him more amenable to a compromise. Du Fournet said he'd think about it and was driven back to Piraeus under royalist escort. The British Legation was filled with Venizelists sleeping on the floors out of fear of royalist reprisals. At five o'clock the following morning Mackenzie was roused by a British marine who, sobbing, described how a Royal Marines detachment had been ambushed by royalist troops from behind the wall of the main Athens cemetery. 'They just shot us down as we were, sir, without a chance to reply.' The stunned marine had been wandering around all night. All that day Athens resounded with the whizzing of bullets. Nevertheless, the Allies managed in the end to seize control of the city and forced Constantine to accept a ceasefire on 28 January 1917. They also compelled the King's government to admit (wrongly) that it had begun hostilities. The government was further humiliated the next day at the Zappeion Mansion where officers of Britain, France, Italy and Russia demanded that the Greek Army make a show of respect to their flags. Prince Andrew, who at the time commanded the 1 Cavalry Regiment at Athens, was chosen to represent the Greek military.[26] In a needlessly offensive 'Apology Ceremony' the Greek detachment of 2,000 officers and men had to march behind a Greek flag that was lowered before the flags of the Allied powers. Andrew, the highest ranking Greek officer in the ceremony, was given credit for maintaining discipline among his men who must have smarted under this blatant humiliation.

The Anglo-French blockade of Piraeus caused immense public hardship. The threat of famine was very real. At a time when Britain and France, as liberal democracies, were battling the autocracy of Kaiser Wilhelm, their harshness towards small countries such as Greece was quite equal to anything the Germans could come up with. Only the influence of Italy and Russia kept the Entente recognizing Constantine's government while – most irregularly – also recognizing the Venizelos administration in Thessaloniki. Then the Tsar was unseated during the revolution of February 1917, and the whole equation changed. Pressure on Constantine mounted, until at last it became intolerable.

In April 1917 a cache of letters by Greek royalists was intercepted by the Allies who published the contents in their newspapers. These letters were taken as proof that the Greek royals were not neutral, as they had always claimed, but some of them were even involved in organizing the royalist reserves who had attacked Allied forces in Athens during the previous year. One of the intercepted letters was purportedly written by Ioannis Metaxas, a colonel on the General Staff, once an ADC of Venizelos but a staunch monarchist and Germanophile; he was chiefly responsible for organizing the royalist reservists, and in August 1916 the Allies had pressured Constantine to transfer him from the General Staff. (Metaxas would play an important role in Greek politics over the next two decades, as we shall see.) The London *Daily Mirror* of 10 May 1917 used this revelation to launch a front-page attack on Prince Andrew. The article featured a photograph of Andrew and (Menelaos) Metaxas in London in 1916, alongside Andrew's sister Maria and her two daughters who at the time were living there. The headline was: 'How Prince Andrew of Greece repays our hospitality' and in the caption Metaxas is described as 'the Colonel on the General Staff who was a prominent member of the Germanophiles and an author of one of the incriminating letters'. As a result, the British government eventually barred Andrew from entering the country, though this did not include Alice, who continued visiting her relatives in Britain. Yet the *Daily Mirror* had committed a serious error in mistaking Andrew's aide Menelaos Metaxas for the latter's near namesake Ioannis Metaxas. Making the misidentification easier was that both were colonels. This slip-up, however, seriously dented Andrew's reputation in Great Britain.

The Allies were now even more determined to get rid of Constantine. The King, in chronic poor health, caved in and agreed to 'provisionally' remove himself from the country as a cooling-off measure. 'A long time ago I had decided to accept any Entente ultimatum by leaving my homeland with my family,' Constantine told his cabinet. 'What I will not accept is for even one drop of Greek blood to be shed for my benefit.'[27] On 2 June 1917, weary and heartsick, Constantine and his family left the palace by the back door, like fugitives.

On that day, troops in Athens that had remained loyal to the king were ready to clash once again with the Allies in an attempt to prevent his departure. But Andrew went to their barracks and talked the officers into accepting Constantine's decision.[28] Replacing Constantine as King at Venizelos' insistence was his second-born son Alexander; his eldest son, Crown Prince George, was deemed too much of a 'Germanophile' to be allowed to reign in Constantine's place. But it was not an abdication in the classic sense. Constantine had merely agreed to step aside so that political passions could cool and hoped to return after Alexander's stewardship (which indeed turned out to be the case). He still considered himself the King, with Alexander as his stand-in. Still, it is usual to style the new monarch King Alexander, as he became the *de facto* occupant of the Greek throne.

Venizelos left Thessaloniki and established his government of a reunited Greece in Athens. At first he allowed Andrew and Alice to remain in the country; Andrew was to stay to advise his nephew Alexander in his new duties. When Alexander took his oath as King, Andrew was there and so was Venizelos. Andrew wrote an angry letter to Alexander's mother Sophia recording that the 'poor boy' Alexander was in a precarious position having to confront Venizelos and the forces of the Allies in Athens; he described the ceremony as a hoax and heaped verbal abuse on the Allies and Venizelos whom he referred to as 'Satan', the nickname the royals would often use for him. Sophia recorded verbatim Andrew's words in a letter she sent to her brother, Kaiser Wilhelm II, to show how badly the Allies and Venizelos were treating Alexander.[29] During the next few weeks Andrew as the only brother of King Constantine still in Athens became a rallying point for the monarchists who were working for his restoration. Of course the government had him under surveillance and recorded all his meetings with the monarchists; Venizelos then decided that Andrew was becoming dangerous for his government and in July 1917 he was asked to leave Greece with his family, which they did.[30] Initially they resided in Italy but soon moved to Switzerland and lived a peripatetic existence between Zurich, St. Moritz and Lucerne for the remainder of the war.

In June 1917 Venizelos' power was at its peak. He could have abolished the Greek monarchy at any time. But the times were parlous. The First World War was still raging. National unity was precarious; the disappointed royalists had to be placated, which is why Venizelos engineered the accession of Alexander. The immediate problems appeared to have been ironed out, but beneath the surface all was not well in the palace. Friends of the King alleged that he and they were suffering political persecution. 'He was a prisoner in his own palace,' wrote his uncle Prince Christopher. 'His orders were disregarded... If he showed the slightest preference for any human being, that person immediately disappeared from the household.'[31] Letters to the King's relatives in exile were intercepted and never sent on. He derived some comfort from his morganatic marriage to an attractive Athenian debutante and his passion for fast cars. But friends (those allowed to see him) noted that his face had become thin and drawn.

Why such hostility? The stridently republican French certainly had something to do with it, having been the prime movers of Constantine I's deposition. It was made plain to Alexander that he was King of Greece on sufferance, probably just to please the British; if the French had their way they would almost certainly have turned Greece into a republic like their own vaunted one. The British were rather more accommodating. They appreciated what they saw in the young and genial, tall and athletic King who was apparently more interested in seeking release from the stifling palace atmosphere behind the wheel of a sports car than dipping in the Greeks' intractable political quarrels and intrigues. Alexander made a point of mending fences with the anti-royalist opposition whenever he could. He truly wanted to heal the deep royalist-republican divisions that had scarred Greece for four years and caused Britain in particular to worry about Greece's potential instability in that turbulent region of the Mediterranean. The Ottoman Empire was on its last legs, and Britain needed to keep secure the all-important connection to India that ran in a southeasterly direction through Greece (and Cyprus).

Though Andrew did not see any fighting in the First World War, the events of those years, and especially the 1917 exiling of the royal family, marked him for the rest of his life. In his eyes Constantine was entirely in the right and Venizelos was responsible for all the misfortunes of Greece and its monarchy.[32] True, there was little love lost between Venizelos and the royals, especially Constantine, but Andrew became the most vocal opponent of the former.[33] Apart from being the most dynamic royal, Andrew had been the most attached to his profession of army officer, and the fact that he was forced to give it up in 1917 fuelled his fury against Venizelos; in contrast Nicholas and Christopher were not so enthusiastic about the military.[34] Andrew considered the Greek Army to have been at its finest in 1915 until Venizelos destroyed it with his breakaway movement and adherence to the Allies; he was particularly critical of those officers who joined Venizelos in Thessaloniki, with some justification considering them opportunists who had rebelled against Constantine solely for personal gain.[35] After June 1917 monarchist officers, many of them Andrew's friends and including his ADC Menelaos Metaxas, were cashiered. Metaxas elected to join Andrew in Swiss exile, after helping the prince sell his cars.[36] Settling into a hotel in St. Moritz, they were not allowed by the Allies to communicate with Greek monarchists or even King Alexander. Alice suffered a further blow when she received news of the assassination by the Bolsheviks of her aunts Elizaveta (Ella) and Tsarina Alexandra.

Andrew threw himself into opposing the Venizelos government by any means available. He gave a multitude of interviews to the foreign press accusing Venizelos of undemocratic rule. On 20 September 1920, one month before the general election that Venizelos had called for 25 October, Andrew sent a detailed report he had drawn up to all the crowned heads of Europe, US President Woodrow Wilson and the prime ministers of Britain and France, in which he accused Venizelos of flouting the people's will in not allowing opposition parties to be heard during the election campaign and of planning to abolish the monarchy.[37] Andrew is also known to have met exiled anti-Venizelist figures on several occasions. But he is suspected of using more radical methods, and in early May 1920 incriminating correspondence to that effect between him and anti-Venizelist officers was published in Greek pro-Venizelist newspapers, with one ex-naval officer mentioned by name as 'Andrew's man in Greece'. Stephanos Paparrigopoulos, an ADC of King Constantine, as a staunch monarchist was cashiered from the Navy by the Venizelos government in 1917 and accused of supposedly plotting to assassinate Venizelos.[38] Paparrigopoulos denied the accusations and a subsequent investigation failed to find conclusive evidence.

As was expected, the government of Venizelos kept a close eye on the exiled royals in Switzerland, monitoring all their activities that had political significance, especially their contacts with Greek monarchists visiting Switzerland or the exchange of messages with those in Greece. A document dated 20 November 1919 and signed by Nikolaos Apostolopoulos, the secretary of Venizelos' political office, reveals fascinating details about these activities and how the government received information about them.[39] The document claims that all the activities of the royals and their contacts were reported to Venizelos' vice-premier, Emmanouil Repoulis, who handled domestic security. However, as this particular document shows, copies of the reports were also forwarded to Venizelos himself. Apostolopoulos' report came to the conclusion that of all the exiled royals the one with the greatest involvement in clandestine and subversive political activity was Alice! There is also reference to Andrew, but Apostolopoulos makes it clear that it was Alice who wrote most of the letters addressed to those monarchists in Greece suspected of plotting against Venizelos. He accepts this as undisputed fact, on the basis that all letters from the royals to recipients in Greece were intercepted and copied by government agents. The copies were then archived and Alice's letters form the bulk of this archive.

One of the recipients of the royal letters, including those from Alice, was Menelaos Metaxas. As we have seen, in 1917 Metaxas followed the royals into exile but was allowed by the Venizelist government to return to Greece some time later. Subsequently Metaxas made several visits to Switzerland and had meetings with Constantine and Andrew. While he was in Athens he kept in touch with the royal family by mail. According to Apostolopoulos, the letters Metaxas received from Switzerland informed him in detail about Constantine's health. However, the letters Metaxas sent to the royals were of particular interest to the government, such as one dated 26 July 1919 addressed to Virginia Simopoulos, Alice's lady-in-waiting, who had accompanied her to Switzerland. In this letter Metaxas informs her that Alice's father, Prince Louis Mountbatten (Battenberg), was to travel to Corfu, and that he had learnt this from 'Admiral Kelley' (in fact Admiral Sir John Kelly). The news was passed on to Alice and the other royals; the intercepted letter, in fact, was how the Venizelos' government learned of Mountbatten's visit which was considered highly suspicious at the time.

Apostolopoulos' report goes on to record that after Metaxas returned from his exile in Switzerland he set up an automobile sales business in

Athens. Was this business a front for Metaxas' real aim of keeping in touch with the royals without attracting suspicion? The government certainly thought so. From intercepted letters that Metaxas sent to a Swiss businessman it appeared that he sought to acquire a car dealership in Zurich and told the businessman that he should contact Prince Andrew to verify Metaxas' own bona fides. The report strongly indicates (without openly saying so) that Metaxas' business premises were being used as a front for clandestine royalist activity. In support of that claim the writer of the report cites an intercepted letter from Virginia Simopoulos to Metaxas to the effect that he was fronting the operation. Indeed, after Metaxas acquired the automobile agency he travelled several times to Switzerland. From there he would write allegedly coded letters to his wife in Athens, indicating that he knew he was under surveillance. Apostolopoulos cites a letter from Alice to a Greek monarchist according to which one of Metaxas' visits to Switzerland 'was greeted by the royals with enthusiasm'.

On his return from his last visit to Switzerland, Menelaos Metaxas was thoroughly searched by the police but nothing suspicious was found on him. Metaxas had with him a packet of fabrics which he said was a gift from Alice to the family of General Pallis (a leading monarchist and aide-de-camp to Prince Nicholas). The police found nothing suspect in the packet, but to Apostolopoulos' suspicious mind it could have contained some sort of subversive message, though he could not specify what that might be. Even Metaxas' sister, who also made several visits to Switzerland, was suspected of being a clandestine royalist courier. Eventually the whole Keystone-cops paranoia evaporated of its own accord.

Yet there was a plot against Venizelos' life, and not necessarily from the royals themselves. The attempt was made on 30 July 1920. He had just signed the treaty of Sèvres in Paris (giving Greece territorial rights in Asia Minor) and was about to board a train at the Gare de Lyon to return to Greece. Two Greek monarchist ex-officers who had been cashiered in 1917 approached him and fired ten pistol shots at him. Most of the bullets missed, but two hit him in the right arm. The would-be-assassins were arrested on the spot by the French police; they claimed that they had acted alone; but the following day the Venizelist section of the Greek press ran stories implicating members of the royal family, zeroing in on Prince Andrew as the alleged mastermind behind the attempt. In revenge, Venizelist fanatics murdered in cold blood a leading royalist politician, Ion Dragoumis, in Athens. (Dragoumis, ironically, had been a moderate who had worked towards healing the toxic royalist-Venizelist rift.) On both sides the fanatics were now firmly in charge.

On 9 September 1920 it was announced that an official investigation discovered evidence that the plot to assassinate Venizelos in Paris had been hatched at a meeting at St. Moritz between Prince Andrew and leading royalist figures. The report (which was careful not to implicate Constantine) claimed that as soon as news of Venizelos' assassination would reach Athens, Constantine's followers would stage a revolt and seize power with the aim of bringing him back, and that Andrew himself would travel incognito to Athens as a representative of Constantine in the meantime; Andrew strenuously denied all such allegations.[40] However, the arrest was ordered of Andrew and fifteen others on charges of high treason. Andrew, of course, was abroad and could not be seized. On 20 September the pro-Venizelist newspaper *Eleftheros Logos* ran a front-page story detailing Andrew's alleged nefarious actions in Venice and included details of two 'mystery men' seen with the Prince shortly before the attempt on Venizelos' life – a clumsy innuendo that Andrew had met the two would-be-assassins. The story was in fact a complete fabrication; all it did was to move Andrew to write a letter of protest to the editor claiming the made-up report was designed to influence the judges in the forthcoming trial of those arrested.

The so-called 'Conspiracy Trial' opened on 25 September. Andrew was tried *in absentia* in the company of other absent royalist politicians.[41] It was the first time in modern Greek history that a member of the royal family was in the dock, and under accusations that were punishable by death if proven. (Two years later Andrew would be tried again, this time in person, on a different charge also technically punishable by death.) At the time, the election campaign had just begun. Royalists denounced the trial as a mere witch hunt on the part of the Venizelists who they claimed wanted to destroy Greece. The political atmosphere, toxic enough after the attempt on Venizelos and the murder of Dragoumis, deteriorated badly. But an unexpected event that took place a week before the opening of the trial had far more serious repercussions.

On the morning of 17 September when Alexander was walking his Alsatian, Fritz, in the Tatoi Palace grounds, the dog began to play with a pet monkey recently brought by the grounds keeper; the monkey thought it was being attacked and turned on Fritz. Attempting to separate the fighting animals, the King received a nasty monkey bite on the ankle. As this was in the days before antibiotics, the wound suppurated. The conventional story is that sepsis set in, but according to ex-King Constantine II, it was the toxic dye in Alexander's sock that entered his bloodstream and poisoned it beyond cure.[42] Alexander died delirious on 15 October after a month of excruciating pain and suffering. He was just twenty-seven years old.

Of course, conspiracy theories abounded. It was common knowledge that it would have meant nothing to the Quai d'Orsay if an obscure Balkan monarch were to suddenly disappear. Then there is the issue of the medical treatment that the stricken King was given. According to the highest sources in the Greek royal family, Alexander could have been saved by an amputation of the lower leg and foot, but the doctors shrank from such a radical solution.[43] Against the theories of mistrust can be set the reasoning that if the French indeed wished to get rid of Alexander physically, there would have been plenty of more efficient ways of doing it with plausible deniability. The untimely death, moreover, solved nothing – in fact, it only complicated the political scene. Hence we can safely discount the rumours of foul play.

But as a consequence of that chance accident in the royal grounds, wrote Winston Churchill later, 'a quarter of a million persons died'. Greece had already begun its campaign in Asia Minor which would end two years later in disaster for its army and the large ethnic Greek population living there. As will be seen, Alexander's death and his replacement by Constantine was a key to that tragedy. The story of King Alexander continues to fascinate. He was a veritable icon of the emerging twentieth century: young and 'with it' (to use a phrase that became common currency much later), and showing every promise of a monarchy adapted to rapidly changing ideas of democratic and parliamentary rule. But this shooting star fell with tragic suddenness, giving an other-worldly aura to Alexander, almost a sacrificial victimhood considering the slights and insults he had to endure from the petty minions of the liberal state, all the time uncomplaining.

Alexander's death threw the contest for the Greek throne wide open again exactly at the time of a general election. The French distrusted Constantine's own first-born, George, as pro-German (even though the First World War had been over for two years and there was no more Kaiser in Berlin). Venizelos suggested sixteen-year-old Prince Paul, Constantine's third-born, but Paul refused the offer of the crown. The elections that had been set for 25 October were postponed until 1 November. The Conspiracy Trial was adjourned. When it reconvened one week before the election, the jury concluded that there was no evidence of a conspiracy and as a consequence all accusations against Andrew and the others were dropped.[44] The 1 November 1920 election was a resounding defeat for Venizelos who was forced out of power. In his place a coalition of anti-Venizelist parties supporting the exiled Constantine formed a government. In 1921 Dimitrios Gounaris, the most prominent of these politicians, became prime minister. The day after the general election Venizelos left Greece for self-exile in Paris, ironically as other exiles such as the Greek royals and many of their supporters were packing their suitcases to return to Greece.

The Greek royal family in exile was jubilant at Venizelos's defeat; Prince Christopher threw a celebratory dinner party which Andrew and Alice attended.[45] Though not as dynamic and vocal as Andrew in his opposition to Venizelos, Prince Christopher through his wealthy American wife, Nancy Stewart Worthington Leeds (aka Princess Anastasia) had made an important contribution to Venizelos' defeat by donating 30 million drachmas to the campaign of the anti-Venizelist parties.[46] The two would-be-assassins of Venizelos were eventually freed in 1923 after writing a personal plea for forgiveness to Venizelos and asking him to intercede with the French premier for their early release, which he did. Prince Christopher had paid the lawyer who defended them in their trial in France, Vincent de Moro-Giafferi, probably Frances's most famous attorney at the time. After they were freed one of them was hired by the Prince as caretaker of his farm in Greece, where he lived until his death at the ripe age of ninety-two.

Chapter 5

Andrew in Danger:
Asia Minor and Court Martial

The Greek government brought in by the 1 November 1920 election was understandably pro-Constantine; George I's widow, the Dowager Olga, became the Regent. (All dates are given in the old Julian Calendar that was used in Greece at the time, which was twelve days behind the Gregorian Calendar in use elsewhere in Europe.) She immediately sent a telegram to her children, Maria, Christopher and Andrew who were in Italy, informing them that they could return to Greece.[1] On 8 November the three siblings boarded a ship at Brindisi, setting foot on Greek soil at Corfu after three years in exile. There Andrew re-opened Mon Repos as his family's residence to prepare for his family's return. At Corinth the party boarded the destroyer *Ierax*, sent by Olga to take them to Piraeus. In charge of the destroyer was Commander Pericles Ioannidis. Princess Maria, whose husband the Archduke George Mihailovich had been killed in Russia by the Bolsheviks, formed an attachment to Ioannidis, marrying him in 1922. Ioannidis (whom some sources indicate was rapidly promoted to admiral) resigned from the Greek Navy and would follow Maria into exile when the Royal Family was once again ousted from Greece that year. In Athens the three royal siblings received a rapturous welcome from thousands of people.[2] These were mostly monarchists, but also there were others who may have supported Venizelos in the past yet had been worn out by a decade of wars and hoped that regime change would finally bring peace to Greece on a permanent basis. A week after Andrew's arrival in Athens, Alice, who was pregnant with Philip, returned to Corfu with her four daughters to settle in Mon Repos.

The main aim of the new government was to restore Constantine to the throne and for this reason, within three weeks of taking power, it organized a plebiscite for 22 November 1920. The result favoured the restoration of Constantine I, who returned to Greece on 6 December to a tumultuous welcome. Many people were tired of seeing their small country as a plaything of the European powers and desired a king to raise the national prestige. In the two weeks between the plebiscite and the King's return, Prince Andrew was Constantine's agent in all dealings with the Greek government. The British, French and Italian governments actively signalled their disapproval, but to no avail. Thus Constantine, rather in the manner of Napoleon returning from Elba, became a symbol of national independence.

But if this was a golden chance to restore the throne's prestige in the eyes of the Greeks, Constantine, to put it quite bluntly, blew it. For in the meantime Greece had got itself embroiled in another war. The defeat of the Ottoman Empire in the First World War had whetted Greece's old appetite for Constantinople, Smyrna and the ethnic Greek territories in the Asia Minor hinterland; here was the 'Great Idea' again, now unhindered by the powerless Ottoman sultan, and here was Constantine, almost miraculously back to fulfil the legendary promise of his name. The old mystic prediction that 'a Constantine would take back Constantinople' appeared to be on the verge of fruition. Greek troops, in fact, had marched into Constantinople already in 1919, as part of a short-lived Allied occupation, and had landed on the Asia Minor coast, having been sent there by Venizelos with active encouragement from British Prime Minister Lloyd George.

Constantine himself well knew that the Allies could not accept him, however much he might assure them of his friendly feelings. Neither could Andrew have much rest, as by now the ill-fated Asia Minor War had broken out. The Treaty of Versailles that ended the First World War had given the Greeks hope that with the Ottoman Empire finally vanquished the age-old Greek communities in Asia Minor could be brought back into the ethnic fold. This hope was given solid encouragement by the Treaty of Sèvres on 28 July 1920, though Venizelos himself had somewhat jumped the gun by sending the first units across the Aegean on 2 May 1919. That force was intended to be an army of occupation to hold Smyrna and the immediate hinterland until the treaty could become effective and hand the territory officially to Greece. The British in the person of Lloyd George enthusiastically backed this dream. At first the Greeks enjoyed some success, advancing through the dry Asia Minor gullies in the direction of Ankara, where a dynamic new Turkish leader, General Mustafa Kemal, was building up his forces for a counterpunch. The Army was not well led; the King had staffed the senior posts with royalists of questionable or no ability and hardly any strategic common sense.

Andrew was reinstated in the Greek Army and promoted to major-general. It was expected at the time that he would play a nominal part in the campaign, showing up at the front to distribute medals or hold a post with no real strategic authority. But he considered himself first and foremost a professional officer, even though he had not yet actually led men into battle. In contrast to Andrew, his brothers, even though all were trained officers, do not seem to have shared his eagerness to get involved in the fighting. Constantine himself was not in good health and thus not expected to actively campaign as he had in the Balkan Wars. Andrew's elder brother George had been living in Paris since the 1909 coup, after having been thrown out of the Navy while his brothers were dismissed from the Army. Nicholas and Christopher, though re-instated in the Army together with Andrew, wore their uniforms only to accompany the King on ceremonial occasions. The fact that Andrew was eager to join the campaign in Asia Minor is undoubtedly to his credit, showing a deep patriotism.

Turkish propaganda was quick to make use of Andrew's enthusiasm. A despatch from a reporter of the London *Evening Standard* at Constantinople quoted Turkish sources as saying that Prince Andrew had been shot in the stomach near Brusa, and had succumbed to his wound in a military hospital shortly afterwards. The report went on to say that Andrew's superior, General Aristotle Vlachopoulos, was also killed. The report, hotly denied by the Greeks, proved to be false. At the time Andrew was not even in Asia Minor but still in Athens, hundreds of miles away. Nevertheless, the bogus report made the front pages of most newspapers throughout the world for the next two days. Some newspapers even printed obituaries of Andrew, causing unnecessary distress to his family and friends outside Greece who only found out the truth some days later.[3]

Almost certainly the Turks had advance information about the Greek plans for the Asia Minor campaign. The Greek 4th Division was about to sail for the front, and it appears that Andrew had been earmarked as its commander. Andrew himself was sure of it.[4] The rumour somehow reached Kemal, whose propaganda machine fabricated the story about Andrew's supposed death on the battlefield. The 4th Division did in fact sail for Asia Minor in April 1921 but without Andrew. The false report may well have dissuaded the General Staff from sending Andrew to Asia Minor at the time; but Andrew himself insisted on being sent over as an active division commander. To mollify him the General Staff offered him the position of deputy commander of the Asia Minor Army – a post that sounded grander than it was, as it carried no real authority and would have forced him to sit in Smyrna, hundreds of miles away from the front lines. Andrew rejected the offer, demanding a 'real' command.[5] Finally, in early May he received positive news that he would finally take command of the 12th Division, to move into Asia Minor from Thrace to take part in a major Greek offensive in the summer.

In March 1921 the Greeks launched an offensive against the forces of Mustafa Kemal with the intention of seizing his headquarters at Ankara by the summer. The offensive, launched on 23 March from Brusa, was designed to take the Turks by surprise, but it was halted by stiff Turkish resistance at İnönü. Witnessing the action was Ernest Hemingway, an American correspondent with the Greeks. His verdict was that the Greek officers 'did not know a god-damned thing.' He saw Greek artillery firing into its own troops and a British observer 'crying like a child.' Another eyewitness was noted British historian Arnold Toynbee, who described the retreating Greeks as 'an interminable procession of troops, mules, ox-carts and lorries crawling along a foundered road.'[6]

However, May 1921 saw a revival of Greek fortunes with the capture of Eskişehir and Afyon Karahisar. At this point Constantine decided to go and take personal command, landing at Smyrna the following month – the first Christian king to set foot in Asia Minor since the Crusades. Other historical analogies abounded; Churchill thought the Greeks were engaging in their 'greatest campaign since Classical times'. 'I am leaving to become the head of my army where for centuries the Greeks have called home,' the King said on 29 May 1921 in a nationwide address. 'The entire past of our race guides our arms.'[7] The wording reveals the almost complete divorce from reality that the King had undergone.

He seems to have come close to believing that he was the legitimate 'Constantine XII' of Byzantium – a thoroughly imaginary connection which, however, carried much weight with many Greeks, especially in the country districts. (It may also have been a subconscious attempt to sweep the 'foreignness' of the dynasty under the carpet in the interests of patriotism, rather like George V of England's changing the royal surname from Saxe-Coburg-Gotha to Windsor.)

The Asia Minor offensive of 1921 is one of the most controversial military moves in Greek history, and it is customary to assign Constantine the blame for adopting an absurd strategy that ended, as it was bound to, in utter disaster. The Greeks pressed on into the vast Anatolian hinterland, incautiously lengthening their supply lines and in effect walking straight into a trap that was eventually sprung with devastating effect. But how much was Constantine really responsible for this? His grandson ex-King Constantine II goes so far as to claim that a reckless advance to Ankara was not the King's intention at all – he simply cannot have been that stupid. He certainly had no further need for military laurels, having gained his in the victorious Balkan Wars. Moreover, Prince Andrew, by this account, also opposed the entire campaign, as did the royalist Colonel Ioannis Metaxas, one of the sharpest minds in the Greek Army.

It was mathematically certain that if the Greeks continued to advance, Kemal would conserve his strength like a coiled spring and eventually roll back the Greek line – with the added inestimable moral advantage of appearing as a national Turkish liberator from Greek aggression. Andrew's diaries, so far unpublished, show that both King and Prince opposed an advance. [8] Then why, it is fair to ask, was it not stopped? Constantine's frail health has been cited as a factor; he was in constant pain from the cancer that would soon kill him. He may well have been influenced by one of his senior commanders, General Anastasios Papoulas, who saw himself in romantic terms as a soldier-liberator and yearned for the distinction of seizing Kemal and Ankara in one blow. Papoulas was often at odds with the King, but almost always got his way.

Then there were the British. The Prime Minister, Lloyd George, actively cheer-led the Greek campaign, in opposition to the French, Italians and Soviet Russians, who had decided to cultivate Kemal. The last Ottoman Sultan, Mehmet V, was weak and hardly a factor in anything.

In Athens huge and unrealistic hopes were pinned on Lloyd George, the victor of the First World War. 'The great man is with us,' it was said, 'and in his own way and in his own time and by his own wizardry he will bring us the vital aid we need.'[9] Rarely have such pious hopes been so brutally dashed.

On 29 May 1921 (old calendar) Constantine left Piraeus for Asia Minor, arriving in Smyrna three days later. He was accompanied by his eldest son George, Andrew and Nicholas, the prime minister and war minister, who wished to evaluate conditions at the front. The party disembarked at Smyrna to a rapturous welcome by the local Greek populace. Constantine tried to emulate the successful example of the Balkan Wars, when he had with him a group of trusted advisors helping him plan tactics that won battles. But Constantine was seriously ill in 1921 and this affected his judgement. He relied to a large extent on his brothers, especially Nicholas, for advice and even physical support so that he could stand up. He thus considered that a younger royal could do what he had done ten years earlier. But Nicholas and Christopher were disinclined to take up active commands, so in the King's eyes Andrew was the natural choice to be assigned a command in the Greek expeditionary force. Andrew would also act as the King's representative on the front and also reap the royal glory on his behalf.

On accompanying the King to the front Andrew was given command of the 12th Division that was incorporated into the III Corps. Andrew's appointment was officially announced on 31 May/13 June 1921.[10] He joined the division at a railway station 270 kilometres east of Smyrna on the way to the front that was outside the town of Afyon Karahisar. Interestingly, as military commander he used the formal title *Vasilopais*, meaning 'Son of the King', instead of the more usual Prince. On the march to Afyon Karahisar Andrew commanded the 12th Division in battles with Kemalist irregulars while seizing important railway stations. Control of the railway line from Smyrna to Baghdad that runs through the interior of Asia Minor was vital for Greek strategy. Between 23 June and 10 July the division captured Inei, Elbanlar, Afyon Karahisar, Çerkez, Ak In and Alpanos.[11] The most important battle was that of Afyon Karahisar which was taken by Greeks on 29 June. Andrew later claimed that the town was captured by his own division and not 4th Division that was also involved in the fight.[12] However, he also noted that the Turks evacuated Afyon in good order. On 2 July, 12th Division was transferred to I Corps, bringing Andrew under the immediate orders of the corps commander, General Kontoulis. So far the division's war record was good, redounding to Andrew's credit.[13] All the evidence shows that he did a competent job and succeeded in the tasks that had been assigned to his division. However, Kemal's forces, far from being crushed, were regrouping east of the Greek lines around Ankara and being supplied with modern weaponry by France, Italy and Soviet Russia.

While 12th Division was stationed at Alpanos, on 10 July Andrew was recalled from the front and told to assume command of II Corps. King Constantine, still in Asia Minor at the time, had called a conclave of generals, prime minister Gounaris and war minister Theotokis to plan the advance against Ankara. At this meeting it was decided to remove the II Corps commander, General Aristotle Vlachopoulos, who unofficially was accused of incompetence at the Battle of Eskişehir and blamed for the failure of the Greeks to continue their offensive against Kemal's forces after taking Kütahya and for not attempting to stop the Turks from retreating.[14] There was a short delay in implementing this decision to allow Andrew to get to his new post as II Corps commander. While driving from Smyrna with an entourage to take up his new command he was ambushed by about two hundred Turks. According to the *Chicago Tribune* four of his staff were wounded.[15] Even in the Greek rear Kemalist forces were active. On 5 August Andrew formally took over II Corps at Seidi Gazi.[16] Constantine would remain in the war theatre for the rest of the summer until continuing ill-health compelled him to return to Athens.

Andrew took over II Corps in time for a major offensive into the Asia Minor heartland planned for later in the summer. The requirements were immense, and needed the abilities of an experienced and talented general. Such, unfortunately, were in short supply and Prince Andrew was not one of them. A photograph of the Greek General Staff in Asia Minor at the time shows Andrew with the other corps commanders and their superior, General Papoulas. Andrew's youthful appearance stands out in contrast to the other generals, all elderly men with grey moustaches. Apart from the age difference, Andrew was indeed on a different wavelength from his fellow commanders, as would soon be demonstrated.[17]

In a book written later (to which we shall return) Andrew asserted that though General Papoulas was a loyal monarchist, he was an incompetent army commander, relying entirely on his staff for all important decisions. He was unstable emotionally, alternating bursts of optimism with periods of depression. However, though Andrew went into great detail about his own service in Asia Minor, he was largely silent on why he was given such an important command – almost one third of the Greek Army in Asia Minor – at a most crucial point in the expedition. The omission is at variance with the detailed and analytical narration of his military involvement. Having been promoted to major-general, and having successfully led a division, Andrew was qualified for corps command; but that did not necessarily mean that he earned the promotion on merit. It was essentially a political appointment. Moreover, 12th Division had fought Kemalist irregulars of questionable quality; Andrew as commander of II Corps would now have to conduct a major offensive against the best Turkish units Kemal could muster.

The King seems to have believed that it would raise the Army's morale if he put a corps under the command of his brother. He harked back to his own morale-raising role in the Balkan Wars nine years before, but failed to read the very different situation of 1921. This time he had very little of a capable and experienced officer corps to rely on; Venizelist sympathizers had been purged and replaced by men of either indifferent calibre or actual mental instability, as in the case of Lieutenant-General Georgios Hadjianestis, whose severe delusions would eventually get him shot. Andrew, with little enough military experience, and in view of his deep misgivings about the whole campaign, cannot have been a great asset. The purged Venizelists, at least, could boast of some experience on the Macedonian front in 1918 and were acquainted with technological advances in armoured vehicles and aircraft. Constantine's men were still fighting the Balkan War against an obsolete Ottoman army, not a dynamic innovator like Kemal.

The planned Greek offensive to take Ankara got underway on 21 August 1921. British liaison officers with Constantine's army were invited to a victory banquet in Ankara once that city was taken. Yet it wasn't Ankara per se that was the Greek objective but the crushing of Kemal's army in the hope that Turkish morale would collapse. But there was disagreement about how it should be done. Papoulas wanted to dig in at Eskişehir and lure the enemy forward to be cut to pieces; the King, on the other hand, wished to push straight on to Ankara in a spectacular move that would please the jingoist press at home. The King's view prevailed, and for ten days the long-suffering Greek troops marched on and on into the wilderness, running out of food and water in the fierce heat. The harsh conditions made worse a lingering financial problem that had plagued the Greek Army from the outset: there were simply not enough state funds to provision it adequately – another sign of incompetent staff thinking,

Kemal waited for the Greeks at the Sakarya River, protected by the loops of the waterway. Poring over maps, he saw the Greek Army as a 'long black dragon' creeping up from the west, 'so much thicker and so much bigger than ours.'[18] Kemal was anxious – in fact he told his aides he was quite prepared to die – but also cultivated a shred of hope that he could outwit the exhausted Greeks through superior tactics. In the opposing army, its commander in chief, General Papoulas, was well aware that his men were exhausted after their 200-mile march through the desert between Eskişehir and the Sakarya River with minimum supplies and in scorching summer temperatures. Though Papoulas had reservations about any further advance against Ankara, it was politics which dictated his tactics on the battlefield. The Greek government expected that the capture of Kemal's capital would force him to seek a peace settlement. Papoulas in the end accepted an ambitious plan for an all-out attack against the entrenched Kemalists at Sakarya drawn up by officers on the General Staff who had little knowledge of the real conditions on the front. It was a high-risk gamble for all or nothing: if the Greeks won they would have taken Ankara; if they were defeated their entire army in Asia Minor could be wiped out by a counteroffensive of Kemal's forces. Papoulas knew that the odds were stacked against him but he was not the sort of commander who would disobey the orders of his political superiors and try to reason with them. The Battle of the Sakarya opened with the Greeks attempting to turn Kemal's left flank from the south, but Papoulas in mid-manoeuvre changed his mind (a result of faulty air reconnaissance) and switched the attack to Kemal's centre, where in fact the Turks were strongest.

After the first clash, both armies hammered at each other fearfully on an 80km-long front for three weeks. The Greeks made repeated courageous but extremely costly attacks on Turkish-held heights, wiping out many defending units. But with Asian stubbornness the hardy Turks held on, though the steely Kemal himself sometimes despaired of the outcome. The Greeks gained twelve kilometres in ten days, a slow rate of progress that enabled the Turks to regroup after each Greek attack. As the opposing armies swivelled like a vast revolving door, it became clear that a long ridge one thousand feet high named Çal Dağ commanding the railway line to Ankara was vital; the Greeks attacked it vigorously, and for four days it changed hands confusingly several times. Kemal and his staff felt 'the iron curtain of doom' descend upon them as news arrived of Çal Dağ's fall; in his army lieutenants found themselves in command of battalions, such was the appalling loss rate. In one particularly fraught moment, 'two soldiers drinking from a spring looked up at one another and ran off in different directions – for one was a Turk and the other a Greek.'[19]

Kemal received unexpected encouragement when one of his generals in the field, Fevzi Pasha, telephoned him that the Greeks appeared to be exhausted. A devout Muslim who never lost his cool, Fevzi Pasha sounded convincing to Kemal, who at once called for more coffee to stay awake to plot his countermoves. Greek units, too, had been decimated, and lacked ammunition. Kemal ordered up reserves to hit the Greeks in the centre, but they were driven back in three days of ferocious combat. His army began to run out of shells. The Greeks were now digging in east of the Sakarya River.

As Kemal watched through his binoculars, a great cloud of dust arose from the battlefield around a conical height called Kara Dağ (Black Peak). 'The Greeks are fighting gallantly,' he told an aide. 'Their artillery is doing its utmost, and sacrificing itself to cover the retreat of the main forces.'[20] The Turks lost half a division capturing Kara Dağ, but the Greek advance was finally halted, and when that became obvious to the high command in Athens, the order came to pull back.

Technically the Battle of Sakarya was a draw. But Winston Churchill was right when he judged that it was a long-term defeat for Greece. The long advance into Asia Minor could only mean anything if the Greeks secured undisputed victory, which, however, was a political and military chimera. Services of thanksgiving were held in Greek churches, but they could not in the end conceal reality. Mustafa Kemal was lionized in Ankara, promoted to marshal (so far he had held no formal rank, commanding an army by his mere charisma alone) and given the honorific Muslim title of Ghazi, or Conqueror.

Prince Andrew's II Corps fought well at Sakarya, suffering disproportionate casualties in comparison with I and III Corps. The gains had been small for such a cost. After the battle there was much recrimination over which commanders had made which mistakes and for such small gains. Andrew as the King's brother drew perhaps more than his fair share of blame. He was accused of squandering men in a futile attempt on the height of Kale Grotto and then ordering a withdrawal without an order from his superior, Papoulas. In his own defence Andrew claimed to have been ordered by Papoulas into an ill-advised assault on Kale Grotto, and had no choice but to obey.[21] Andrew despised Papoulas as an incompetent martinet prone to hasty decisions. In the face of his corps' severe losses he had withdrawn it on his own initiative, ordering it to re-form behind I Corps in case the Turks went on the offensive. When Papoulas heard what the Prince had done without orders, he sent him the following stinging message: 'I am surprised that you have abandoned your positions and order the [II] Corps to remain in place. I, as the Army Commander, am the only one authorized to judge and take decisions.'[22] Two days later, however, Papoulas changed his tune and duplicated Prince Andrew's original order to re-form behind the I Corps.

This phase of the battle of Sakarya remains controversial to this day. Many writers (mainly Greek) have claimed it was Andrew's direct disobedience of Papoulas' orders that turned the tide at the Sakarya and robbed the Greeks of victory and the chance to capture Ankara which was Kemal's main base and capital. (As we shall see, that was what one of the witnesses, Colonel Ptolemaios Sarigiannis, testified at Andrew's court martial in 1922 and was highlighted in the newspapers at the time.) Other Greek writers, while not agreeing that Andrew's disobedience had any significance on the outcome of the battle as it had already been decided, assert that his order for the retreat of II Corps endangered I Corps by denuding its right flank of protection from the large Turkish force that was opposing it at the time. Whatever the truth of this assertion, Andrew was adamant that he did the right thing, as his men had been exhausted from the action of the previous days and had already suffered high casualties, besides lacking food and ammunition. The truth appears to be somewhere in the middle: Andrew did order his men to retreat, indisputably without such an order from the Army commander and this may have put I Corps at a disadvantage. However, the Turks did not make any move against I Corps, and it should be noted that until the end of Andrew's command the Greek Army had not suffered any major defeat even though the Battle of Sakarya was a stalemate. In Andrew's recollection, even Stylianos Gonatas, the I Corps chief of staff (and one of the leaders of the 11 September 1922 revolt, see below), agreed that the II Corps attack at Sakaraya could not have been implemented, and that whoever drew it up had no idea of the conditions on the front at the time.[23] (Andrew kept copies of all the orders he received from Papoulas and the General Staff and would publish them in a tell-all book several years later.)

As a reward for his exertions Prince Andrew on 1 September 1921 received Greece's highest decoration for valour (the Aristeion Andreias) from his brother the King. The medal appears conspicuously on his uniform in a photograph taken of Andrew, Alice, their four girls and baby Philip at Mon Repos on Orthodox Easter Day (3 April) 1922.[24] That, however, was scant comfort. Because he had acted without orders, Andrew was a convenient scapegoat for the stalemate of the Battle of Sakarya. Papoulas himself did not accuse Andrew of any dereliction of duty or have him arrested and court martialled; in fact Andrew remained in command of II Corps for a month more. But his superiors' displeasure made itself felt almost immediately, as on 28 August his chief of staff, Colonel Gaballias, was transferred to rear-echelon duties. Andrew knew Gaballias was a scapegoat for himself, whom Papoulas hesitated to touch because of his royal status (which is exactly what Papoulas would say at Andrew's court martial a year later). The Prince got the message, however, and immediately asked to be relieved of II Corps command, but Papoulas refused.[25] On 18 September 1921 Andrew requested and received a three-month leave; his second-in-command, General Digenis, temporarily took over the corps.

Between September and November Andrew relaxed at the family home at Mon Repos on Corfu. He finally was able to get his first view of his three-month-old son Philip, who had been born a few days after Andrew had left Corfu to join his brother's entourage in Asia Minor. Finally, a boy! Because of the Salic laws governing succession in the Greek monarchy, only males could succeed to the throne. Therefore large segments of the public were overjoyed at the addition of another male to the royal family tree, and Prince Andrew's own prestige would be raised another notch. As the next eldest sibling, Sophie, was already seven years old, little Philip was naturally pampered.

The name Philip was new to the Greek royal family and believed to be connected to Andrew's nephew, the deceased King Alexander. After all, Philip II of Macedon and his son Alexander the Great still shone brilliantly in the firmament of world history. Shortly before his death, Alexander learned that his wife Aspasia Manou was pregnant and expressed the wish that if his child were a son he would like it to be named Philip. Following the king's death, Aspasia Manou left Greece and gave birth in March 1921 to a girl she named Alexandra after her late father. Therefore it was Prince Andrew's son, born two months after Alexandra, who was picked for the honour of fulfilling the late king's wish.[26] On 24 October 1921 Philip was baptized at Corfu during a ceremony attended by all the local dignitaries and civilian-military authorities. The ceremony was a splendid official affair. Philip had two godparents, one of them symbolic in the form of the Municipality of Corfu represented at the ceremony by the mayor and other senior officials. The other godparent was his grandmother Olga, who could not attend, being represented by her namesake granddaughter, the daughter of Prince Nicholas.[27] Crown Prince George had been scheduled to attend, but had to go urgently to Smyrna on war duty. His wife, Princess Elizabeth of Romania, sent toys as baptism presents to baby Philip.[28]

Andrew returned briefly to Asia Minor in December 1921, still as commander of II Corps and a member of the Supreme Army Council at Smyrna that planned grand strategy. However, he did not actually return to Eskişehir, to take over from General Digenis, as by that time he seems to have decided that the whole Greek enterprise was doomed. He found a kindred spirit in staff Colonel Ioannis Metaxas, who, though an officer loyal to the monarchy, had refused to take command in Asia Minor, presciently advising the King that the campaign would never work. Andrew wrote Metaxas that the position of the Greek Army was precarious, and that if Kemal should make a major push, the Greeks would be overwhelmed. Better, he said, that the Greeks get out of Asia Minor before disaster struck. He also had little love for most of the influential Greeks of Smyrna, calling them unredeemed Venizelists hostile to the King and ungrateful for the blood already shed on their behalf.[29]

He did not mince words and undoubtedly put pen to paper under great stress. He was lucky indeed that the letter was kept away from the press, as it might well have brought down a charge of high treason on his head. Indeed, some of the more extreme Venizelist newspapers tried to make a case that Andrew inadvertently helped Kemal win the war. Andrew, on the contrary, blamed Venizelist officers conspiring in the ranks. He was no doubt sincere, but with his blast at 'Venizelism' he had made the cardinal mistake of diving into Greek petty politics. Andrew's incautious words were effectively turned against him by republicans and leftists in later years to discredit him along with the royal family.

Andrew's frustration with what was going on in the Greek Army in Asia Minor led him to request a new command. He was given that of V Corps in Epiros and the Ionian Islands, about as far away from Asia Minor as it was possible to get.[30] There was no fighting in Andrew's new post but nonetheless his foes charged that Andrew had been sent to Epiros to suppress their party as the previous military commander in the area was considered 'non-political' and hence too lenient with the Venizelists.[31] Again, this time despite himself, Andrew was being used as a pawn in the political tug-of-war.

When Andrew left Asia Minor the situation on the front was deteriorating fast. For Greece, Sakarya was what Stalingrad would later be for the Germans – the blow that turned the tide. Kemal's forces staged their grand counter-offensive in August 1922. Andrew's former command, II Corps, suffered a catastrophic defeat, many of its men killed and captured. Few of the prisoners were to survive and return home years later. The most illustrious captive was General Trikoupis, who had replaced Andrew as corps commander and had just been upped to commander-in-chief on the very day of his capture. (Interestingly, two decades later at Stalingrad, General Friedrich Paulus, commander of the German Sixth Army, would receive his promotion to field marshal on the very day of his capture by the Soviets; Paulus learnt about his promotion a few minutes before his capture, while Trikoupis learned it from his well-informed Turkish captors). Kemal and Trikoupis sat down to a soldierly discussion of tactics. Then Kemal, according to an account by Lord Kinross, held out his hand to the Greek general.

'War is a game of chance, General,' he said. 'The very best is sometimes worsted. You have done your best as a soldier and as an honourable man. Do not be distressed.' Whereupon Trikoupis declaimed theatrically that he ought to commit suicide, but didn't have the courage. Kemal narrowed his eyes at this lack of spirit. 'That,' he replied, 'is a thing that concerns you personally.'[32] Trikoupis' attitude, long on emotion and short on logic, illustrates the illusion the Greek command was under, and tends to buttress Prince Andrew's view that the Army leadership was incompetent.

The Greek Army, thoroughly demoralized, retreated chaotically to the Aegean coast to be evacuated; with them across the sea to mainland Greece went nearly a million ethnic Greek refugees. Smyrna was sacked and burned (Kemal's forces were accused of doing it), and its once-prosperous Greek population was either massacred or forced to flee destitute across the Aegean to mainland Greece. The war – ever since termed the 'Asia Minor Catastrophe' in Greek annals – ended with the Treaty of Lausanne of 1923. Never before had Greece been so humiliated. And to one middle-grade officer who had gone through the whole campaign in the front line, somebody would have to pay – namely, the incompetent commanders and ultimately King Constantine and his lackeys.

This was Colonel Nikolaos Plastiras, the commander of the 5/42 Evzone Regiment, which in 1921 had been under Prince Andrew's command. Plastiras was an anti-monarchist by conviction, one of the few officers who were. He had extricated his men from Asia Minor as best he could, with minimum casualties. On 11 September 1922 he and another colonel, Stylianos Gonatas, helped by a naval detachment, decided to move on Athens. A few days later a military aircraft droned over the city dropping proclamations calling on the King to abdicate. Constantine responded by proclaiming martial law, which had not the slightest effect on events. In mid-September Gonatas led an insurrectionist march on

Athens from the port of Lavrion 70 kilometres away. (One wonders whether it could have served as an inspiration for Benito Mussolini's famous 'March on Rome' that took place about a month later.) But Plastiras was the real force behind the revolt. The only reason he had been able to keep his post despite his political convictions was that he was a superlatively good soldier and popular with his men. He had been present in every conflict since 1912, distinguishing himself throughout. As Greece nursed its wounds, many erstwhile royalist officers – including General Papoulas, who was the supreme commander of the Greek Asia Minor Army but replaced a few months before its catastrophe, and Colonel Gonatas – switched sides and became fanatically Venizelist.

The people's bitter disappointment at the disaster in Asia Minor was cleverly exploited by Plastiras in his campaign to discredit the monarchy and all who served it. Plastiras lost no time in setting up a 'Revolutionary Committee' to run the country. Britain, of course, took an active interest in the proceedings, always on guard for any move that might threaten the Greek throne. No doubt there were many in the new government who wanted to abolish the monarchy altogether, but it was Constantine personally, not the crown as an institution, who was in Plastiras' gunsights. The leaflets dropped from the air on an unsuspecting Athenian population expressly mentioned Crown Prince George as the preferred replacement for Constantine. The distinction was carefully kept on 4 October, when the Committee issued a statement stipulating as 'enemies of the country' all who supported 'Constantinism' and urging their 'exemplary punishment.' The opaque reference to 'Constantinism' rather than royalism was no doubt deliberate, seeking to heap on one man the failings, real and imagined, of the royal system.[33]

Constantine at first did not intend to go quietly. Before Plastiras and Gonatas could march on Athens, the King's men sent messages to the villagers of the communities east of the capital, in the interior of the Attic peninsula, most of whom were firmly royalist and prepared to fight for their king – but not before they could bring in the grape harvest! Thus lacking support from the countryside, royalist officers were arrested wholesale. By mid-September Constantine saw that further resistance to the Revolutionary Committee was hopeless; on 14 September he departed for his second (and final) exile. In the absence of clergy of the requisite rank, a simple priest swore in Prince George as George II. There were, however, plenty of royalists left among the people, and when Plastiras saw the delirious crowds hailing the new king and government ministers hiding themselves away, he ordered a wave of arrests. The protagonist of these arrests was Pangalos, the old classmate of Prince Andrew. This second ejection worsened Constantine's already frail health. He had reigned just six years, but those years had been exhaustingly tumultuous ones. He was just fifty-five but looked a lot older. Four months later in Palermo, he succumbed to a massive stroke (some claim the killer was cancer; it could have been both).

It was clear that sacrificial victims were needed to slake the Greek press's thirst for blood. Making a mess out of the fabled 'Great Idea', howled the editorials, was nothing less than a national crime. So when Plastiras and Gonatas promised 'exemplary punishment' in their proclamation, they knew exactly whom they were going to punish and how. They were five former politicians in Constantine's government plus the commander-in-chief in Asia Minor on whose watch disaster had struck, Lieutenant General Georgios Hadjianestis. Before even the advance on Athens the insurrectionists meeting on board the battle cruiser *Limnos* had already decided to execute them after a fig-leaf court martial. Added to the list of those who required 'punishment' was Prince Andrew on the grounds of his supposed disobedience at Sakarya. As Andrew was also the only royal who held any command in Asia Minor, he was fair game.

Andrew felt he had nothing to apologize for. What really mattered to him was what the Greek people thought of his record. In later years he spent much time researching and writing a book in defence of his actions at the Battle of Sakarya, which he published in Greek in 1928 with the title *Dorylaion-Sakarya 1921* (republished as an English edition in 1930 with the title *Towards Disaster: The Greek Army in Asia Minor in 1921*). In his book Andrew analysed all his actions during and immediately after the battle of Sakarya. He tried to show that he did his utmost in trying to serve Greek interests in Asia Minor. But at the time his critics, who relentlessly attacked his record at Sakarya, were many and powerful.

Another cause of Andrew's unpopularity was his absence on a long period of leave in Athens during the summer of 1922, away from his post as military commander of Epiros at Ioannina. Though he was no longer on the front lines in Asia Minor, his absence from another crucial military post at a time when the Greek Army was suffering a disastrous defeat (August–September 1922) was noticed even by the British ambassador to Athens, who in a telegram to the Foreign Office recorded the criticisms levelled against Andrew from many different quarters.[34] At the time Alice and the rest of the family were returning to Greece from England where they had attended the wedding of Alice's brother, Louis (Dickie) Mountbatten to one of the wealthiest women in Britain, Edwina Ashley, on 18 July.[35] Thus while Andrew was blotting his copybook with the Greeks, his family was making quite a positive impression in Britain. His daughters, the four sister-princesses, were bridesmaids at the wedding. The British magazine *Tatler* on the cover of its 12 July 1922 issue ran a group photograph of the princesses lined up by age. It was one of the magazine's most successful covers and drew favourable comments from the British public, which appears to have forgotten its previous mistrust of Andrew over his record during the First World War. Pictures of the girls as bridesmaids at Louis Mountbatten's wedding appeared in many newspapers and magazines in Europe and the United States.

The infant Philip was taken with Alice and his sisters to Britain; during his uncle's wedding he was left in a nursery.[36] This was not Philip's first visit to the country, as Alice had brought him with her when he was a mere three months old in September 1921 for her father's funeral. At that time the baby prince was hardly noticed, but ten months later, in the shadow of his sisters, Philip did receive a measure of publicity. For example, on 30 July 1922 the *Buffalo Courier* of New York state ran a front-page story headlined: 'What is an English Wedding to this little Greek Prince?', accompanied by a large photograph of Philip as a cute toddler with a winning smile. The caption read:

Prince Philip, the one-year-old son of Prince Andrew of Greece, seems to think this wedding stuff is a huge joke. He recently arrived in London with his two sisters who were bridesmaids to Miss Edwina Ashley. Little Prince Philip is the only son and a great favorite with his sisters, but just between him and the photographer he thinks it is a good joke that they had to bring him all the way from Greece for the big wedding.

This was almost certainly Philip's debut in the international mass media.

However two months later these happy days had become a distant memory for Andrew, Alice and their family. On 5 October 1922, the Revolutionary Committee set up an investigative commission for the Asia Minor catastrophe headed by General Pangalos and including two colonels. The commission issued warrants for the arrest of prominent politicians and high-ranking officers charged with responsibility for the catastrophe. Andrew was told that he would not be arrested if he resigned from the Army and left the country immediately (as reported by the Greek press on 8 October).[37] The Prince resigned his commission but instead of going abroad, he returned to Mon Repos as a private citizen to be with his family. A few days later one of the colonels on the commission, Haralambos Loufas, was sent with the destroyer *Aspis* to fetch Andrew from Corfu to Athens. Loufas had a distinguished war record as one of the few commanders who had managed to extricate his unit (in his case 23 Regiment) from Asia Minor in one piece. The colonel took Andrew in custody and accompanied him back to Athens on 13 October 1922 to testify before the commission. The Prince may well have wondered if he was going to see his little son ever again.

As for the new King George II, Prince Philip's cousin, it was made clear to him that he would be wise to expect his reign to be a short one, and that during that time he had better keep quiet, to maintain the lowest of low profiles. George's hasty coronation came as something of a shock to him. His uncle Prince Nicholas noted in his diary that 'all these events, coming one on top of the other with amazing speed, have bewildered us to the point where we can't feel much any more.' George himself appeared hardly aware of the crown thrust upon him. 'By upbringing and nature very disciplined, he felt aggrieved that a group of upstart Army and Navy officers could take it on themselves to topple the legitimate regime.'[38] The new King justifiably felt all but helpless, residing in the summer royal residence at Tatoi and rarely venturing into Athens.

While in detention Andrew was told he was required to testify at an upcoming court martial of senior politicians and officers charged with treason, though it was clear he was not himself accused of anything – yet. One of the accused was General Hadjianestis, who was in fact the brother-in-law of an Englishman, Edward Law, who had been Viceroy of India in the early twentieth century and was a highly respected figure in the British establishment. Law's first cousin, Andrew Bonar Law, was actually Britain's prime minister at the time. Hadjianestis' sister had made desperate attempts to save her brother, backed up by Bonar Law himself and repeated representations by the British ambassador, Sir Francis Lindley, but to no avail.

It was a travesty of a trial, as Lindley knew it would be even before it got started. Under British and French pressure, Plastiras initially hesitated to press for capital punishment; but such was the counter-pressure from the extreme anti-royalist press that howled that the 'enemies of the country' be punished with exemplary severity, that he dared not display any leniency. Hadjianestis and five ex-ministers (including three ex-prime ministers) were in the end indicted on fifteen counts of high treason, all punishable by death. From the opening of the sensational trial on 31 October in the packed Old Parliament building there was little attempt to provide a level legal playing field; prosecutors and press alike called the defendants 'criminals' and worse. The deck was definitely stacked against them.

The trial brought out all the dirty washing, the strategic and logistical incompetence, of the ill-fated Asia Minor campaign. Hadjianestis, whose mental instability (he had bouts of believing his legs were made of glass, to mention just one of his delusions) was all but an open secret in Athenian society, blamed the war's outcome merely on bad luck. On the eighth day of the trial the British foreign secretary, Lord Curzon, made a point of meeting Venizelos on the sidelines of negotiations in Lausanne, Switzerland, for a Greek-Turkish peace treaty and argued forcefully that there should be no executions. Venizelos could do little; in self-exile at the time, he had no hope of changing the minds of the hardliners in Athens. On the eleventh day of the trial the prosecutor demanded the death sentence for the defendants; Lindley called on the minister of the interior and threatened to rupture diplomatic relations. Radical officers on the other hand staged demonstrations with the slogan, 'Death to the traitors!' At the stroke of midnight on 14 November the tribunal retired to decide on the verdict. Lindley made a final desperate effort to save the defendants' lives with a last-minute appeal to Plastiras, but the grizzled colonel dismissed him roughly. In the early hours of the following day the verdict was issued: death by firing squad for Hadjianestis and the five civilians. King George had little choice but to sign the order.

Early in the morning the condemned were roused from their cells and put into two Army lorries for the ride of a few miles to a small pine wood behind the Sotiria sanatorium hospital in the Athens suburb of Goudi where the firing squad waited. One more final humiliation awaited Hadjianestis before his end: his dishonourable discharge from the Army. Before anyone could approach him to remove his insignia, he threw them away along with his braid-encrusted hat, shouting that his 'only shame' was that he 'commanded fugitives.' One of the ex-ministers opened his cigarette case and took out a last cigarette, with instructions that the case be given to his son. Another handed over his wedding ring to be given to his wife. All refused the option of a blindfold. A few final blessings by a priest, and the volley rang out.

Greece and all Europe were in shock at the news. A furious Sir Francis Lindley demanded his passports and boarded a train to leave Greece that night in a fury, after sending the Greek government a blistering letter all but severing diplomatic ties forthwith (however, a chargé d'affaires was left to run the embassy). The United States government warned Greece that the American Relief Societies that were doing much to alleviate the plight of the Asia Minor refugees might be obliged to curtail their charitable activities. Strong protests also came from France, Italy, Spain, Belgium, Romania, Serbia, Poland, the Netherlands and Sweden. Diplomats from all those countries were instructed to limit their dealings with the Greek government. *The Times* of London on 29 November carried a detailed report of the executions with the comment that they had badly harmed Greece's relations with the rest of Europe. Yet the hard men running Greece appeared to care little about what the foreigners thought.

Historical minds would have harked back to 406 BC, when Athens had tried and put to death six generals for incompetence during the naval battle of Arginusai against the Spartans during the Peloponnesian War. The condemned included a son of Pericles. The historian Xenophon's account of the trial has an uncanny parallel with that of 1922. Both were essentially political theatre staged for the benefit of the angry masses. In both cases the accused were deprived of adequate due process. And in both cases the result was preordained.

In Athens Andrew was not exactly jailed, but fairly close to it. He was told he could stay at his brother Prince Nicholas' vacant mansion. But by the time Andrew had arrived at Athens, the mansion had been taken over by the Red Cross to house refugees. So Andrew found a room in the home of General Pallis, Prince Nicholas' former ADC. Pallis himself had been arrested by the Revolutionary Committee as a chief suspect in the Asia Minor debacle.[39] Andrew was not allowed any contact with the outside world and had a guard at his door. The only other royal allowed briefly to visit Greece was Prince Christopher, who wished to donate money to the Asia Minor refugees.[40] Prince Christopher has described in his memoirs how Andrew was clamped in solitary confinement with a guard at the door and not allowed any visitors. Andrew could communicate with friends and relatives only through messages scrawled on cigarette papers used by his valet.[41] Pangalos saw fit on 17 October 1922 to publicly explain on the front pages why Andrew had been taken into custody even though he was not one of the accused. 'Andrew's transfer to Athens', Pangalos claimed, was dictated by 'the need for his presence here for the more complete conducting of the inquiry' and because the 'evidence made it necessary to impose his enforced detention and non-communication with others as ordered by... General Pangalos'. On 27 October the commission of inquiry decided it had enough evidence against Andrew's conduct in the recent war to send him to trial. The official indictment records that:

'Commanded on 27 August 1921 by Order No. 10531-6239/3/26-8-21 (2140 hours) of the Asia Minor Army, he failed to obey the order in the face of the enemy, specifically refusing by his Report No. 1491/27-8-21 (0730 hours) to the Army command and [instead] ordering the Corps to move in another direction'.[42]

If he were to be found guilty, the only sentence the court could deliver would have been death. It looked bad for Andrew, since the new regime clearly showed that it had no qualms in physically eliminating those it considered responsible for the Asia Minor disaster. Pangalos, as minister of war, had wide-ranging influence. According to Prince Nicholas, before the trial and execution of the six, Andrew was brought under guard to the office of Pangalos who interrogated him about the political and military personnel who had been arrested for the Asia Minor Catastrophe and were on trial. During the interrogation, Pangalos asked Andrew how many children he had. When Andrew told him, Pangalos reportedly said: 'Poor things, what a pity they will soon be orphans'.[43] That was the first hint that after the six, Andrew was to face the court martial and a possible death sentence.

However, unbeknownst to Andrew, even though the members of the Revolutionary Committee were unanimous that the six should be condemned to death and shot, there were disagreements among them about what Prince Andrew's fate should be.[44] This led to the decision to leave the matter entirely to Plastiras, the regime strongman.[45] Andrew's fate was thus in the hands of a colonel who in 1921 had been under his command. Plastiras was implacable in his desire for no mercy for those deemed responsible for the Asia Minor defeat.[46] It is generally believed that it was the intercession of a British naval officer, Commander Gerald Talbot, with Plastiras which saved Andrew's life. As we will see, however, Andrew's nephew King George II played the crucial role in this.

Nearly all the members of the Greek royal family had gone into exile with Constantine in September 1922. But Princess Alice had stayed at Mon Repos under police surveillance. When Christopher left Athens on his way to Italy, he called at Corfu and found Alice with her five children in great anxiety over Andrew's fate. Alice wanted to go to Andrew in Athens but Christopher could not accompany her as that would violate his agreement with the Revolutionary Committee and he feared he might be apprehended. He left Corfu for Italy and from there went to Paris.

Alice decided to go to Athens to be with Andrew at his forthcoming court martial. Her loyal friend and lady-in-waiting, Virginia Simopoulos, met her at Piraeus and accompanied her to where Andrew was confined; they were not allowed to see him and went to stay with Menelaos Metaxas at his house. Earlier that same day General Hadjianestis and the five politicians deemed responsible for Greece's defeat in Asia Minor had been executed; the news sent Alice into shock, as she now expected that Andrew would be next.

The trial of Prince Andrew opened on Saturday 19 November/ 2 December (old and new calendars respectively) 1922 in the Old Parliament Building, the same place where the unfortunate six received their death sentence four days before. Relatively few people attended, as the press had been told not to high-profile the event. Foreign reporters noted the lack of attendance; their photographs show no more than about fifty people in a room that could hold seven times that number. An unusual aspect was the relatively large number of women among the spectators, not common in trials of the time. Perhaps an aura of glamour had arisen around Andrew thanks to the fact that he was a prince, his conspicuous military service and attractive wife. There is no record of Alice's having been present at the trial, and neither, as far as is known, did she ever mention it in later life. However, the royalist newspaper *Esperini* reported on 19 November that Alice had requested permission to attend Andrew's trial and that her request had been granted by the Revolutionary Committee. She most probably did attend, as while Andrew was awaiting the verdict she accompanied him to the Pallis house. The experience might well have deeply scarred her, which could account for why she never referred to it. In one of the photographs of the trial a woman – very likely Alice– can be seen in the audience looking at Andrew with a worried expression.[47]

A hitherto unpublished photograph from the trial shows over twenty officers seated as tribunal members – almost all Revolutionary Committee supporters – next to and behind the president of the court and the prosecutors. The sight of the sheer weight of brass would have been intimidating to Andrew, the sole defendant. It would certainly have been for Alice, assuming she was present. Four witnesses for the prosecution testified at Andrew's trial, including General Papoulas and the division commanders of II Corps present at the Sakarya. Among the witnesses was Colonel Ptolemaios Sarigiannis, who had been on the General Staff of the Asia Minor Army and had helped plan the 1921 offensive.[48] The only witness for the defence was a journalist named Nikolaos Karvounis, who in August 1921 had been with Andrew's staff on the front line.[49]

Remarkably, the testimony of the prosecution witnesses, with the exception of that of Colonel Sarigiannis, tended to support Andrew.[50] The correspondent Karvounis asserted that Andrew's conduct in Asia Minor as commander of 12th Division and II Corps had been impeccable.[51] The assertion was backed up by a letter from a subordinate, Major Ioannis Tsangarides, who had been seriously wounded during the Greek advance on Kale Grotto; this officer had asked to testify at the court martial but his request was denied. So he wrote a letter in Andrew's defence which Karvounis read out in the trial.[52] Tsangarides' letter seemed to impress the judges. especially as he had been an ardent supporter of the Plastiras revolution. But the tribunal president threw it out as evidence as 'expressing personal views not relevant to the case being tried'.[53]

It was Sarigiannis who pinned all the blame for the defeat at Sakarya on Andrew's decision to withdraw II Corps from the front line. According to Sarigiannis, Andrew's precipitate action prevented the Greeks from seizing Ankara. He also described Andrew as incompetent and deliberately insubordinate.[54]

The Prince was in civilian dress in court, prompting an American correspondent to remark that 'he failed to give the impression of a virile general defending his actions during the war.'[55] But this was to be expected, as Andrew had already resigned from the Army. Foreign journalists also noted that the defence of Andrew, conducted by a noted lawyer named Damaskinos, was very competent (something that does not appear in the Greek press reports). Photographs show that next to Damaskinos sat a colonel keeping notes; one photograph shows them conversing. It is likely that this officer had been assigned as Andrew's military defence counsel, as this was a court martial, not a civil trial.

Andrew defended himself stoutly, rebutting the prosecution's charges. According to foreign press reports he was rather emotional at the start of the trial but as the hearing proceeded he became more relaxed in cross-examining the witnesses. At the close of the trial he read out a statement in which he refuted the charges and pleaded that he did his best at Sakarya under difficult circumstances. However, the way that Andrew read the statement gave the impression that it had been written for him and that he was seeing it for the first time.[56] Photographs from the trial show Andrew holding a paper – possibly his statement – and gazing at it. His main point was that as a royal he was simply a figurehead and should not be considered as a 'normal' professional general officer. It was frankly casuistry, and foreign press reports hinted at something of the kind.[57] Yet it seemed to carry weight with the tribunal.[58]

At 8pm the judges retired to consider the verdict, which was delivered at 11.15pm.[59] Not surprisingly, the tribunal unanimously found Andrew guilty as charged. However, instead of the death penalty he was given the unusual one of lifelong banishment from Greece and deprivation of military rank. In the words of the tribunal president:

> Whereas this hearing has proven that the accused royal son Andrew committed the act attributed to him, ... and as all the circumstances show clearly and conclusively, that the accused was not entirely bereft of common sense to the point at which a failure to completely and legitimately adhere to orders would be justifiable in case of inexperience in the command of large units and other circumstances in which he found himself... Therefore [the court] unanimously proclaims the accused royal son and Lieutenant General Andrew guilty [and] condemns him to lifelong exile and divestiture of his rank, and imposes on him the costs of his personal detention.[60]

The verbiage of the verdict strongly suggests that it had probably been prepared even before the trial. There is evidence that it was written by members of the Revolutionary Committee in accordance with the advice of Venizelos, who was in Geneva at the time. A few days before the trial Venizelos had appealed to the Committee to wind up the Prince's trial within forty-eight hours and impose exile for life. In a telegram he sent them he even told them: 'We must scrupulously avoid any ceremonial cashiering [of Andrew] from the military'. A document in the Venizelos Archives shows, in fact, that Andrew's court martial was essentially a show trial for public consumption, with the verdict a foregone conclusion. Venizelos received a top secret telegram from Athens signed by Konstantinos Rentis (the Foreign Minister at the time, who was also Minister of Justice) on 2 December (new calendar) and marked '21.30 hours' that included the phrase: 'The trial of Andrew that began this morning is ending, [and] the verdict is according to your instructions'.[61] At the time the judges were still in conference, supposedly deciding on the verdict! As a sentence, banishment for life was not on the Greek law books, and hence was unconstitutional and illegal. Moreover, Andrew as a Greek citizen could not be legally exiled as long as he retained his citizenship.[62] Even worse for Andrew was the fact that he had no right of appeal.

The sentencing was a hurried business and the speed with which it was concluded took even the reporters by surprise. The great majority of the press assumed the trial would last for several days at least. The text of the verdict may or may not have been drawn up by the Revolutionary Committee, as there are some elements in it that point even to Andrew himself as a possible source. In particular, his reference to being simply a figurehead in the Asia Minor Army and not a 'normal' commander was included in the verdict of the court martial; this was taken essentially as an extenuating circumstance to be able to avoid handing down the death sentence even though Andrew had been found guilty as charged. In his later book Andrew tried to brush off this potentially embarrassing point, trying hard to show he was not a mere Army figurehead. His old ADC Menelaos Metaxas, who had since retired from the Army, may also have had his hand in the trial's outcome.

In Metaxas' archive is a copy of a letter written by one of the public prosecutors at Andrew's trial containing a list of names of the officers selected for the tribunal.[63] It is unclear how this key document ended up in Metaxas' hands and what use he may have made of it at the trial. Did he want to contact some of the officers beforehand, as he certainly would have personally known some of them, and hence would have known whom he could try to win over to Andrew's case?[64] Yet as Andrew complained in his book, none of his former colleagues except Major Tsangarides made the slightest effort to defend him.[65] Sarigiannis' hostile testimony in the end was given the greatest weight.

The day after the trial the Greek newspapers printed the official press release of the process but were not allowed to add any independent reportage apart from technical details such as the times of recesses. There was no mention, for example, of Tsangarides' letter. From the press release it is clear that the tribunal focused on the main weakness in Andrew's case – that he had no experience in divisional command, and got his post only because he was a brother of the King, which gave him the confidence to disobey the orders of his superior General Papoulas.[66] The verdict was delivered to Andrew and Alice at the Pallis house[67] by one of the prosecutors and the court martial secretary.[68] Some newspaper reports claim that the Director of the Athens Police accompanied them. (But one story, that Pangalos delivered the message personally, can be discounted.)

The terrible hours Andrew's family endured as they waited for news of the verdict have been well described in his memoirs by Prince Christopher, who went to Paris to be with his mother Queen Olga and his sister Marie (Minnie) in their time of distress:

> I found my mother and sister worn with anxiety over Andrew, whose so-called trial was just drawing to its conclusion. Day after day we waited for news in an agony of suspense. Reporters besieged us every hour, clamouring for interviews… All night we sat up… The next morning my mother, wan and haggard, went to the Russian church to pray. At ten o'clock the telephone rang. My hands shook so that I could hardly lift the receiver. It was a reporter, a *New York Herald* man. 'Your brother is to be exiled, not shot,' he told me.
>
> My sister and I drove at top speed to the church. My mother was just coming out. The colour drained from her face when she saw us, and her hand flew to her heart. 'He's safe, he's safe. It's all right,' we called. She turned back towards the church, made the sign of the cross and burst into tears.[69]

According to Prince Nicholas, he and Constantine were closely following what was going on in Greece from their own exile at Palermo.[70] Horrified by the execution of the six, they feared Andrew would share the same fate. Andrew's court martial would indeed prove to have a traumatic effect on him and Alice over the years, with serious repercussions for the entire family. Though Andrew was stripped of his rank, his penalty did not include dishonourable discharge from the military, and thus he was spared that humiliating ritual. As we have seen, Venizelos had also interceded with the government urging that Andrew not be subject to it.

The day after the trial, on 20 November/3 December, Prince Andrew and Alice boarded a British Royal Navy gunboat, HMS *Calypso*, at Phaleron. Driving to Phaleron in the same car was Commander Gerald Talbot, a British naval officer who arrived in Athens to try and save the lives of the six and Andrew (see below). Behind them was a second car, that of General Pangalos, the minister of war, with a posse of armed soldiers. Talbot had requested the armed protection as he feared an attack on Andrew on the way to Phaleron. Pangalos, to allay his fears, accompanied them himself.[71] As soon as Andrew, Alice and Talbot embarked on HMS *Calypso* it set out for Corfu where they picked up their four daughters and little Philip, now eighteen months old. Philip was reportedly carried to the vessel in a makeshift crib made out of an orange box.

It is not generally known that George II was actually the one who did more than anyone else to save his uncle's life – even if he was forced to sign the death warrant of the six who were tried for treason only a few days before. George threatened to quit Greece if Andrew were shot, and so the Revolutionary Committee was forced to sit up and listen; they needed the monarchy, though quiescent, to retain their relations with the European powers. His threat had alarmed Venizelos to the point that on the day of Andrew's court martial, he cabled the King from Geneva sympathizing with George's distress over the forthcoming trial of his uncle, but pleading with him to show restraint and not jeopardize the country and his throne, and reassuring him that soon the worst would be over.[72] Venizelos was certain that Andrew would not be executed, but of course he could not say that in his telegram to the King. A few days before the trial George had met with one of the judges on the tribunal.[73] There can be little doubt that he would have talked to him about his uncle's case. Yet George had not lifted a finger to save the unfortunate six. Some of those lined up before the firing squad had been his personal friends and supporters. And even though Venizelos was definitely not one of Andrew's favourite people, to his credit he pleaded with the revolutionary government in Athens asking that the Prince's life be spared.

If there was someone who knew with certainty who had intervened to help Andrew avoid the death penalty, that was General Pangalos. In a statement to the press in 1935 he revealed that it was only because George II threatened to abdicate if Andrew were condemned to death that the Prince was spared; the Revolutionary Committee wanted to avoid at all costs the controversy of an abdication. Pangalos went on to assert that George made no effort also to save the six condemned men, all of whom had been loyal supporters of the royal family, and only cared about his uncle. Pangalos thus implied that George could also have saved the lives of the six if he really wanted to. He said the Revolutionary Committee completely ignored Commander Talbot's pleas for Andrew's life, and only George's intercession saved him. As for why Pangalos accompanied

Andrew and Alice from Athens to Phaleron to board HMS *Calypso* and leave Greece, it was only because George had asked him to.[74]

However, a decade before, on 18 February 1924, in a speech to the Greek Parliament, Pangalos had told a completely different story. There was no intervention by George II, he said this time. Andrew was spared only because a nameless 'English agent' (Commander Talbot) had promised 'a lot of financial incentives' for Greece (i.e. favourable loans from Britain) in exchange for Andrew's life; these promises, however, remained a dead letter after the 'agent' left the country with Andrew. As Pangalos was speaking, the foreign minister interrupted him and denied any knowledge of such a deal. Pangalos, the minister of war at the time, assured the house that Andrew's guilt had been proven beyond a doubt and read out Colonel Sarigiannis' testimony in Andrew's court martial. He went on to say that Andrew would have been shot but was spared because of unspecified 'external dangers'. After Pangalos spoke, the prosecutor at Andrew's trial told the Parliament that Andrew would have been indeed condemned to death had not Pangalos intervened in the judgement process.[75]

Was Prince Andrew really in danger of execution? No doubt he and his family genuinely feared it. But objectively speaking, public opinion would not have been on the Revolutionary Committee's side. Public ire was centred against those in charge in 1922, the year Asia Minor was lost, not the campaigns of the previous year in which Andrew had been involved. The execution of the six satisfied a vengeful public opinion. By contrast, even though Andrew was a prince and the brother of Constantine, his trial did not draw the same amount of attention as the 'big' one of the six. In fact, it lasted barely a day, and the evidence is that the verdict was determined before the trial was concluded. Anything else must remain in the realm of speculation. Andrew's ordeal permanently scarred his psyche for life, and by extension that of the Greek royal family and even the British one.

It is worth a closer look at Prince Andrew's war record and public image in Greece in 1922. It was never proven that he had actually made any fatal tactical mistakes at the Sakarya – in fact it could be argued that he made fewer than other high-ranking officers. Nobly, he never attempted to dissimulate or deny reality, unlike his superior Papoulas, who after his arrest by the Revolutionary Committee hastily dropped his royalist allegiance and joined the new order to save his career (and possibly his skin as well[76]). Andrew was therefore the perfect scapegoat for the Revolutionary Committee to present the Greek royals as guilty of meddling in military affairs that led directly to the Asia Minor defeat. They drove home the point that Andrew was appointed to corps command merely because he was a prince; there appears to be some truth to the later assertion that though he was a competent officer, he was not up to the task of corps commander as he lacked campaign experience. Following Andrew's safe escape from Greece, Venizelos telegraphed to the Greek government that Lord Curzon, the British representative at Lausanne, had expressed the satisfaction of his government with this development and that it would help along the peace negotiations with the Turks.[77] All went according to plan. On 21 November/4 December (old and new calendars respectively) the Greek Government Gazette published the order cashiering Andrew from the Greek officer corps.

What the revolutionaries wanted to avoid at all costs was to turn Andrew into a martyr by having him executed. On the contrary, the six who were actually executed were not seen as martyrs as most Greeks, rightly or wrongly, held them responsible for the Asia Minor disaster which after all had happened on their watch. It was enough for the regime to embarrass and humiliate Andrew by including in the court verdict the allegation that Andrew was a mere figurehead commander of II Corps at the battle of Sakarya and not the *de facto* one. This last point would weigh heavily on Andrew but also the rest of the family. Half a century later, in the early 1970s, classified documents of the Foreign Office relating to Andrew's trial were released to the public. One included an addendum to the ruling which mentioned as 'extenuating circumstance' Andrew's lack of experience in commanding a large unit. According to Parker, Philip felt that such criticism was unjust for his father and would have preferred that it had been withheld from the public 'as people might think it was true'.[78]

The relative leniency of Andrew's sentence came in for sarcastic comment in some of the British press. For example, an ironic comment in the *Illustrated London News* of 16 December 1922: 'Terrible punishment for Prince Andrew of Greece. That is what I read as a headline. To me it seemed that banishment from Greece just now was a blessing...' Interestingly, after Andrew's trial the regime halted all prosecutions linked to the Asia Minor War. Though a number of other military and political figures had been arrested and were to stand trial, in what was called 'a spirit of national unity' they were amnestied and released. Plastiras and his associates figured that the execution of the six had slaked the public thirst for blood. There was also Venizelos, who from exile was negotiating a peace treaty to officially end the state of war with Turkey and required calm on the home front.[79] Two men who had been sentenced to life imprisonment by the same court martial that condemned the six to death had their sentences reduced to one year. Among those pardoned was the convicted murderer of a Venizelist newspaper publisher.

In subsequent interviews Andrew asserted that his life was in direct danger and that he was saved by the intervention of the British government after King George V made a personal plea to the Greek revolutionary government. Later reports claimed that he had actually been condemned to death at his trial and saved at the last moment by the intervention of the British monarch.[80] This theory was adopted by members of the Greek royal family. George V of England could have been haunted by regrets that he had not allowed his doomed cousin, Tsar Nicholas II of Russia, and his family to take refuge in Britain from the Bolsheviks; therefore, he may have urged British intervention to evacuate what remained of the Greek royal family, who were also his relatives, so that there would be no repeat of what had happened in Russia. However, there is no evidence that he did anything in particular about Andrew except send a telegram to the exiled former King Constantine at Palermo stating that he would do all he could to save the Prince.[81] It would have suited George V to present himself as Andrew's saviour. And he wasn't the only one; King Alfonso XIII of Spain and Pope Benedict XV had both sent envoys to try and avert the executions of the six, though in vain, but they are believed to have had some influence in saving Prince Andrew's life.

Andrew thanked George V publicly, but he could hardly do the same for his nephew on the Greek throne who, given the atmosphere of the time, could hardly show his own hand. After all, he was the one royal who had to stay in Greece. Commander Talbot, a former British naval attaché in Athens who has often been cited as intervening on the part of the British government and George V to save Andrew, was, in fact, sent to

Greece on the personal request of his close friend Venizelos; the British government appears to have had no formal part in the mission. Failing to save the six, Talbot was instructed by Venizelos to intercede for Andrew. Talbot can be none other than the 'mystery man,' in the words of Philip's sister Margarita, whom her mother said many years later had been sent by Venizelos to save Andrew's life.[82]

Andrew himself was grateful to the British government for helping him leave Greece on the *Calypso*. However, there were questions in Britain on why the government should have taken the trouble of ferrying a Greek prince and his family outside Greece when there was no such apparent solicitude for its own people. For example, the *Northampton Chronicle and Echo* of 7 December 1922:

> Cruiser to Greece to provide a passage for Prince Andrew. Unemployed British workmen might be regarded as having at least an equal claim with unemployed Greek Princes. The whole business of fetching Prince Andrew is a little unsatisfactory.

There was even bigger backlash when it became officially known from the Admiralty that this action cost the British taxpayer £1,200 (a considerable sum at the time).[83] A Labour Party member asked Parliament: 'Are we to understand that a government which can pay to save Prince Andrew of Greece cannot pay to save the miners of this country?'[84]

Some members of Parliament argued that as Andrew was in no real danger of being executed, there was no need to send a British warship to take him out of Greece; instead, the argument ran, the money would have been better spent on Britain's poor and unemployed and not on some foreign royal. *Forward* of Glasgow, a socialist newspaper, asserted on 16 December:

> There's a shortage of cash for the unemployed workers of Britain. When recently Prince Andrew of Greece got the sack, the British Government sent a cruiser at a cost of £1,200 to take him from Greece to Brindisi.

Some newspapers asked why Britain had intervened to save the very man who during the First World War had supported his brother Constantine's pro-German neutrality. Thus mocked the *Kirkintilloch Gazette* on 15 December 1922:

> There was another fellow who lost his job last week – Prince Andrew of Greece, relative of King Tino, who during the war was the friend of Germany. The Government sent a cruiser to lift Andrew.

On 5 December 1922 (new calendar), Andrew and his family disembarked from the *Calypso* at Brindisi and from there went to Palermo to join Constantine and the rest of the family. Five days later they were in Rome to thank the Pope for interceding on behalf of Andrew by sending a personal telegram of appeal to Plastiras. As soon as he left Greek shores Andrew threw himself into campaigning against the Greek revolutionary government. On 6 December he gave an interview to foreign reporters at Rome, the first after his banishment.[85] Leading European newspapers ran the interview, such as *Le Petit Parisien, Il Giornale d'Italia* and the *Daily Telegraph*. It showed that Andrew had been traumatized by his arrest and court martial, saying he was certain he would have been executed. He added, however, that he was treated well in Athens, contrary to reports that he was imprisoned as recorded by later, mainly British, writers.[86] He concluded his interview by thanking the British government for intervening and saving him from certain death.

The interview embarrassed the Greek revolutionary regime, as Andrew appears to have promised his old nemesis Pangalos not to interfere in the country's politics. King George also was placed in a squirmy position. The regime's response was to censor the interview, stopping the presses of the Athens newspapers at the last minute. Phrases critical of the government were blanked out. For example, the Athens daily *Ethnos* ran the story pointing out that Andrew's statements in Rome indicated he was 'pleased' with his treatment in Athens and mentioning nothing about his trial and brush with death! In the following months, however, Andrew gave other interviews to the international press where he took off his kid gloves and directly accused the Greek government of incompetence. These did not have anything positive about the Greek government. Pangalos hit back by accusing Andrew of undermining stability in the country at the time of deep social crisis in the wake of the Asia Minor disaster.

From Rome on 8 December Andrew and his family moved on to Paris where they met up with Christopher and his wife, Nancy Leeds, who had recently arrived from the United States, and Queen Olga.[87] A series of photographs taken at the time by a French news agency show Andrew and his family arriving at the Gare de Lyon greeted by Christopher, other relatives and friends, and French officials. Though Andrew was exiled, Greece was still a monarchy, and as Andrew was the uncle of that country's king, there were official welcomes by the governments of the countries he visited. One photograph shows the family ready to get into a car with Queen Olga smiling at Princess Cecile. A few days later the royal party disembarked at London with the intention of establishing residence there, to be near Alice's relatives, the Mountbattens.[88] Two known photographs show the family in their London home; the first one shows Andrew with Alice, joined in the second photo by their eldest daughters Margarita and Theodora. All are wearing travel clothes and appear tired and anxious. The photographs are recorded as having been taken on 1 December 1922,[89] but that is hardly possible, as that was the day before Andrews's trial and thus he could not have been in London with his family on that date. The correct date is probably sometime in mid-December. Yet Andrew for some reason was soon dissatisfied with London and moved across the Channel to Saint-Cloud on the outskirts of Paris. Their new residence was a small house loaned to them by Andrew's wealthy sister-in-law, Marie Bonaparte (Princess George of Greece).[90] As he and his family had been stripped of their Greek nationality, they travelled with Danish passports.[91] Money was short and they had to depend on their relatives for financial support. *The Illustrated London News* on 16 December 1922 in its story headlined 'The World of Women' dealt with the financial condition of Andrew and Alice after their banishment:

> Neither she [Alice] nor the Prince has much money; both are said to have good brains, and to intend to use them to earn money. Princess Andrew has a pretty talent in dress-designing, and will probably take it up as a profession. Her sister-in-law, Lady Louis Mountbatten, is said to be the richest heiress in England, and being a real good sort, will doubtless help all she can.

On 1 January 1923 Commander Talbot was knighted by George V in the New Year Honours. He was named a Knight Commander of the Royal Victorian Order for essentially saving Andrew's life.[92] The description of his action in Athens in many British newspapers tended towards the sensational, portraying Talbot as a James Bond–esque figure dashing to save Andrew from angry revolutionaries through a hail of gunfire. The description run by the *Daily Express* of 29 December 1922 and copied almost verbatim by other British newspapers, rivals anything Ian Fleming could have dreamed up. 'THE GREEK EXECUTIONS. SAVED PRINCE'S LIFE,' the headline blared. 'NAVAL OFFICER AS ENVOY. RACE AGAINST DEATH DESCRIBED.' The report claimed to be

> the story of how [Talbot] was able to save the life of Prince Andrew of Greece after a dash across land and sea, and failed by twenty minutes to rescue the Greek ex-Ministers from their fate is described for the first time. Commander Talbot made his historical dash to Athens on the instructions of the Foreign Office as soon as it was seen that the lives of the ex-Ministers and Prince Andrew were in grave danger. The story of this exploit forms a dramatic episode rarely equalled in recent history....The man for the job was quickly chosen...his instructions were handed to him...Every moment now was precious – it was a race against time for the lives of the men in jeopardy. The Revolutionary Committee were then debating the issues of life and death. Too late to save six.'

Other British newspapers, however, claimed that Andrew's life was never in real danger and that Talbot's intervention was not all that necessary. The fact that Venizelos and not the British government asked Talbot to go to Athens was conveniently ignored, if it was known at all. [93]

On 30 December it was announced that Andrew's family was planning to go to America; they set sail on 13 January 1923.[94] This visit was duly covered by the international press and on arrival at New York six days later, Andrew was interviewed by the American press about conditions in Greece.[95] His reason for travelling there was to seek financial support from Christopher and his wealthy American wife, Nancy Leeds. However, there were almost certainly political motives as well. Andrew appears to have tried to win the support of the thriving Greek community in New York to preserve the monarchy in Greece. It was while travelling to the USA that he received the news of ex-King Constantine's death in Palermo. Constantine's passing delivered a seemingly fatal blow to Andrew's ultimate objective of enabling the royal family to return to its country.[96]

Andrew's movements abroad, of course, were closely monitored by the Greek government and also by Venizelos in Geneva, as reported by the British press.[97] For example, in the Venizelos Archive in Athens there is a telegram by the Greek ambassador in London, Georgios Melas, to the Greek Foreign Ministry reporting that Talbot met George V who had asked to be briefed on Andrew's trial and also the latest political developments in Greece.[98] Someone in the Foreign Ministry scribbled a note in pencil to the effect that no political significance should be attached to this meeting, which apparently was simply to inform the English King about one of his relatives.

Chapter 6

A Family in Pieces

Wilhelm II, now Germany's ex-Kaiser exiled to the Netherlands, harboured a delusion that one day the new German republic would collapse and he would be recalled to his throne. After George II had abdicated Wilhelm wrote to his sister Sophia suggesting that she visit him: 'Why don't you come? Is it perhaps because those idiots in the Greek royal family have influenced you? Can't you see that your son Georgie will never return to Greece unless I return to Berlin and again be leader of the Germans?'[1] Both those predictions, of course, proved delusional; 'Georgie' would eventually return to Greece as king, and the Germans would presently indeed have a new leader – a *Führer*. But in 1924 the horizon looked bleak for the Glücksburg dynasty. Prince Andrew and Princess Alice, having 'had their fill of Greek politics,'[2] settled down with their children on the estate at Saint-Cloud near Paris. Here the Prince would have plenty of time to think about the curiously hazardous position the monarchy has always had in Greece.

Greece's modern kings have always been termed not 'King of Greece (or Hellas)', but 'King of the Hellenes.' There is a crucial difference. The former appellation suggests that the monarch reigns over a specific territory with specific borders, like the Queen of Great Britain or the King of Norway. In the case of Greece, when Otho and then George I assumed the throne, Greece was limited essentially to the lower half of the Balkan Peninsula; there were a great many ethnic Greeks living beyond the borders in the Ottoman Empire, and the kings considered themselves monarchs of those people, too – not just 'of Greece' but also 'of the Greeks'. It was a powerful subconscious reminder that Greeks everywhere, even on the other side of the world, had a royal father figure to look up to. Those Greeks in the East Mediterranean, the Balkans and above all Constantinople might reasonably expect the King of Hellenes to come and liberate them and take them under his wing. The notion was a powerful reinforcement for the Great Idea, and no doubt was an indirect cause of the unfortunate wars of 1897 and 1920–22, when the king of the time signally proved unable to do what his title told him to do.

There is no sign that anyone in the chancelleries of Europe at the time recognized the implications of any of this. In 1922 Greece was not high on their list of priorities. As we have seen, Britain and France were preoccupied with recovering from the losses of the First World War, Germany was more or less prostrate, Italy under its new leader Benito Mussolini was busy punching its way back to major influence, the Soviet Union had begun its relentless campaign of trying to communize the world, while the United States retreated into isolationism. Few were moved by the fate of a small Balkan royal house.

Andrew, Philip's father, had learned the hard way how insecure the Greek throne actually was. The experiences of the past ten years had been most didactic. George I, Constantine I, Alexander and now George II had to keep figuratively looking over their shoulders; anything, at any time, might blindside them or worse. George I, whose reign was the longest and seemingly the most successful, fell to a madman's bullet while taking a walk. (Fifty-four years later Constantine II would be taken equally by surprise by the Colonels' coup of April 1967 which, though he had no way of knowing it then, sounded the death knell of the modern Greek monarchy.) Such a sense of insecurity could be justified by the volatile nature of Greek politics, though it's hardly a recipe for a throne to survive in the long term. The kings might have as their motto 'My Strength is the Love of My People,' but too often it would turn out to be codified wishful thinking.

The events immediately after 1922 fully justified this pessimism. George II reigned as a puppet of the Revolutionary Committee for eighteen uneasy months. That period was not a total loss. In July 1923 the Treaty of Lausanne between Greece and the new Turkish republic put to rest the issues lingering from the Asia Minor War; thanks to the help of Britain's Lord Curzon, Greece agreed to finally and irrevocably abandon its claims to the lands east of the Aegean Sea and to Constantinople (now Istanbul). A month later Mussolini's navy bombarded Corfu in retaliation for the murder of an Italian general that he tried to pin on the Greeks. The League of Nations, confronted with its first major crisis, forced Mussolini to withdraw his warships, though Greece had to pay an indemnity for the slain general. In the words of C.M. Woodhouse, 'Greece had learned what it meant to be small and friendless in a post-war world.'[3]

Towards the end of 1923 Venizelists and moderate monarchists tried to work out a *modus vivendi*, but the stalwart monarchist Ioannis Metaxas attempted to derail it by a failed coup. Prince Andrew was suspected of being a prime instigator. Though George II almost certainly had nothing to do with the attempt, it added nothing to his public image either. In a December 1923 general election the Venizelists and republicans scored an overwhelming victory. King George as a formality invited Venizelos to return from exile and form a government; as for a period of two years he had been married to Princess Elizabeth of Romania, he also wrote to the princess's mother in Bucharest, who knew Venizelos personally and, it was hoped, could persuade him to return. Nothing happened. In fact the Revolutionary Committee, alarmed at this sign of royal initiative, felt bold enough to take a page out of 1917's book and ask the King to quietly 'remove himself' for three months while a new constitution was being worked out. Declining not-so-subtle demands to abdicate, an embittered George and Elizabeth were escorted to a warship on 19 December and told not to come back unless asked. Which, as many on the republican side hoped, would be never.

On 25 March 1924, the 103rd anniversary of the proclamation of Greek independence, the Revolutionary Committee saw its chance and pushed through the Parliament a harsh resolution by which it declared 'the Glücksburg dynasty finally deposed,' banned its members from living in Greece, stripped them of their Greek citizenship and confiscated their property.[4] In vain did Venizelos protest from Paris that the decree was overly harsh, treating the royal family like common criminals. Greece thus became a republic, which was endorsed by plebiscite on 13 April 1924. The venerated Venizelos returned to try and put some order into the chaos, but was upstaged by Prince Andrew's old foe General Pangalos, who in 1925 set himself up as a short-lived dictator (the first one in Greece, but not the last).

Britain and the other major powers immediately recognized the new Greek republic under its figurehead president, Admiral Pavlos

Koundouriotis, who had achieved fame in the Balkan Wars when in his flagship, the armoured cruiser *Averof*, he had almost single-handedly driven the Turkish fleet from the Aegean Sea. But under him, chaos reigned. There was a series of attempted coups and counter-coups, moderated only by the calming influence of Venizelos. The Treaty of Lausanne, which settled outstanding issues with Turkey, was about the only real success of those years. With the volatile Pangalos in the saddle, Greece was rash enough to send an army to invade Bulgaria in October 1925 after a series of border incidents, only to be forced to withdraw by the League of Nations and pay a humiliating indemnity.

Pangalos had called a general election for January 1926, but after the Bulgarian debacle he changed his mind and decided to rule by decree, dispensing with niceties such as a Parliament and a free press. To meet a currency crisis, he ordered all banknotes sliced in half. Judging that women's skirts were too short in the current flapper fashion, he decreed a minimum length for them and actually sent police into the streets with tape measures (an interesting parallel with 1967, when the Colonels condemned mini-skirts). The venerable Admiral Koundouriotis resigned in protest at these inanities. Pangalos then got himself 'elected' President of the Republic in April 1926, serving at the same time also as prime-minister (as Hitler would do a decade later in Germany).

During those years, Andrew, exiled in France, had no intention of living in comfortable retirement in Europe but remained actively involved in trying to reinstate the monarchy in Greece. He also must have undergone an identity crisis of sorts, as he had been trained as a professional soldier, with the result that in exile he did not have any profession to follow. As he made clear in 1928 in his published recollections of his participation in the Asia Minor campaign, 'my military stage has ended for ever.'[5] He was still young and energetic, in his forties, and never lost his love of his country and the mental legacy of his military training and experience. He had to occupy himself with something and what came naturally to him was to make it possible for the monarchy to return to Greece and have his and his family's status restored. Naturally, all the Greek royals nursed hopes of returning, preferably to their previous privileged positions. But none was as vocal as Andrew, far more than the very restrained ex-King George II. Andrew was active among Greek emigrés in France plotting against the republic, closely following the political situation in Greece and communicating with local monarchists either by mail or their visiting him outside Greece. Andrew could not hide his contempt for Venizelos and his supporters. His trial, of course, had radicalized him but he was, in any case, extreme in his politics by nature. Pangalos denounced the Prince in Parliament as the main agitator for a restoration of the monarchy, alleging that Andrew had promised not to antagonize the Greek government but had reneged on the promise. In February 1925, shortly before becoming dictator, Pangalos in a speech in the Parliament called Andrew an 'idiot' who was unable to utter a word to defend himself at his trial, and could only accuse his own people who had made him a general and given him his command in Asia Minor.[6]

The period 1922–1924 was almost a replay of 1917–1920, when the royal family had been exiled, leaving behind only one of its members as king. But this time the game had changed. Instead of returning, in 1924 the monarchy was abolished and replaced by a republic, the first time such a regime change had occurred in Greece. All the family lost their titles – a severe blow. Though actual prospects for a return were minimal, they still had a few cards and kept their hopes up. A large percentage of the Greek population was still monarchist at heart, though Venizelos gained many supporters from Asia Minor and other Greek lands lost to the Asia Minor debacle who tended to blame Constantine I for their sea of troubles. Moreover, the period from 1924 to 1928 was one of economic and political instability that did not reflect well on the republic.

Andrew believed passionately in his role as the republic's nemesis. Of all the members of the royal family it was Andrew who bore the burden of the fight. He considered himself indelibly Greek, as did his wife and family. Though Philip was too young at the time, his sisters were old enough to be able to adopt an identity. Andrew had fought for his country and led men on the front, many of whom were killed, and he could never allow himself to forget it. Traumatized by his court martial, he was obsessed with the way his foes were running the country and hated them with a passion. His brothers were not so fervent; though they were technically military, they had not had real commands as he had in 1921 during the Asia Minor campaign. Of the brothers, George appeared to show little interest in Greece. Nicholas and Christopher did get involved in a few political gestures, but only after Andrew asked them; they were cosmopolitans now, having settled in Europe or America and not really needing the restoration of the monarchy.

The only real gain from Andrew's trip to America in 1923 (see above) had been the fact that Princess Christopher – who would die just a few months later in London in August 1923 – arranged to pay for Andrew's children's school fees, enabling Philip to enrol in the exclusive MacJannet American School in Paris, a kindergarten for the privileged. Among Philip's classmates were the children of Princess Margarethe of Denmark, Philip's cousins. In 1928 a photo of the royal children doing archery practice was published in several American newspapers; Prince Philip appears second from left.[7] Andrew and his family continued to depend on the charity of relatives and friends to feed, house, clothe, and educate the members while in exile.

Alice has given us a fascinating account of how little Philip grew up at Saint-Cloud and acquired traits of character he would retain for the rest of his life. Fast-forwarding to 1953, as Alice was about to leave Athens to travel to London for Elizabeth's coronation, a reporter asked her about Philip as a child. Alice opened her heart and told him intimate things about her son. She made the point that she loved Philip a lot because he was her last child and also the only boy. As a result, even as a little child he always wanted to show his worth and that was why he turned out to be so dynamic. Looking back, she sometimes regretted that she may have been a little too strict with him when he was a child but she was like that, and she treated him thus so that when he grew up he could do something worthwhile with his life. His upbringing was difficult (compared to that of his sisters) as he was a mere eighteen months old when he was exiled, and consequently grew up without a country and real happiness. Alice claimed that Philip found it hard to learn Greek, a language which she loved so much that it took her only two months to master. Philip was different (in character) from his sisters because they grew up in a royal household. In contrast to them, Philip only knew exile and that was why he had so little respect for protocol and traditions and became so unconventional.

As a child growing up at Saint-Cloud, Philip was boisterous and constantly played in the garden, summer and winter; he would play only with older children or adults, never with children of his age or younger. At the time, the family was living in a small villa on the estate of Prince George, Andrew's brother. Next to the estate was a villa belonging to a French woman whom Alice describes as a 'variety actress'. This lady had many gentlemen callers and would throw wild parties until very late in the night; Alice and the rest of the family could sometimes hardly sleep because of the music and cars arriving and leaving the villa next door. By day this French woman would ride a horse around George's estate or be driven in open cars by men courting her. Alice says that little Philip became fixated with her and every time he saw her out and about he would leave everything he was doing and stare at her for a long time. He would then ask Alice many questions about this woman, questions which she 'did not find pleasant'. Alice concluded by telling the reporter that because of this French woman the entire family had a quite miserable time at Saint-Cloud.[8]

Andrew in exile was continuously plagued by bad luck and affected by events he could not control. As time passed it became clear he could not return to Greece. When on 25 March 1924 Greece became a republic, as we have seen, all the possessions of the former royal family, including Mon Repos, were to be confiscated.[9] At the end of that year his reputation suffered a blow through no fault of his own but because of a namesake royal cousin. On 10 December Prince Andrew Romanov of the former Russian royal family was declared bankrupt, owing the huge sum for the time of £14,000 pounds. The Russian Andrew had lost all his assets in the Bolshevik Revolution, and what was left abroad had gone to financing the anti–Bolshevik Whites during the subsequent civil war. Seeking asylum in Britain, with what little money he had left he tried his luck in various business ventures, all of which failed, and he was declared bankrupt and penniless in July. In the years following, Andrew Romanov would live in Britain almost in penury and his wife, Princess Xenia, would resort to designing and selling bags to survive, even though they were still mentioned in the society columns of the British press as princes and 'Royal Highnesses'. The problem for Andrew of Greece was that the day after the bankruptcy court in London pronounced its verdict on his Russian cousin, some British newspapers erroneously reported on their front pages that Prince Andrew of Greece had become bankrupt!

Even those reports that simply mentioned 'Prince Andrew', without specifying further, automatically suggested the Greek Andrew, who after all was much better known in Britain.[10] Though the Greek Andrew was not considered wealthy, he was never bankrupt, and this misreporting of the British press gave rise to the story of the 'penniless prince' that would pursue him until his death, and even rub off on Philip before his marriage to Elizabeth.

When in 1925 General Theodoros Pangalos, Andrew's old schoolmate, rival and nemesis, established his dictatorship, there was a flurry of speculation in the international press that he might reinstate the monarchy, and that Andrew was the main candidate for the Greek throne.[11] Such reports were at the least bizarre, taking into account that Pangalos throughout never abandoned his stern opposition to monarchy and had denounced Andrew as its main champion. Moreover, in June 1926, while Pangalos was still in power, an official government announcement said Mon Repos would be repaired and used as a summer retreat for the President of the Hellenic Republic – that is, Pangalos himself.[12] The plan eventually did not materialize, but at no point could it ever be seriously considered that the irascible dictator was secretly plotting the return of the monarchy. The reports may have been started by friends of Andrew, or even by himself, to test the waters, citing as source a 'diplomatic correspondent' who, of course, could have been anyone. The collapse of the Pangalos dictatorship in August 1926, however, gave birth a year later to an even more bizarre plan – that of installing Andrew in Greece as President of the Republic. The idea very likely originated with Alice who, according to her biographer Hugo Vickers, contacted influential people, up to and including Britain's King George V and Sir Eric Drummond, the first secretary-general of the League of Nations, asking them for their endorsement and help.[13] Andrew had approved it as a possible way of calling a plebiscite at the close of his putative term to bring the monarchy back to Greece. Though the plan appeared to be bizarre, it did in fact have a successful precedent seven decades earlier. In 1852, after a term as first President of the Republic of France, Louis-Napoleon Bonaparte held a plebiscite for changing the polity from a republic into an empire, as it had been until 1815 under Bonaparte's much more illustrious namesake and uncle. Winning the plebiscite, he had become Emperor Napoleon III.

The rather involuted reasoning was that since the Venizelists had taken power in 1922, Greece had suffered a string of coups and political unrest; only if someone from the opposite faction were to take the reins, someone as internationally famous as Prince Andrew, might the country find the stability it needed to attract foreign loans and build up an infrastructure. The growth in the economy would help raise the living standards of the people, especially the many thousands of refugees from Asia Minor who were still living in squalor. The plan admittedly verged on the fantastic, considering that Andrew was a well-known staunch opponent of republicanism; he was also the least liked of the royals by the Venizelists who at the time were a majority of the Greek electorate. It would have been like making a Buddhist pope.

Andrew and Alice shared their thinking with Greek politicians in order to familiarize the country with the idea. These politicians were not confined to the traditional monarchists, most of whom were now in the Populist Party under the leadership of Panagis Tsaldaris, and the few followers of Ioannis Metaxas who after a brief period in exile following his 1923 coup had been amnestied and allowed to return to Greece. The most influential politician who was informed was Spyridon Merkouris, a fanatic far-right monarchist; others were Theodore Ypsilantis of a well-known old family connected with the Greek War of Independence, who had founded Greece's first fascist party, the Union of Greek Fascists, in October 1922 and one Efstratiadis, a leading member of Ypsilantis' party. Alice and Andrew saw Merkouris and Ypsilantis in Vienna and wrote to Efstratiadis in Athens. [14] These were new men on the Greek political scene. Why did Andrew try to co-operate with far-right politicians or even fascists? It is likely that at this early stage of the plan Andrew avoided informing his mainstream monarchist friends who would most likely have dismissed out of hand even the idea of making him President. By contacting the fascists, Andrew may have been testing the waters. In 1927 the fascist movement was still relatively new; Mussolini had taken power only five years earlier. In Greece the fascists represented an insignificant power and remained so; even if they had supported the plan for installing Andrew as President, they did not have the political power to follow it through. In the end the plan was stillborn, as except for a few on the far right it had little support. There also wasn't much foreign backing. But this failure did not dissuade Andrew who remained active in exile politics, receiving in Paris in November 1927 a visit from Tsaldaris, the leader of the Populist Party. Venizelist newspapers at home blasted Tsaldaris for even deigning to meet the Prince.[15] Greece's monarchists, on the other hand, held up Andrew as their champion.[16] How, after all, could a true-blood prince deign to become a mere president?

Outside politics, Andrew and Alice led a life of leisure with visits to royal relatives. They were frequently seen in society events and vacationed in summer on the Riviera, the Lido and Romania. They do not seem to have had economic difficulties, though on 3 December 1927 the weekly British newspaper *The Graphic* reported that Alice opened a high street shop in Paris selling silks, perfumes and other luxury products from Greece. There is a photograph of Alice with her eldest daughter, Margarita, in the shop along with three Greek ladies. A text accompanying the photo asserts that Alice opened the shop and was working there for an actual livelihood.[17] On the other hand, of course, Alice is more likely to have run the place simply to be doing something. Her association with Greek products was symbolic in that they included top-end silken garments made by Alice's old School of Embroidery. The shop also may have been a means of staying in touch with monarchists in Greece and the shop itself was appropriately named 'Hellas'.[18]

It was at this time that Andrew thought a great deal about his controversial role in the Battle of Sakarya and put forward his thoughts in the book we have mentioned several times already.[19] The stigma of his conviction by court martial was too heavy for him to bear. The prologue of the book brings this out; it was written in Greek and hence addressed to a Greek readership as he did, after all, remain a Greek at heart. He began work soon after settling at Saint-Cloud and published it six years later, in 1928, under the title *Dorylaion-Sakarya 1921*. The detailed and well-written narrative shows Andrew to have been a competent writer and to have spent many months working on it. One of the book's strong points is the ample use of official documents that Andrew had in his possession from the time he commanded 12th Division and then II Corps. Andrew had deemed these documents important enough to take with him into exile in 1922 with his few belongings. It is likely that he had held on to these documents in the hope that he could one day appeal his conviction.[20] The narrative dwells much on military matters such as army movements and logistics and demonstrates Andrew's deep knowledge in this sphere. Yet it appears to have been written for experts in military matters and makes boring reading for the layman. On top of that, it is clear from the start that it is an exercise in self-justification as Andrew tries hard to divert blame from himself as a military commander. In particular, the book is an attempt to exonerate himself of charges that his disobedience of orders had directly resulted in the defeat at Sakarya. It delivers a scathing accusation of Plastiras and the other officers who had led the September 1922 revolt that eventually toppled the Greek monarchy. According to Andrew, those men were the 'real traitors' who had handed Greek Asia Minor to Kemal on a silver platter, while he, the 'patriot' Prince Andrew, was exiled. Andrew claimed to have made no mistakes while in command during the Asia Minor campaign and that at every step he was surrounded and hobbled by incompetent and treacherous officers.[21]

In that respect Andrew named only Nikolaos Plastiras; we might have expected that his hatred would have been centred on Pangalos instead. Plastiras had become a legendary figure in the Greek Army, and even Andrew acknowledged his bravery and concern for his men. But, he said, all the regimental commanders under him were brave as well. He attributed Plastiras' subsequent fame to government propaganda. There is some contradiction here, as Plastiras was a known Venizelist and the (royal) government had tried to replace him, but his men had threatened to mutiny. Plastiras' fame had been first cultivated by the very same government that wanted to replace him on the Asia Minor front! The accusation that Andrew had disregarded the order of his commander-in-chief, General Papoulas, which landed him before a court martial, was the poignant subject of almost one third of the book as he tried to justify his actions.[22] Andrew's conclusion reveals that he had remained a fanatically patriotic Greek even after these events.

The book was published in Paris by Agon (Greek for 'struggle'), a pro-monarchist imprint. Its circulation was permitted in Greece, where it became a great sensation but at the same time provoked attacks against Andrew by the Venizelists. Their main arguments were that Andrew presented himself as the only one who did his job properly during the

Asia Minor campaign in 1921, while the other officers were incompetent and undermining one another. Yet all those supposed incompetents from November 1920 onwards were loyal monarchists and had been appointed to their posts by King Constantine. Nearly all Venizelist officers, with the exception of Plastiras and a few others, had been replaced by royalists. Therefore, the argument went, if in the summer of 1921 Andrew found himself on the Asia Minor front surrounded by incompetent and treacherous officers, he only had his own political friends to blame.

By the time Andrew's book was in print, he and Alice were starting to travel in Europe separately, Alice making frequent visits to her relatives in Britain. Philip and his sisters became accustomed to seeing less of their father at Saint-Cloud. In the late 1920s many members of the Greek royal family took their summer holidays in Romania,[23] where ex-King George lived with Queen Elizabeth, his Romanian consort. There were serious tensions in that marriage, however, as George disliked Romania, especially as he had to depend financially on his wife. Moreover, it transpired that his wife could not conceive. That meant that if George were ever reinstated as king in Greece he would not have a son as successor.

The problems came to a head in 1930, with George's divorce from Elizabeth and his move to Britain; his cousin George V had personally intervened to allow him into the country, though the British government opposed it. George settled into a hotel in Piccadilly, bringing him closer to the British establishment in which he felt increasingly at home. Among the Greek royals who vacationed in Romania in 1927 and 1928 were Philip, his sisters and Alice, but not Andrew. His cousin Michael, just six years old, had just become the King of Romania after the death of his grandfather Ferdinand. As Philip was also six, the two boys became close friends. According to newspaper reports, Philip and Michael played together building sand castles and staging wars with Michael's toy soldiers.[24] Philip taught Michael some American slang he had picked up from his American school in Paris while Michael taught him how to swim.[25] Philip introduced cowboys and Indians, a game which the other royal children took up with gusto. One newspaper in 1930 quoted Philip as telling Michael: 'My father never stays at home much, but at least I have a father. I never see yours around at all'.[26] It was a telling testimony to the emotional insecurity of royal youngsters in all ages.

Nevertheless, there is strong evidence that Alice and Andrew were still very much attached in the late 1920s. In 1928, the couple celebrated their silver wedding anniversary with all members of the family present at Saint-Cloud (see below). Alice also identified with her husband's cause – to eventually return to Greece, preferably after a regime change from republic to monarchy. In this context she took her own initiatives and tried to influence her many contacts in high places to support the cause. Alice also translated Andrew's book into English, in which edition it was published in 1930 with the catchy title *Towards Disaster in Asia Minor* under the Murray imprint. The book, with its many details and military terms, cannot have been easy to translate, even for someone fluent in both languages. It is likely that Alice began working on it before it was first published, when the writing was in its final stages.[27] Andrew appears to have been interested only in the Greek edition so that his compatriots could read his side of the story of the campaign in Asia Minor in 1921. If he had intended to publish it in English as well, he would have issued both editions simultaneously. Alice must have spent a long time translating it, very likely helped by her husband as it included many military terms she is unlikely to have been familiar with. Alice penned the prologue for the English edition in which she faithfully echoes Andrew's assertion that he committed no errors in the campaign and was plagued by incompetent officers who conspired against him and who later organized the 11 September 1922 coup that led to the expulsion of King Constantine and eventually to the abolition of the monarchy. The epilogue in the Greek edition of Andrew's book is full of such accusations,[28] which Alice uses in her prologue. Her words, in fact, go beyond her husband's claims: she goes into detail about Andrew's court martial and his brush with death even more than he does, but most likely the detail is spurious at best. She did not intentionally write falsehoods; what she was told was what she wrote. We should also bear in mind that Alice at the time of Andrew's court martial was in a wretched psychological state and may well have uncritically accepted as fact every rumour she heard surrounding this event. Between the lines the prologue shows that until 1930, at least, Alice was very much attached to Andrew and was his staunchest defender.

The Murray publishing firm took out full-page advertisements for the book in *The London Illustrated News* and *The Times*, indicating possible high-level influence. In Greece the news of an English book by Andrew sparked intense interest among both monarchists and anti-monarchists who waited to see what it would say. Some thought the English work would be a new book, as the title was different from the Greek; moreover, the catchier English title gave the impression that the 'new' book would reveal hitherto unknown facts and secrets about the Greek defeat in Asia Minor. The Greek newspaper *Ethnos*, which supported Venizelos, reviewed the English edition, concluding that it really did not contain anything new, and ran a Greek translation of Alice's prologue countering her points one by one. Its headline, 'Alice's over-the-top defence of Andrew – Her Prologue for the English Edition of her husband's book – How everyone is at fault except him,' spoke volumes.[29] It would appear that the Venizelists became angrier with the English edition than the Greek one, as Alice had added in her prologue spurious 'facts' about Andrew's court martial. On this topic the British ambassador to Athens, Sir Patrick Ramsay, cabled the Foreign Office reporting that the book had caused an uproar among the Venizelists who at the time were in government.[30]

As the 1920s were drawing to a close it seemed less and less likely that Greece would revert to monarchy. Andrew continued to be seen as the champion of the monarchists, even if to most Greeks he was fighting for a lost cause. But ex-King George was of a different stamp. George appears to have had the mental robustness to be able to handle his exile without ill effects. As a boy, as we have seen, he was the most serious-minded of the princes, as his preference for toy soldiers shows. He also owed something of his personality to his austere German tutors, which made it possible in 1909 for him to graduate from the Greek Military Academy (Scholi Evelpidon) with the rank of captain, at the age of nineteen. That same year he moved to Germany to become an officer in the Kaiser's 1 Garderegiment zu Fuss (Foot Guards' Regiment). Three years later he transferred to the Second Squadron of the 3 Uhlan Guards Regiment of cavalry, though he was permitted to wear the uniform of the 1 Garderegiment zu Fuss. When the First Balkan War broke out George returned to Greece to serve on the staff of his father Crown Prince

Constantine, the commander-in-chief of the Greek armies. He saw
action at the Battle of Elassona against the Ottomans on 2 October 1912.
A few months later, in the Epiros sector he helped his father recapture
Ioannina. At Bizani, just short of the city, the army received a visit from
Prime Minister Venizelos. The Turks, seeing a group of high-ranking
officers and officials on an eminence, opened up with their artillery.
Constantine and Venizelos ducked behind the wall of an old church,
while Prince George and a general threw themselves to the ground. A
Turkish shell burst nearby, wounding one of the prince's staff.[31]

The outbreak of the Asia Minor War saw George at his father's side
in the general staff, just as in the Balkan Wars nine years before. This
former officer of the 1 Garderegiment zu Fuss would go up to advanced
positions to see for himself the situation and encourage the troops. Several
times his anxious father would send out search parties to bring him back.
Mere days after the devastating Greek defeat, on 14 September 1922, he
found himself taking the oath of King. The situation for the royals had
not improved. King George was 'alone, kept like a prisoner in his new
royal palace, haunted by the shades of his parents and surrounded by
hostile revolutionary police.'[32] The uncomfortable fact was that George
was the head of an unravelling family.

For the next five years Andrew and Alice, as we have seen, were
apart far longer than they were together. Both travelled a lot in Europe,
staying with royal relatives, enjoying the social amenities of London and
showing up at the occasional royal wedding or funeral. It was an idle life
of no real purpose. There was a final reunion for their silver wedding
anniversary on 8 October 1928 at Saint-Cloud. It was a cloudless autumn
day commemorated by a special group photograph in the garden. But
psychological pressures on Alice were mounting, and two weeks later
she decided she'd had enough; she renounced her Protestant faith and,
following most of her royal relations, converted to the Greek Orthodox
Church. A few months after that, the seven-year-old Philip was sent to
live with his mother's Mountbatten relatives in Britain.

By this time Alice was starting to develop what appeared to be
psychological problems. It appears that the intense labour involved in
translating her husband's book and also the bad memories it brought
back, especially Andrew's arrest and court martial with the threat of the

death penalty, were decisive factors in making her condition worse.[33] A few weeks after she had finished working on the book, in early 1929, she went to London where she arranged for its publication by Murray. She returned to Paris bringing with her books on mysticism. This did not trigger any alarm in her family, as Alice had developed an interest in mysticism also in the past; during the family's first exile, she and her brother-in-law, Christopher, had participated in seances to try and communicate with spirits.

However, this time Alice's family noticed that she had also become extremely introverted. By spring of 1929 she was described as 'intensely mystical' and would lie on the floor to receive divine messages. She claimed to be able to heal with a laying on of hands, and to control her thoughts like a Buddhist. This was enough for Andrew to stay away from her for months. Alice wrote to her mother that soon she would have 'a message to tell the world'. She became convinced she was a saint, and carried sacred talismans about the house to banish evil spirits. The 'bride of Christ' was how she described herself. In a secular age such phenomena are usually taken as signs of serious mental imbalance. Yet it can be argued that Alice was merely duplicating mystic traits of holiness already well known in the Greek and Russian Orthodox Churches and Roman Catholic Church. Her flight from Protestantism was a search for something deeper and more authentic in the Christian experience. She gave up the worldliness and materialism of being a princess, feted by society but essentially doing nothing creative, in favour of her true vocation, which was to live the life of the spirit in the manner of the great saints and Christian mystics, whose faith unleashed huge powers.

Many years later, in 1953, the largest Athens daily newspaper, *To Bima,* described how Alice decided to convert to Orthodoxy; it is likely that the source of this story was Alice herself. One night in 1927 she happened to be walking outside the Greek Orthodox Cathedral of Saint Sophia in Moscow Street, London. She entered the church and inside there was only a priest conducting vespers. After he had finished, Alice approached him and asked him in Greek if he was willing to hear her confession, even though she was not Orthodox; that was the moment she decided to convert.[34]

Of course, Andrew and his relatives didn't see it so charitably at the time. He summoned Alice's gynaecologist for a diagnosis, as well as her sister-in-law, Princess Marie Bonaparte of France (the mother of Prince Peter). Marie Bonaparte was close to Sigmund Freud, and arranged for Alice to see one of Freud's former co-workers, the psychoanalyst Ernst Simmel, near Berlin. She was promptly admitted to Simmel's clinic and eventually diagnosed as a 'paranoid schizophrenic' suffering from a 'neurotic-prepsychotic libidinous condition,' whatever that was supposed to mean.[35] Freud himself was consulted and prescribed 'an exposure of the gonads [ovaries] to X-rays, in order to accelerate the menopause,' presumably to calm her down. Typical of secular medicine, the doctors totally discounted the spiritual side.

Most writers attribute the condition to a combination of Alice's congenital deafness, the ordeals in Athens, separation from her children, a traumatic menopause and a bipolar tendency. There was also talk of an erotic infatuation with an unnamed married Englishman, which, however, remained purely platonic.[36] The phrase 'religious crisis' has also been tossed in, without defining what the term means. The question naturally arises: was Alice consulted about what was to be done for her? Probably not. Despite treatment at the Simmel clinic, Alice's condition did not change, and on 2 May 1930 she was taken involuntarily to the Bellevue private psychiatric clinic at Kleuzlingen in Switzerland. Her once-close family life was now finally over, though she and Andrew never went through the formality of a divorce. A disillusioned Andrew closed the family home at Saint-Cloud and moved to the south of France, where he squandered the rest of his life drinking, gambling away what money he had, and womanizing. At the risk of indulging in pop psychology, one might say that Andrew's entire post-Greece life was engaged in a subconscious search for another identity to replace what he had lost. A prince in name only, he had nothing left inside. One relation called him 'a deeply unhappy man.'

Alice, oddly enough, followed a more meaningful course. She, too, was profoundly affected by the loss of her Greek identity and self-image. But she did not give in to despair. Her apparent mental illness was, in fact, the point of entry into a new strength, a more profound identity, a mystic Orthodox Christian, one along the lines of the great Russian saints. It had far more meaning for her than the artificial princess world she had inhabited, and sustained her through the rest of her long life as her husband sank helplessly into decadence.

The girls, aged nineteen to twenty-nine, were mature enough to handle it all and by now had families of their own in Germany (two of them ended up marrying German Nazis). Philip was still only nine when his mother was institutionalized and his father all but abandoned him. Said his sister Sophie: 'Then we all sort of disappeared and the house in Saint-Cloud was closed down.'[37] Philip would have little contact with his mother for the rest of his childhood, which was spent living with his mother's relatives in England and attending boarding schools in England, Germany, and Scotland. As for Andrew, as we will see, he entered a period of strange personal rebellion: scarred by recent events, he became estranged from Princess Alice and took up residence at Monte Carlo – in hotels and on yachts – with a young French mistress, the Countess Andrée de la Bigne.

In those years Philip was more or less thrown on his own emotional resources. The events in the family during those years would help shape his character later on. Doubtless his parents' adverse experiences in Greece, as told to him, left a bad subconscious impression. Though his family was royal, it was by no means rich; he depended on the charity of relatives and friends. Matters were certainly not helped by Alice's confinement in an asylum. But there was a lingering confusion about Philip's identity: a Greek prince living in France and educated in Anglo-Saxon institutions. The boy could be forgiven for wondering exactly who he was. As he explained later: 'If anything I've thought of myself as Scandinavian, particularly Danish. We spoke English at home. The others learned Greek. I could understand a certain amount of it. But then the conversation would go into French. Then it went into German, because we had German cousins. If you couldn't think of a word in one language, you tended to go off in another.'[38]

In 1928 Philip went to Britain for the first time to attend Cheam School, under the care of his maternal grandmother. As we have seen, he appears to have been a somewhat boisterous child – not uncommon in cases of absent parents – who required a certain measure of discipline. Alice wrote to the school in 1929 asking his tutors to form a Cub Scouts company for her son. The letter carries a hint of anxiety. 'The training would have such an excellent influence on him... I should be infinitely grateful if you could manage it as soon as possible.' [39] Yet young Philip led a pillar-to-post kind of existence, spending some time at Saint-Cloud in the less-than-ideal family environment, chronically short of money and being clothed in hand-me-downs. In later years his great benefactor would turn out to be his maternal uncle, Lord Louis Mountbatten. Yet the tender ten-year-old would receive no word from his mother between 1932 and 1937. When Philip was asked about this in later years his reply was stoic and pragmatic: 'It's simply what happened. The family broke up. My mother was ill, my sisters were married, my father was in the south of France. I just had to get on with it. You do. One does.'[40]

In the aftermath of this disintegration, the British part of Philip's family took a large share of responsibility for his care. His maternal grandmother, Princess Victoria, sent him to live with his uncle George, the Marquess of Milford Haven, who was to be Philip's guardian for the next seven years and a surrogate father to him. Philip would become close friends with George's son David (who would be the best man at his wedding to Princess Elizabeth). The two boys attended Cheam School where Philip excelled at sport. The Marquess would often come to watch him and his son play in school matches. The Milford Havens gave Philip a sense of stability that was lacking elsewhere but he remembered the upheaval as confusing. When he was later asked what language was spoken at home he replied, 'What do you mean, at home?' [41] A telling comment indeed. Philip had never had much of a home in the conventional sense. He had spent only the first year of his life at the Mon Repos palace on Corfu, his birthplace, and can hardly have been expected to have any fond memories of it. The other places in his life, from Saint-Cloud to Cheam, were mere temporary accommodation.

When Philip was a pupil at Cheam School, the headmaster was a clergyman, the Reverend Harold Taylor. He cared for the welfare of his pupils but at the same time he was a strict disciplinarian, and when the boys were caught breaking the school rules he used to beat them with a cane and even a cricket bat. Philip was no exception and he had his fair share of spanking.[42] The result was that while he was at Cheam he did not hide the fact that he did not like Reverend Taylor.[43] But after he left the school he came to appreciate that the discipline regime at Cheam School had been beneficial for him and played a large part in building him into an independent and self-disciplined adult (especially as he had been a boisterous child).[44] However, Philip had also impressed Taylor as in 1947 the latter told Mike Parker – Philip's best friend at the time – that:

> when he [Philip] was 12 my wife and I said he would make a good king, thinking then of him as King of Greece, not as a husband for Princess Elizabeth. He has two vital qualities, leadership and personality.[45]

Philip for years stayed in touch with his old headmaster, as can be seen in a hitherto unpublished letter he wrote to him in March 1947, almost twenty years after he had been a pupil there. In it Philip apologizes for not attending a school reunion party but expresses his fond memories of the school:

> Thank you very much for your letter and kind invitation. As far as the invitation to the party is concerned, I am sorry to say that I will be away on leave at the time and so will be unable to attend. I have been meaning to run over and visit you for some time but what with one thing and another I seem to have been rather rushed for time recently. However I shall definitely be over someday soon. I am delighted to hear that everything is going so well at the school though naturally the weather has not been particularly helpful. I received the piece of cake safely and enjoyed it immensely although my recollections of Mrs Sawyer are rather vague. Please remember me to Mrs Taylor[46] and any of my old friends (or should I say masters?) who are still with you.[47]

In fact Philip did keep his promise in his letter to Reverend Taylor and visited Cheam later in 1947 with Princess Elizabeth; he introduced his old headmaster to her as 'the man who used to cane me'.[48]

Back in Greece, in 1928 Venizelos won a resounding election victory; as a result the main pro-royal opposition, the Populist Party (Laikon Komma) pledged its loyalty to the republic. Even that staunch royalist officer Ioannis Metaxas appeared to assent to it. As conditions began to stabilize in Greece, it seemed that royalty was definitely a thing of the past and that the members of the royal family would remain in permanent exile.

In the case of ex-King George II, no West European country had initially cared to host him, so he had settled down with his wife, Elizabeth of Romania, at the sumptuous Villa Cotroceni in Bucharest, later buying their own home on the city's Galea Victoriei, a major avenue. At the same time the King's sister Helen married Crown Prince Carol of Romania, the son of King Ferdinand, cementing the Romanian link. But there was soon trouble in paradise. 'Neither marriage could be called an impassioned love-match,' writes Arthur Gould Lee, an expert on the Greek royal house. George was serious and reserved by nature, unlike the vivacious Elizabeth; their fourteen-year marriage would have no offspring. Elizabeth's brother Carol shared her spirited temperament, gradually alienating Helen. Above all, both George and his sister were ill at ease with the excessive pomp and pageantry of the Romanian court, having been used to the far more spartan and informal surroundings of the Greek court. Helen tried to scale down her own level of luxury, but Prince Carol didn't appreciate it, and that marriage, too, hit the rocks in seven years.

As George and Elizabeth drifted apart, he began to travel widely, seeking a place where he could feel at home. He did not have many needs; sports and study were his main occupations. Not caring overmuch for social life, he could often be found in a corner of a room buried in a book while others were making merry.[49] Prince Andrew, as we have seen, never managed the equilibrium, and his son Philip was repressing his own youthful insecurity by just 'getting on with it'. George found such a place in Britain, whose countryside he loved and whose people's character most chimed with his own. He especially appreciated the controlled and understated elegance of the British upper class, from whom he carefully picked his limited circle of friends. He settled in London, where he bought a car and went to the races and lived the quiet and comfortable life he craved. Though he doubtless followed the sometimes turbulent events in Greece, at no time did he ever indicate he wished to return to Greece or its throne.[50]

One prince, nostalgic for the past, did have a burning desire to see up close what was happening in his homeland, and that was Prince Paul, George's younger brother. In 1930, aged twenty-nine, he got to know a Danish couple in London who were planning a yacht trip to Corfu. Paul joined them on the trip, growing a beard so that people wouldn't recognize him, passing himself off as a Dane named Peter Wesel. The yacht touched at Corfu, ports in the Peloponnese, and finally Phaleron, the seaside of Athens. He was careful to avoid the city proper, but as luck would have it he was recognized – he was a head taller than most Greeks anyway – by a retired naval officer in the street. The officer at once rushed to tell his wife, who (fortunately) flatly disbelieved him. Thus ended 'Peter Wesel's' brief Greek adventure.[51] Later Paul, essentially without resources, was forced to seek work. King George's brother laboured first as a mechanic in the Ford Motor Company in the USA, and then in Britain as an aircraft mechanic. He never to anyone's knowledge blew his own trumpet or insisted on any 'royal' honours, and was known to all as a genial and easy-going man.

Andrew was thus very much left alone to carry on his crusade for a royal restoration. None of his brothers had his degree of commitment and even former King George appeared to have become complacent. Andrew was fighting a campaign on his own and the result was that Alice and the rest of the family took second place to this objective. He also had to find a way to keep Philip in a safe environment as he could not look after him. This he did by parking him in a noted school in Germany, then a rising power and home of many of the royals' distant and not-so-distant relatives.

Chapter 7

What To Do With Young Philip?

In the eight months between December 1930 and August 1931 all four of Philip's sisters got married, all to German nobles from prestigious local royal houses. This had the trappings of a Hollywood romance – four princesses for four princes! The fact that the girls married in quick succession, and that these marriages were arranged soon after Alice was institutionalized, gives the impression that they may have been engineered by Andrew to rid himself of some of his paternal burdens. On the other hand, this does not appear to be the case, as all four German men were young, wealthy, and quite good-looking. Nevertheless, as the girls, belonging to higher-tier royalty, in fact married beneath them, there is no doubt the husbands got the better of the deal.

The first to get married was sixteen-year-old Sophie, on 15 December 1930, to Prince Christian of Hesse, who later joined the Nazi Party and the SS. Next came Cecile, 20, who on 2 February 1931 married Prince George Donatus of Hesse-Darmstadt, another future Nazi Party member. Margarita, the eldest sister at twenty-six, on 30 April married Prince Gottfried of Hohenlohe-Langenburg. Finally, on 17 August twenty-five-year-old Theodora married Berthold, the Margrave of Baden, whose father had been imperial Germany's last chancellor and who was rather less of a Nazi than the others, though he would serve his country in the coming war.[1] All four weddings took place in Germany, attended by Andrew and Philip (but not Alice). This meant that young Philip spent much of 1931 sojourning in Germany.[2]

In 1933 Theodora reappeared in Philip's life and set him down the path towards a different education, introducing him to the noted German-Jewish educator Kurt Hahn. Hahn had been her father-in-law's personal secretary and was known to the family. He was a fervent German patriot who had been involved in negotiating the 1919 Treaty of Versailles. He had been so upset at the Allied treatment of post-war Germany, especially by

The first known photograph of Andrew (1886); he is four years old and clutches a toy gun that the photographer, Petros Moraitis, gave him to hold. (*Published in A. Ξανθάκης, Ιστορία της Ελληνικής Φωτογραφίας 1839/1970, 67*)

Photograph by Carl Boehringer made into a postcard showing second lieutenant Prince Andrew (right) with his fellow officer and future ADC Menelaos Metaxas in 1902-1903. (*ΕΛΙΑ Archive. Reference no. 1E40.001*)

Group photograph by Carl Merlin of Andrew (back row, second from the right) and some of his fellow cadets at the Greek Military Academy (*Schole Evelpidon*) in Athens in 1898. (*ΕΛΙΑ Archive. Reference no. KOU 1.087*)

Andrew and Alice photographed on the Royal yacht *Amphitrite* on the day of their arrival at Piraeus, Christmas 1903. (*EΛIA Archive. Reference no. 04.16.3.038*)

Alice photographed on the Royal yacht *Amphitrite* on 24 April 1904, dressed up in Andrew's cavalry officer uniform and wearing his spectacles as well. (*EΛIA Archive. Reference no. 04.16.3.046*)

A group photograph from 1910 depicting the families of Andrew (standing, right) and his brother Nicholas. Nicholas and Ellen had three daughters while Andrew and Alice at the time two, as Cecile and Sophia had not yet been born. Andrew and Nicholas had been dismissed from the Greek army in the previous year and are photographed in civilian clothes. (Tatler, *30 March 1910*)

A photograph taken by Italian photographer Luca Comerio in 1907 showing the car driven by Andrew arriving outside the palace at Tatoi with Vittorio Emanuele III and George I in the back seat. Next to Andrew sits Vittorio Emanuele's bodyguard. (*Private collection*)

Photograph of Andrew and Alice which appeared on the cover of *Tatler* during the First World War, 12 January 1916.

The front page of *Daily Mirror* of 10 May 1917 attacking Prince Andrew and accusing him of being a Germanophile and ungrateful to the British people.

Andrew (centre), with his siblings Maria and Christopher photographed on the deck of the Greek warship *Ierax* in November 1920 while returning to Greece from their exile. The Naval officer next to them is Perikles Ioannides commander of *Ierax* and future husband of Maria. (*Pinterest: https://gr.pinterest.com/pin/417286721719744646/?nic_v2=1a4geF3GG*)

Andrew (centre) photographed in 1921 in Asia Minor with other Greek commanders. (*EΛIA Archive. Reference no. 2643*)

Andrew on the Asia Minor front in July 1921 photographed outside his tent next to a pelican. (*France. Agence Rol*)

Andrew as a lieutenant General in Athens in 1921 after he had returned from Asia Minor. (*France. Agence Meurisse*)

Andrew with his baby son, Philip.

Photograph of the judges at Andrew's court-martial in 1922 as its president is about to announce the verdict. Andrew and his attorney, Damaskinos, are seated opposite the judges' bench. (*France. Agence Rol*)

Andrew playing around with Philip's tricycle at Saint-Cloud.

The cover of *Tatler* of 12 July 1921 with Philip's four sisters who were photographed in London where they attended Dickie Mountbatten's wedding as bridesmaids.

Andrew, Alice and their two eldest daughters, Theodora and Margarita, are photographed in London in December 1922. (*France. Agence Rol*)

A photograph of Alice (far right), her eldest daughter, Margarita (forefront), and three unidentified Greek ladies in the shop 'Hellas' which Alice ran in Paris, selling silks, perfumes and other luxury products from Greece. (The Graphic, *3 December 1927*)

Andrew (centre under the banner) photographed at Halandri, Athens, on 21 May 1936 during his visit there to a gathering of monarchists. (Ellinikon Mellon, *22 May 1936*)

Alice's tomb in Jerusalem. Pinterest. (*https://i.pinimg.com/1200x/2c/41/1d/ 2c411d2430ff83fd6b87b3d75b31b099.jpg*)

Photograph of Philip as a smiling toddler on the front page of the *Buffalo Courier*, 30 July 1922.

Seven year old Philip -second from left- with other pupils of the MacJannet American School in Paris, practicing archery. (Standard Union, *7 May 1928*)

A group photograph of Greek royals on vacation at the seaside in Romania with the local king, Michael, and his mother. Seven year old Prince Philip (second from right) sits next to his cousin, Prince Paul, the future king of Greece. (London Illustrated News, *15 September 1928*)

Philip photographed by Emile Markovitch at
Paris in 1930. He is dressed in the traditional
costume of a Greek evzone, the elite palace
guards in Greece. (*Private collection*)

Philip (far left) and three other pupils of Gordonstoun photographed during the rehearsals of the School's production of Macbeth in 1935. (*Aberdeen Press and Journal, 3 August 1935*)

Prince Philip as the sentry at a play of Hamlet at Gordonstoun School in 1936. (Aberdeen Press and Journal, *28 July 1936*)

Philip in the Nativity play of Gordonstoun School in December 1938 as one of the three kings, offering his crown to baby Jesus. (*Photograph in the* Decatur Herald, *24 December 1938*)

Gordonstoun School hockey team in 1936. On the front row, first to the left is Prince Philip as captain of the team. (Aberdeen Press and Journal, *13 March 1936*)

An action photograph of Philip on the hockey team of Gordonstoun. (Aberdeen Press and Journal, *9 March 1938*)

Gordonstoun School Cricket team in 1938. Pictured in the centre is Prince Philip as captain of the team. (Aberdeen Press and Journal, *21 July 1938*)

A still from the newsreel of the funeral of the Greek Royals in Athens in 1936 showing Philip walking in the procession behind Andrew who is wearing his ceremonial uniform as Greek general (next to Andrew is Christopher, also in the uniform of a Greek general). Philip is talking to his brother-in-law, Prince Gottfried of Hohenlohe-Langenburg, who is wearing his uniform as officer of the Luftwaffe. (*Private collection*)

Philip in Venice during late summer 1938. He is photographed with Mrs de Levigne. (The Tatler, *21 September 1938*)

Philip having drinks with Cobina Wright Jr and Sir Robert Peel. (Tampa Bay Times, *7 December 1941*)

Photograph of Cobina Wright Jr. with the caption 'Prince Philip is upset'. (Daily News, *16 January 1940*)

Photograph of nineteen year old Philip published in *The Australian Women's Weekly*, 20 April 1940. Philip looks identical with his grandson Prince William when he was of the same age.

The article in the *Daily Telegraph* of 7 April 1940 describing Philip as 'Mystery Man' and treating him as if he were a wanted criminal with his photograph so that the public will be able to identify him.

Philip in naval uniform dining out in 1944 in London with childhood friend Georgina Wernher. There were rumours at the time that they had a relationship, something, however, which both denied. (The Tatler and Bystander, *26 July 1944*)

PRINCE AT LUNA PARK

Photograph of Philip (foreground) and other officers of the HMS *Whelp* in civilian clothes enjoying themselves in a revolving barrel in Sydney's Luna park. (Daily Telegraph, *5 December 1945*)

Photograph of Philip on the cover of *The Sketch* of 18 September 1946. The caption bears the title *Greek Sailor Prince*.

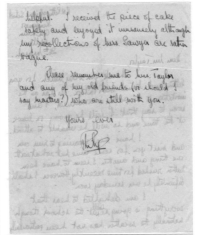

Photograph of an unpublished letter Prince Philip sent in 1947 to his old school master at Cheam, the Reverend Taylor, with references to his time there as a pupil. (*Private collection*)

Philip and Elizabeth on the
Acropolis in Athens in 1950 with
King Paul of Greece in the centre.

The Church of Saints Philip and
Elizabeth at Nikaia in Athens.
(*Authors' archive*)

The mayor of Athens, Pafsanias
Katsotas and members of the Athens
municipality council smash the
plaque commemorating Philip and
Elizabeth at their namesake church
at Nikaia. Photograph published
on the front pages of various Greek
newspapers in May 1956.

France, that he helped coin the term *Kriegsschuldluge* (the war-guilt lie), that would ironically be employed by the fanatically anti-Semitic Nazi Party as its explosive slogan to justify revenge and rearmament. In 1920 Hahn and the Baden family founded a school at Schloss Salem in Baden-Württemberg and it was here that Theodora sent Philip in autumn 1933.

It was an anxious time to move to Germany as Adolf Hitler had recently come to power. Hitler had been in office only for a few months but it was enough to create political tensions; Hahn himself was arrested for taking part in anti-Nazi protests. For Philip the move was bad timing. 'He wasn't really integrated into the community,' one of the masters at Hahn's school had to admit. 'He had little opportunity to make real friends, and he spoke very little German. He was really very isolated.'[3] The Nazis naturally promoted the school's own Hitler Youth, whose members used the Nazi salute. Philip would wryly note that the salute was the same gesture that the boys at Schloss Salem used to ask to go to the toilet.

Hahn was ejected from Germany and moved to Scotland, where he set up Gordonstoun School. Philip moved there in September 1934, and received the benefit of Hahn's radical and innovative teaching methods. Hahn believed that adolescents should be respected, but at the same time they were susceptible to the corruptions of society. Hahn had a theory that civilization decayed in six stages, which he saw reflected in young people if they weren't careful. The stages of decay were first in fitness, followed by initiative and enterprise, memory and imagination, skill and care, self-discipline, and lastly compassion. Gordonstoun pupils were taught to counter the degenerating tendencies. For instance, they rose at seven o'clock every morning, donned shorts and ran barefoot for three hundred yards to the washroom where they showered in cold water, winter and summer. Unlike at other British secondary schools, most of the students' free time went into tough physical training and chores, something hitherto unheard-of for an exclusive private school such as Gordonstoun. The hardy, energetic and competitive Philip flourished under this tough regimen. In his last year he even became head boy. Under Hahn, first at Salem and then at Gordonstoun, Philip received an education and training unique for a scion of the Greek, or any royal family. In that respect he was exceptional. Gordonstoun, and being under the wing of the Mountbattens and Milford Havens, seem to have given Philip that vital sense of stability that was so lacking in his young life so far.[4]

A turning point in Philip's life came with the marriage in November 1934 of his cousin Princess Marina, the daughter of Prince Nicholas, to George, Duke of Kent, the brother of the future King George VI. Philip attended the wedding at the Greek Orthodox Cathedral in London. One of the bridesmaids was Princess Elizabeth, the bridegroom's niece. Marina's wedding meant that Philip was no longer referred to in the British press simply as 'Prince of Greece' but more importantly, as the cousin of the Duchess of Kent. It was an appellation that elevated his position vis-a-vis the British aristocracy. As far as Greece was concerned, however, the marriage became a rallying-point for the Greek monarchists, who were working openly to bring back their George II. But the whole royal family was by no means united on this: the moderate and artistic Prince Nicholas, for example, made clear his utter lack of interest in Greek politics. Moreover, the British government had deemed it necessary to reassure the Greek government that the marriage was in no way an act of interference in Greek domestic affairs.

In 1935 Hahn introduced a course in 'coastal duties' and hired as instructor a retired naval officer, Lieutenant Commander J. H. Lewty.[5] The *Portsmouth Evening News* made explicit mention of Philip as one of the students who attended the obligatory twice-weekly course to qualify the pupils as coast guards.[6] Lessons were usually taught by the sea on the Moray Firth. As part of their training the pupils observed a display of life-saving at sea by the Lossiemouth Rocket Life-Saving Brigade. Philip was one of the pupils who took part in the display.[7] In December of that year, Philip as a British Sea Scout helped build a watchman's hut on the Moray Firth coast.[8] He and other pupils on the seamanship course sometimes shared duties with the coast guard, especially in bad weather.[9] In August 1937, when Gordonstoun closed for the summer holiday, twenty-four of its pupils took a three-week cruise from Scotland to Norway on board the school's ketch-rigged sailing boat *Henrietta*. Among them was Philip.[10] The pupils on this cruise received training at sea to supplement the training they had acquired at Lewty's courses on the Moray Firth. Thus introduced to seamanship, Philip by then had already made up his mind to pursue a naval career. His maternal (Mountbatten) grandfather and uncles had a tradition of service in the Royal Navy and this would have played an important role in inspiring young Philip. Undoubtedly his schooling at Gordonstoun brought his dream of a career as a navy officer closer to realization – that is, as an officer in the Greek (or Royal Hellenic) Navy.

Lieutenant Commander Lewty was a capable instructor and taught Philip and his fellow pupils many details of seamanship. Philip had a natural talent in the field and with the help of Lewty his progress was rapid, as can be seen in the instructor's reports. Through his studies at Gordonstoun Philip acquired basic naval skills early in life. A few years later this acquired knowledge and ability would put him ahead of the other cadets at the Royal Naval College at Dartmouth.[11] It is not clear if Hahn introduced the seamanship course at Gordonstoum as a nod to Philip and his relatives the Mountbattens, or simply because his new school was very close to the sea. Philip's grandmother Victoria, Lady Milford Haven, wrote to Dickie Mountbatten on 5 November 1935, mentioning that Andrew told her about a naval officer [Lewty] who was 'a sport master etc.' at Gordonstoun and who would turn Philip into someone able to serve in the Navy.[12] This does not necessarily mean that the seamanship course had been introduced at Gordonstoun specially for Philip's benefit. Nevertheless, the Mountbattens may well have lent their support as Lady Milford Haven was invited to officially name the ship that the school used for the course. This she duly did in February 1939 during a ceremony in Hopeman harbour with Philip and his seamanship tutor Lewty by her side.[13] A few days later Philip graduated from Gordonstoun and went on to Dartmouth.

The school helped Philip bring to the fore other skills besides seafaring, such as sports and amateur dramatics, which Hahn wanted all his students to cultivate. Though not one of the top academic achievers at Gordonstoun, Philip turned out to be a good all-round athlete and a competent actor. A month after arriving at Gordonstoun he took part in a hockey game against Inverness. A newspaper reported that 'he played a strong, forcing game as right half-back and was prominent'.[14] The team was not quite the top of the league, though in later years its standing improved thanks to Philip's good performance as a centre forward.

On 9 March 1938 the *Aberdeen Press and Journal* celebrated Philip's contributions to the team's victories as a centre forward by publishing his photograph taken during a hockey game captioned, 'An action picture of young Prince Philip of Greece, centre forward of Gordonstoun School, Duffus, hockey team'.[15] On 12 November 1938 he was the big scorer with two goals in another impressive 4–1 victory over Aberdeen in the Highland District League.[16] Philip remained on the team until graduation.

But it was cricket that Prince Philip excelled in. In 1938 and 1939 there were frequent reports in local Scottish newspapers about the cricket games of Gordonstoun School and Philip's participation and performance.[17] Philip was usually the first to bat during these matches. The team scored a spectacular victory in July 1938, thanks partly to Philip's contribution, prompting the *Aberdeen Press and Journal* to run a story headlined: 'Gordonstoun School – This Moray school team are building up a fine reputation as cricketers in the North'. In the photograph of the team, Philip is seated in the middle of the team and named as captain.[18]

On 10 June 1935, his fourteenth birthday, Philip just managed to squeeze under the age limit for the high jump.[19] There is no evidence of his participating in such competitions in later years at Gordonstoun, but according to the *Tatler and Bystander* of 30 April 1941: 'At [age] 17.5 in the Plymouth Command Naval Sports, [Philip] staggered everyone when he beat all the full-grown champions at the ancient Greek sport of throwing the javelin'. If the recorded age of Philip is correct in the article, then the high jump should be dated to about the time he started his studies at the Dartmouth Royal Naval Academy. Later on, as a midshipman in the Royal Navy, he threw the javelin at an 'inter-port sports meeting'.[20] Apparently Philip performed better in team sports rather than individual athletics, and was good at inspiring and encouraging team members.

In the sphere of dramatics, he acted in school plays with considerable success. On 1 August 1935 Gordonstoun students staged Shakespeare's *Macbeth* – the quintessential Scottish play – in an open-air performance. This performance, attended by some three hundred people, was given in conjunction with Scotland's Garden Scheme in aid of the Nursing Association funds.[21] Philip played the part of Donalbain,[22] his debut on the stage.[23] It is likely that Philip was chosen for the role of Donalbain as he had much in common with this character. Both were princes who had been exiled from their countries following tragic events suffered by their respective fathers. Donalbain represents moral order in *Macbeth*, and the father-son motif is strong.[24]

In the play Donalbain eventually returns to Scotland and helps his brother, Malcolm, take the throne seized by Macbeth. Philip may well have been aware that the Greek republic was fading after the crushing of a Venizelist coup in March 1935, and that it was only a matter of time before the monarchy was re-established (which it would be, in November, see next chapter). Philip's parents were almost sure to return to Greece, and Philip himself would be a prince of Greece in fact as well as in name.

The part of Donalbain involves long periods where the character performs without necessarily having to speak – rather fitting for an athletic boy. Photographs of the cast were taken at Gordonstoun on 1 July 1935. They show that the cast rehearsed for at least a month before the production. They also show that Philip was the youngest member of the group of pupils performing in the play.[25] As we have seen, even as a child Philip tended to play with children older than him. Rather inaccurately, on 31 July 1935 several Scottish newspapers reported that Philip was cast in the play as Malcolm.[26] Had he in fact been switched to the role of Donalbain at the last minute? Yet on 23 August, the *Central Somerset Gazette* reported that Philip played the part of Malcolm,[27] though it appears probable that this publication simply copied what had been printed almost a month earlier in the Scottish press. Actually, Philip might well have found the role of Malcolm even closer to his situation than that of Donalbain: Malcolm is exiled from Scotland, finds refuge in England and is helped by the English to reclaim his throne and kill Macbeth. It may be worthy of note that the performance took place in August, when schools were closed and the students were with their families. The following year, the Gordonstoun students performed *Hamlet*, with Philip playing the part of the sentry. Unlike the 1935 performance of *Macbeth*, the Gordonstoun students' *Hamlet* does not appear to have attracted much press attention, with the single exception of the *Aberdeen Press and Journal*, which in its 28 July 1936 edition published a photograph of Philip performing in the play.[28]

In December 1935 Prince Philip took part in the Nativity play of Gordonstoun which was performed at the seaside village of Hopeman on the Moray Firth just over a mile from the school. The proceeds from the tickets went to finance the coast-guarding service that the students had inaugurated a week earlier.[29] Most of the ordinary people attending, such as fishermen and mariners, knew the students, as they had often worked together with them. One of Hahn's principles had been that of working for the local community, with the privileged students giving something back to the lower classes.[30] (Except for Prince Paul, Philip may well have been the first Greek royal to have experience of working alongside ordinary labouring people.)

In subsequent years Philip took part in other Nativity plays, all duly noted in the local press. But it was the international press that took note of his final Nativity performance in December 1938. This was in the Town Hall of Forres for the benefit of the local hospital.[31] Philip played one of the Three Kings. It is likely that here, too, the role given Philip was influenced by the fact that he was a prince and at the time a viable candidate for the throne of Greece, which would naturally attract global media interest. Many newspapers in the United Kingdom and the United States carried reports and a photograph from the play showing Philip on his knees offering his crown to baby Jesus.[32] The photograph may well have been released by Hahn for publicity for his school. Besides, Philip was by then Gordonstoun's most famous pupil. But there were shadows. In May 1940, as German troops were sweeping through Europe, Hahn and his school would be suspected by the British authorities of being pro-German. Five masters and eleven of its students would be interned as enemy aliens and Hahn questioned about his activities. Hahn would issue a statement defending himself and Gordonstoun and strongly emphasizing that Prince Philip – now a Royal Navy officer – had been a graduate of the school.[33] At the time of the 1938 Nativity play and the press coverage it received, the Americans had another kind of special interest in the seventeen-year-old Greek prince, which will be related later.

Hahn's philosophy had a great impact on Philip; many years later Philip called on the educator to help found the Duke of Edinburgh's Award programme, a scheme active today in 144 countries, and based on Hahn's six-stage theory. Philip even arranged for his first son Prince Charles to follow in his footsteps and study at Gordonstoun (which, in contrast to Philip, Charles hated). When Hahn died in 1974 Philip read the story of the Good Samaritan at the memorial service. Philip also developed a deep affection for Scotland, as evidenced by his official title as Duke of Edinburgh. It appears that Scotland became a surrogate country for the Prince at a time when he was not sure what his country actually was. Scotland had apparently replaced Greece as his home. During his years there he became essentially isolated from the rest of his extended royal family. In the school register of Gordonstoun school Philip was listed under his Christian name and travelled by train to his cousin's Princess Marina's wedding to the Duke of Kent as 'Mr Philips'.[34] He may well have taken other trips under that surname.

Disappointingly, during his entire five years at the school, neither George Milford Haven nor Philip's other British guardian, Lord Louis ('Dickie') Mountbatten, visited him. He would have remembered with nostalgia his holidays at Constanza on Romania's Black Sea coast. There is a photograph of him taken there in the summer of 1928; the blond and sunburned prince squints into the camera, flanked by Greek and Romanian royals, while Prince Paul places a protective arm around him and a small terrier nestles at his feet. It is the very image of a boy who for a long time didn't know where he belonged.

Chapter 8

Lucky Royals, Unlucky Andrew

The year 1935 turned out to be a watershed, not only in modern Greek history but also in Philip's young life. Eleven years of a republic had not made the country any more governable or stable. The 1920s had witnessed a bewildering succession of attempted coups and counter-coups more reminiscent of comic opera than serious politics. The egos of ambitious and self-important generals overlaid the perennial royalist-liberal conflict that stubbornly refused to go away. Venizelos himself had tried to moderate the more extreme phenomena, with some success. As prime minister after his landslide victory in the general election of 1928, he signed a non-aggression pact with Mussolini's Italy that same year (accepting Italy's occupation of the twelve Greek islands of the Dodecanese) and a ground-breaking one with Turkey's President Atatürk (as General Mustafa Kemal had now become) in 1930, cemented by a triumphal visit to Istanbul and Ankara. That Venizelos and Atatürk were contemporaries, writes Woodhouse, 'was a fortunate conjunction for Greece and Turkey.' Was the age-old conflict with the Turks about to draw to a close? There was every reason to believe so. Moreover, diplomatic moves were afoot to regularize relations with Albania and Yugoslavia (though Bulgaria held aloof).

On the surface it appeared that Venizelos had put some order into the ever-unpredictable Greek politics, and that a monarchy was no longer required as a stabilizer. A republic on the European model was what many Greeks seemed to want, and for a time they had one. Yet few could have predicted at the time of Venizelos' triumphant reception in Turkey in 1930 that Greece within five years would have its king again, and in the person of George II, the only Greek monarch to be exiled three times and return to his throne twice. The reason lies largely in Venizelos himself; he has been described as a 'romantic nationalist, not a political economist.'[1] He lived in the world of the Versailles Treaty, where the nations of Europe could work out their own borders and identities under the liberal gospel of the idealistic American president, Woodrow Wilson.

That time, however, had long passed (if it had ever existed). Greek political intrigues took no account of ivory-tower theories of international cooperation. There was still a large royalist element in the population, always at odds with the Venizelist liberals, a situation that stoked extremism on both sides. A huge influx of ethnic Greek refugees from Turkey after the Asia Minor War and the effects of the global Great Depression placed huge strains on the state mechanism. With the country on the verge of bankruptcy, Venizelos travelled cap in hand to Europe's capitals, was largely rebuffed, and had to partly default on loans to foreign bondholders in 1932. Faced with withering criticism, in desperation he attempted to muzzle the press, which was his undoing. Forced to resign in May 1932, he intrigued with liberal military officers to prevent the return of the royalists. These latter had formed the Populist Party (Laikon Komma) headed by Panagis Tsaldaris. Ever since 1922 Tsaldaris had always made a point on his trips abroad of calling on the exiled royals, in particular George II and Prince Andrew, to keep them abreast of political developments at home. In a gesture of political realism, however, in 1932 he had issued an official statement pledging allegiance to the republic; he in fact stuck to his pledge in the face of fierce opposition from within his own party until 1935, when the monarchy was reinstated.

A general election on 6 March 1933 gave the Populist Party a parliamentary majority. Extreme liberals took fright; Plastiras staged an inept coup attempt that fizzled through a lack of popular support, forcing him to flee to France, that haven of all opponents of crowned heads. The Populist government sent strong signals about its monarchist intentions, whose effect was only to further ignite passions on both sides. Venizelos escaped another assassination attempt (described below) and retired in bad grace to his native Crete.

As we have seen, Andrew had been the most vocal and energetic of all the exiled Greek royals in the campaign to have the republic abolished and the monarchy reinstated. In such a case his family could return to its homeland and he could play a meaningful role as a senior royal. In 1932, however, only a minority of the Greek people harboured any real hopes of a restoration. Even Tsaldaris, the leader of the pro-royalist

Populist Party, the second biggest in Greece, and a monarchist himself, had bowed to political reality. The sharp rift between the Venizelist republicans and the royalists still existed, but the latter had lost much of their power and influence, especially after the failed royalist counter-coup of 1923 and the abolition of the monarchy the following year. Over the next eight years all the political turmoil in Greece had been caused by the Venizelist-republican factions fighting for power among themselves. The royals were simply observers from afar, one imagines not without a certain *schadenfreude*.

There was, of course, still a great deal of interest aimed in the opposite direction. A great many Greeks at home retained a keen interest in the doings of the royal family, but this interest was largely confined to the content of the society columns of the newspapers. There was much sympathetic coverage, for example, of the engagements and weddings of Andrew's four daughters in 1931 – even in the Venizelist press. This sympathy, however, dried up when it came to Andrew's occasional interviews with the foreign press, where he outspokenly insisted that only the restitution of the monarchy would help Greece solve its serious social and economic problems. The Venizelist press would sharply attack those comments, usually with heavy doses of sarcasm. (The pro-royalist press, of course, would give them great and adulatory prominence. There was no such thing as even-handedness in the media of the time – or any time).

In 1931 Greece began to experience the severe effects of the Great Depression. As the country had received large foreign loans in order to resettle the many thousands of refugees from Asia Minor and Eastern Thrace, it suffered rather more than other European countries except Germany. Greece defaulted in the following year, with the economic crisis becoming acute enough to see off Venizelos' last majority government. He briefly resumed power in early 1933 but only as the powerless head of a caretaker government. The crisis in fact gave great impetus to the monarchists, boosting their claim that only a regime change could help the country. On 4 June 1932 Andrew lambasted Venizelos in a letter to the Greek royalist newspaper *Proia*, blaming him for Greece's seas of troubles. Andrew pinned responsibility for the infamous 1922 executions personally on Venizelos himself, calling it a crime against innocent men and 'martyrs'. The letter can be considered a direct intervention in

Greek politics on Andrew's part, as he had sent it only a few days before a scheduled general election. It also reopened old wounds by referring to the executions. Naturally, the republican faction had a field day with it, declaring in their own newspapers that Andrew posed a direct threat to the republic and the stability of the country.[2] In particular, the Venizelists' most influential newspaper, the *Eleftheron Bima,* in an editorial on 4 June 1932 insisted that Andrew's letter broke the most important rule for a royal, that is, not to take the side of any political faction. It also increased the risk of another expulsion of the royal family if politics should enable it to return. The article ended by telling Andrew that if he thought calmly about his actions he would realize that it was such interference in Greek politics that had led to the expulsion of his family from Greece in the first place.

Andrew was now seen by friend and foe alike as the main spokesman for the monarchists, unlike George II, who in exile kept himself carefully above the fray and remained wisely silent. Andrew's statements and actions were of course keenly scrutinized in Greece, both endorsed and condemned by the respective press factions. Venizelist fears that Andrew might return to Greece and plot against the republic reached a high pitch during the summer of 1932. On 15 and 16 August, Edward, the Prince of Wales, and his brother George, the Duke of Kent, officially visited Corfu on board the battleship HMS *Elizabeth* accompanied by other ships of the Mediterranean Fleet. They received a warm welcome by the government (headed by Venizelos in a caretaker capacity), but a rumour quickly got around that the 'real' purpose of the visit by the two British princes was to secretly disembark their relatives Andrew and Alice on Corfu. This facetious tale gained wide acceptance among both royalists and Venizelists for their own respective purposes, and the Greek and British governments had to issue strong denials.[3] It was a sign that Andrew was making the Venizelists edgy, especially during the worst economic crisis in the history of the country which was eating away at the public.

In fact, Andrew at the time was stepping up his efforts to win the Greeks over to the idea of restoring the monarchy as the solution to all their problems; his letter to the press had only been the first shot. In Greece he had staunch allies and friends who helped in the campaign. One of them was his former ADC, Menelaos Metaxas, who in 1921 had retired as a cavalry colonel. Unlike in Andrew's first exile in 1917, Metaxas did not accompany the family abroad this time, remaining in Greece as a civilian to look after the Prince's estate, most of which was confiscated by the republic – except Mon Repos, the ownership of which would be decided by the courts, which as we saw eventually ruled in Andrew's favour. Therefore Metaxas set up his own business importing automobiles from Germany. He then moved on to importing photographic materials and cameras and supplying gyroscopes and other instruments to the fledgling Hellenic Air Force.[4] In December 1932 Alice's two sisters-in-law, Edwina, the wife of Dickie Mountbatten, and Nada, the wife of Georgie, called at Athens after a long tour of the Middle East. In Athens they met Menelaos Metaxas who looked after them and acted as their chaperone.[5] The fact that in late 1932 Metaxas accompanied the Mountbatten wives in Athens shows that he was always regarded as a close associate and confidant of Andrew and Alice. It is likely that Edwina and Nada may have conveyed information from Metaxas to Andrew to avoid sending it through the mail and having it possibly intercepted by agents of the Venizelist government.

However staunch a monarchist Menelaos Metaxas was, remaining in touch with Andrew, he refrained from involving himself in politics until 1933, when on 30 June of that year he appeared in Thessaloniki as the 'representative' of Princes Andrew and Nicholas at Populist Party rallies for prospective monarchist parliamentary deputies.[6] This was duly noted in the Venizelist press, which linked his presence there with the strengthening of royalist circles in Greece's second largest city – and of course feared a 'a threat to the republic'. The republicans were right to be worried; three months earlier, that old warrior Plastiras had attempted a coup whose failure was partly attributed to action by royalists in northern Greece. Plastiras himself was forced to flee the country. To add to the confusion, Thessaloniki was the base of Georgios Kondylis, the former fanatic Venizelist general who in 1932 changed sides and began supporting the restoration of the monarchy, co-operating with elements inside and outside Greece to achieve this goal.

The victory of the Populist Party in the 6 March 1933 elections was a big step towards the restoration of the monarchy. However, the newly elected Tsaldaris government failed to address any of the serious problems that it had inherited from Venizelos' final administration, as its parliamentary majority was too slender. In June machine-gun-toting hitmen fired on Venizelos' car as he was being driven into Athens from the northern suburbs. In a scene that could have been lifted from a gangster movie, the assailants chased the ex-prime minister in their own car for some kilometres; Venizelos' automobile was riddled with bullets that narrowly missed him and his wife but mortally wounded a bodyguard. Suspicion at once fell upon a purported far-right 'deep state' supposed to include police officials and Populist Party figures. The Athens Chief of Police, Georgios Polychronopoulos, and other police and army officers were arrested as suspected accomplices in the Venizelos' assassination attempt. Ironically, before his arrest, Polychronopoulos had been put in charge of the police investigation.

Naturally the factional struggle took on fresh intensity, reminiscent of the violence of two decades before. Andrew stepped up his attacks on the republic and the Venizelists, culminating in an interview to the *Laikos Agon* (People's Struggle) weekly on 29 December 1934.[7] In it he claimed that he received hundreds of letters and telegrams a day from monarchist supporters calling for a restoration. The weekly itself maintained close ties with Andrew, often reporting on his activities, including his regular denunciations of Venizelos and his faction. However, Andrew's choice of media appears to have been an unfortunate one, as *Laikos Agon*, far from belonging to the mainstream press, was a recently-established fringe publication that from the outset took an extreme monarchist position, alienating even the moderate majority of monarchist supporters. Its front page was regularly emblazoned with royalist slogans.

Its publisher, in fact, happened to be the son of Georgios Polychronopoulos, the police chief accused of complicity in the Venizelos assassination attempt. Early issues of *Laikos Agon* claimed that its sole purpose was to clear the name of Polychronopoulos and the other officials who had been arrested as suspects. Yet it soon revealed its overt royalist colours, loudly calling for a restoration; in 1934 its leading articles urged that a right-wing dictatorship be set up. This stand tended to identify the publication with far-right and 'deep-state' elements, real or imagined. The impression was reinforced by open calls for its readership to murder Venizelos, and included several exquisite suggestions as to how it might be done.[8] Some leading articles went so far as to declare all-out war against Venizelos' supporters everywhere, including physical elimination. Understandably, Prince Andrew's public image after contributing to such a publication took a dive and it was natural that in the eyes of many he would be identified with the shadowy far right.[9] Was he aware of this? If he was, it seemed not to bother him too much. George II kept himself carefully away from any such controversies.

The British ambassador in Athens, Sir Sydney Waterlow, reported to the Foreign Office that what the 'disreputable' Andrew had done was a serious error.[10] Waterlow added perceptively that Andrew's actions were in danger of undermining any prospects of George II's restoration, an aim the British government was actively backing. The Venizelist *Eleftheron Bima* on 30 December 1934 in a front page editorial rebutted Andrew, declaring that if the monarchy were ever reinstated, the monarchists would get rid of their opponents and then divide the public asset spoils among themselves. Venizelists, it said, would rather fight and die than have the 'pack of royal wolves return to devour what little Greece had been left with...They will fight tooth and nail to prevent the restoration of the monarchy and the persecution of half the Greek population'.

Andrew's indiscretions also played into the hands of the Greek Communist Party (KKE), which had its own revolutionary reasons for wanting to get rid of the bourgeois republic and replace it with a Marxist state. The communists, however, saw pro-monarchy sentiment getting stronger by the day and decided that it was the main foe. In August 1935 the KKE issued a manifesto accusing Prince Andrew of dividing the Greek people:

> The scion of the deposed dynasty, Prince Andrew, publishes articles in newspapers, preaches national division and promises material compensation [for the monarchists] which of course will be given immediately [after the restoration] and will burden the working people with new taxes of millions.[11]

The event that finally brought down the republic was an unwise and abortive coup by Venizelos in March 1935 that discredited the old Cretan statesman for good and soaked his movement in disrepute. The republic by now was on very shaky legs. Another cause was the Tsaldaris administration's lack of a strong governing majority, and the threat of the last president of the republic, Alexandros Zaimis, to resign. In the first half of 1935 the Athens press was rife with speculation that if Zaimis went ahead with his threat and resigned, Prince Andrew or Prince Nicholas might become regent in anticipation of George II's return.[12] There were also wider reasons for wanting the king back. As the 1930s progressed, the darkening European stage made many Greeks think that the country needed a strong royal figurehead who could unite the country. Mussolini's Italy was flexing its muscles, while the advent of Adolf Hitler was jangling nerves across the continent. Greece's only reliable ally at the time seemed to be Great Britain, where George II was living, and with his restoration, it was widely believed, Greek-British ties would be cemented yet further. This threw fervent republicans such as Plastiras – still in exile in France since his 1933 failed coup – into a panic. He managed to talk Venizelos into lending his name to the abortive March 1935 coup, which forced Venizelos to seek refuge in France. He and Plastiras were sentenced to death *in absentia*, two generals were shot (one of them was Papoulas of Asia Minor fame – or notoriety) and a host of other officers cashiered. The effort effectively boomeranged in that all it did was increase public backing for the monarchy.

The monarchists were by now certain that it was only a matter of time before the republic collapsed and George II could return to Greece as king. Among them were some members of Tsaldaris' cabinet who were becoming impatient with him as they thought that he was stalling the regime change. Andrew in exile also lost his patience and wrote two long articles about what Greeks should expect from the restoration of the monarchy. He sent both articles to the newspaper *Ellinikon Mellon* (Greek Future) which published them on the front page of its editions of 8 and 9 August 1935. These articles were even more extreme than the interview Andrew had given to *Laikos Agon* eight months earlier. *Ellinikon Mellon*, like *Laikos Agon*, was staunchly monarchist, anti-republican and on the far-right fringe of the Greek press. Though not as extreme as *Laikos Agon*, *Ellinikon Mellon* was dead against any compromise with the Venizelists.

In his articles Andrew called on 'old comrades', meaning Greek friends of the monarchy which included many in the ruling Populist Party, to fight for the royal cause. He went on to assure those who had suffered under the republic that as soon as George II became king again they would be financially compensated. Andrew set his face against any reconciliation with the 'criminal' Venizelists and claimed to know very well exactly who they were; he warned them against trying to pass themselves off as royalists, as they would be discovered and rooted out. Yet he struck a note of conciliation of sorts by asserting that there were followers of Venizelos who were 'as Greek as himself' and did not rule out a deal with those who repented for previous errors. Yet it was clear that the crushing of the March 1935 Venizelist coup had added to Andrew's extremism and intolerance of those he considered to be his Greek foes.

Andrew's articles created a huge uproar in Greece. He came across as nursing vengeful feelings against a large percentage of his countrymen who supported Venizelos' Liberal Party. His views were condemned not only by the Venizelist press, as was to be expected, but also by newspapers that were trying to be politically neutral or even moderate supporters of the return of the monarchy. Their main criticism was that Andrew was planning to start a civil war as soon as the monarchy was reinstated in Greece by tolerating or even inciting far-right violent attacks on key members of Venizelos's Liberal party and its followers. Two leading Venizelist newspapers, *Athinaika Nea* and *Eleftheron Bima*, reprinted Andrew's articles on their own front pages on 9 and 10 August 1935, and rebutted them point by point. Both newspapers warned their readers that if Andrew got his way a dreadful civil war would result that would destroy the entire nation. (Which actually would happen ten years later.) The *Athinaika Nea* of 10 August called Andrew a great liability for the return of the monarchy. It addressed George II, telling him that if he ever returned to Greece he would have to be king not of just his royalist friends but of all Greeks.

The message appeared to be lost on Andrew, who clearly associated the monarchy with a single party, the Populists. On 11 August 1935, a leader in *Eleftheron Bima* rubbished Andrew's claim that there were also 'real Greeks' like himself among the Venizelists by simply denying that he was a 'real Greek'! *Estia*, a neutral newspaper, also blasted Andrew and the 'uncivil' tone of his articles as painting a not-so-encouraging portrait of Greece under a restored monarchy. 'Today's National Division,' its leader said, 'will pale in significance compared to the troubles that will be caused by the attacks of the royalists against the majority of Greeks who support Venizelos and the republic'.

However, Andrew's intervention in Greek politics did not stop at just writing inflammatory articles for the far-right press. In early autumn 1935 staunch monarchists in Greece were fed up with Tsaldaris stalling the King's return and decided to launch a coup against him. So far it had been republican and Venizelist officers who had a predilection for organizing coups; this one, a monarchist one, was well organized and involved the three service chiefs: General Alexandros Papagos of the Army, Admiral Dimitris Ekonomou of the Navy and General Georgios Reppas of the Air Force. The nominal ringleader was ex-General Georgios Kondylis, vice-premier of the Tsaldaris government. On 10 October 1935, as Tsaldaris was being driven from his home to the opening session of the Parliament after the summer recess, he was forced at gunpoint to go back home and resign. That same day Kondylis appointed himself prime minister and brought to the Parliament a bill to abolish the republic and reinstate the monarchy.

Three days before the coup of 10 October *Athinaika Nea* ran an article according to which Princes Andrew and Nicholas had met George in Paris and talked with him about the best way the Greek monarchy could be put back on its feet. There was some disagreement. The King's view was that only the people's vote through a plebiscite would truly legitimize his return; on the contrary, Andrew and Nicholas thought George could be restored to his throne by act of parliament alone, and if that were not possible, a military coup might be needed. *Athinaika Nea* as a Venizelist paper had no love for the monarchy but this article shows that it had a good source of information within the royal household; it also shows that Andrew (and Nicholas) had contacts with major figures in the monarchist camp in Greece who kept him informed about their moves including the coup they were preparing for 10 October against Prime Minister Tsaldaris.

In October 1935, Parliament proclaimed Greece once again a constitutional monarchy, to be ratified by a plebiscite. This was held on

3 November and returned a verdict of nearly 98 per cent in favour of the King's return. The figure reflects a pronounced degree of rigging, including voter intimidation and ballot-stuffing – one authority calls the vote 'the most rigged in modern Greek history.'[13] But even without such tactics the vote would have swung the King's way anyway. Most Greeks were simply fed up with political insecurity and wanted the crown back. An official delegation travelled to London to inform George of his restoration at the Greek embassy in London. Returning via Paris and Rome, he arrived in Athens on 25 November 1935, after a twelve-year absence, to frantic rejoicing. The people may have been ready, but the palace itself wasn't. When George walked through the door he found that nothing had been done to prepare the place for his arrival. In the intervening years it had been used for state banquets and diplomatic receptions, but most of the furniture had gone. In fact, George had to sit on his suitcases in a corridor while a bedroom was hastily prepared for him.[14]

Included in the baggage which George brought from Britain was a deep and abiding mistrust of the Greek political class. Forty-five years old and at the height of his powers, he nevertheless knew that he would be called on to perform a difficult political tightrope act if he was not to suffer a third exile. Among his first acts was to pardon the republican coup plotters of 1 March 1935 and approve a general election for January 1936 that would serve to democratically legitimize his own restoration. That election for the first time brought into the equation the Greek Communist Party (KKE), which gained fifteen seats in the Parliament and became a power broker. As the Greek centre-left appeared willing to work with the communists, the King appointed a veteran monarchist to head the government. This was Ioannis Metaxas (cousin of Menelaos), who throughout his career had remained loyal to the crown and was seen as the most reliable guarantor of order.

The appointment came as a surprise, as Metaxas was the head of a small party; yet he had a record as a brilliant staff officer and was one of the sharpest minds of the country and one of its most incorruptible men to boot. Metaxas had little use for either the communists or the wealthy business class, and showed it. Conveniently, in early 1936 Venizelos died in exile (though not before urging his followers to accept the King as a factor in stability). His death in March 1936 cut the ground out from under the hardline republicans, but in their place the KKE had emerged as the main left-wing adversary of the royal family and conservative camp. Events in Spain were already demonstrating the dangers of excessive left-right strife. Bloody labour riots in Thessaloniki in May 1936 displayed the communists' growing disruptive power. Metaxas asked for and gained the approval of the Parliament to provisionally rule by decree. By 4 August the situation had deteriorated enough for Metaxas to ask George to dissolve the Parliament and indefinitely suspend some articles of the constitution; the King consented, and on that date the four-year dictatorship of the Fourth of August began under Ioannis Metaxas.

George has ever since been accused of acting unconstitutionally, rubber-stamping a grab for power by Metaxas, who proceeded to put in place a fascist-type corporate state which, however, had the approval of much of the peasant and middle classes. The economy rebounded. But the King had never been an autocrat or fascist by conviction; his backing of Metaxas was motivated purely by his deep contempt of ordinary time-serving politicians plus the growing threat of communism which the politicians' antics, he felt, were actually favouring. Greek democracy had too many weaknesses for him to feel fully comfortable with it. Did he exaggerate the threat of anarchy, as many claim? By nature austere and reserved, brought up in a Germanic tradition though an admirer of British decorum and restraint, he was unhappy, for example, with the establishment of the National Youth Organization (EON) which he thought was modelled too openly on Germany's *Hitlerjugend* (Hitler Youth), even down to the Nazi-type salute its members were taught to use.[15] Yet in his eyes it was better than the alternative of anarchy – or a Spanish-type civil war. Moreover, George was aware that Metaxas knew Germany intimately, and was aware before many other leaders of what Hitler's real intentions were.

George's restoration to the throne meant that Prince Andrew could at last return to Greece after a thirteen-year exile. But when George set foot again in Athens on 25 November 1935, Andrew was not with him. At the end of October 1935, Andrew had gone to London to meet George and arrange for their return to Greece. However, at a dinner held there on 28 October with the British Ambassador Sir Sydney

Waterlow, Crown Prince Paul and Prince Nicholas, Andrew heard with astonishment that he and Nicholas would not be returning to Greece with George and Paul.[16] Waterlow considered Andrew and Nicholas as a liability for the restored monarchy. In fact, in a cable to the Foreign Office a few days before George's return he made clear that his reign was almost certainly doomed if he had with him Andrew and Nicholas.[17] Waterlow's anxiety stemmed from the fact that the Venizelists would not tolerate the return of Andrew and to a lesser degree of Nicholas. We have already seen how Andrew had become a red flag for the Venizelists. Nicholas may have not been as active as Andrew against the republic, but the Venizelists suspected that while in exile he had been in contact with hardline monarchist plotters in Greece. Back in 1926 Prince Nicholas had published his memoirs, and also a book in 1928 based on his diaries about the events of 1914–1917 (*Political Memoirs 1914–1917. Pages from my Diary*) in which he pinned all blame for Greece's ills on Venizelos and his supporters. In contrast, the other two brothers, 'Big' George and Christopher, were not suspected of being involved in Greek politics; both lived permanently abroad and were not that eager to return to Greece.

All this, of course, was already well known to George, who had no need to learn about it from the British ambassador. George had made up his mind to return to Athens without the old guard of relatives who were reminiscent of the worst days of the National Division, which he wanted to end as soon as possible. The day after the royals dined with Waterlow, the Greek press received a communique from 'royal circles' in London that George's uncles, Andrew and Nicholas, would not be coming back with him just yet, but at an unspecified date in the future.[18] This announcement was published three days before the plebiscite of 3 November in an attempt to allay Venizelist fears that the bitter and vengeful Andrew might reappear. While Andrew was in London he saw his mother-in-law, Victoria, and told her that he would not return to Greece with King George, saying it was what he really wanted. But was he being honest? Andrew also told Victoria that George had 'sensible ideas' and that the only reason why he [Andrew] wanted to return to Greece on a later date was just to be seen by the people and so 'wipe out the shameful departure after the 'fake' court martial'.[19]

However, in another twist, on 30 November, five days after George's return to Greece, Athens dailies printed an 'official announcement' that Andrew, who was widely expected to be in Athens on the previous day, had postponed his visit until 'after the political crisis has ended'. Both the Venizelist and moderate royalist press that same day ran front-page leaders urging the King not to listen to the fanatics in his camp who wanted to start a civil war with the Venizelists.[20] The implication was that Andrew was indirectly associated with these fanatics and that George did not want him around in case his presence was a red flag to the liberals. There was also another point: in 1922 Andrew had been sentenced to perpetual banishment, a decision that would not be revoked until January 1936. But the overriding reason for his continued absence was that the King did not want to take even the slightest risk of dynamiting the process of reconciliation with the Venizelists that he had started, and this was the only way that they would accept his reign.

George returned to find no political party with a governing majority in the Parliament, and the country run by short-lived caretaker administrations. It was hoped that a general election scheduled for 26 January 1936 would solve the problem; George worked hard with the leaders of the two major political parties, Panagis Tsaldaris of the Populists and Themistocles Sophoulis of the Liberals (who had replaced the absent Venizelos) to find a way out. George's security on his newly acquired throne depended on achieving political stability; he knew very well that continuous political crises might well drive him again into exile, and needed to cultivate the supporters of Venizelos who had little love for him and the monarchy. Venizelos himself, after his abortive 1935 coup collapsed and his flight into exile, finally publicly accepted the restoration of the monarchy as a way for the Greeks to reunite.

As for Andrew, he in no way moderated his views in this crucial period. He had been too radicalized by his experiences of 1917–1920 and court martial in 1922, and unhesitatingly added his voice to the hardliners. In this he was seconded by the senior general Georgios Kondylis who had once been a fanatic republican in the mould of Pangalos and Plastiras, but in 1932, almost overnight, decided that his interests would be best served by switching sides and becoming a staunch monarchist. Kondylis, a key player in the campaign for the restoration of the monarchy, was the war minister in Tsaldaris' government, which gave him the advantage of influence with the military. He was instrumental in putting down the March 1935 Venizelist coup against the government of Tsaldaris. Then on 10 October 1935 he toppled Tsaldaris to speed up the transition to the restored monarchy. After the Greek Parliament had endorsed the restoration of the monarchy in October 1935, Kondylis proclaimed himself Regent in anticipation of the 3 November plebiscite which would ratify the King's return. He was widely believed to have been behind the rigging of the plebiscite. But if Kondylis had any hopes that he would retain his position as the strong man in the new regime for which he had fought so hard and unscrupulously, those hopes were soon dashed. As soon as the King returned, he publicly humiliated Kondylis by refusing to hear a welcoming speech the general had prepared, and not letting him ride into Athens with him in the open royal limousine.

One of George's first acts as King was to strip Kondylis of all power and influence, which probably helped cause his death two months later. Why was the treatment of the general so harsh? The fact is that George intended to quickly and decisively act to promote reconciliation between the Venizelists and royalists, and Kondylis had made it clear that he was strongly opposed to such a policy. Kondylis also appears to have believed fondly that the King would meekly toe his own line. To the King, however, he was a potentially dangerous extremist. George had the political acumen to realize that the only way that he could secure his throne was by promoting national unity; had his own father, Constantine I, not lost his throne twice because of the deadly virus of national faction? He took very seriously the lessons of 1917 and 1922 and was determined not to share his father's fate. To bolster his position on all sides, George issued royal amnesties and pardons for hundreds of Venizelist officers involved (or so suspected) in the March 1935 attempted republican coup. Many were freed from prison or allowed to return from exile. All pending prosecutions and investigations linked to the event were dropped. It came as a shock to the extreme monarchists who had hoped that many of their Venizelist opponents would spend the remainder of their lives in prison or exile. George, however, did not go too far in his magnanimity; ensuring that his potential foes would no longer present a threat, he did not reinstate the cashiered officers in the military. (Some ended up working as unskilled labourers to survive.)

Kondylis' fate entailed the question of what to do about troublesome Andrew. The last thing the King wanted was his uncle back in Greece making a nuisance of himself slamming the Venizelists and undermining the King's carefully-constructed policy of reconciliation. Reports began to appear in the press that Andrew intended to return to Greece after the general election of 26 January 1936, but that date came and went and still he did not return. Andrew also appears to have agreed in public that it was his personal wish to stay away for a while so as to keep the domestic political scene calm. In February he was telling the international press that he had not yet decided on the move.[21] Perhaps as a mark of appreciation at home, in that same month his property in Greece that had been confiscated was restored back to him by law.

But by May 1936 Andrew had still not returned, and many people – especially staunch monarchists – were anxiously wondering why. Both friend and foe agreed that of all the members of the royal family Andrew was the 'most Greek' in sentiment and allegiance. He had been the family's most vocal and active spokesperson and agitator during the 'bleak years' of the republic. If anyone was expected to return with the family, that was certainly Andrew! His daughters had all been married to Germans and had permanently settled in Germany, but where was Alice and what about young Philip, whom the Greeks hardly knew? On 20 May 1936 the Greek press ran a brief announcement from the palace that Andrew had arrived in Greece four days earlier on board the yacht of a friend, on a visit intended to be strictly incognito and solely for recreation. He had dined with the King, taken in the sights with his friend, and the next day he would go to the provincial town of Nafplion in the Peloponnese to visit the archaeological site of Mycenae, and from there leave directly for Turkey. The report also quoted Ioannis Metaxas, the royalist ex-general who was now the caretaker prime minister, saying that he had no information about Andrew's visit but that he was free to come and go whenever he liked.[22]

The newspapers noted the qualification as a clear signal that Andrew would not make any public appearances while in Greece; there was speculation, mostly justified, that George II and Ioannis Metaxas did not want him upsetting the applecart. The 'strictly incognito' phrase was a subtle signal for Andrew's Greek friends to keep their distance from him.

The fact also that Andrew arrived in Greece on the yacht of a friend also emphasized the private nature of the visit. However, the far-right *Ellinikon Mellon*, which a year earlier had published Andrew's most controversial articles, did not just print the announcement about Andrew's visit but also included a detailed report of it. Andrew was travelling on the yacht *Davida* with an Australian friend called Townsend; certain other details in the report make it clear that Andrew was the source. Andrew's first stop was Corfu, where he spent two days trying to avoid public contact; it appears that no-one who happened to come across him recognized him. In rather sentimental terms the newspaper described how the Prince went to his villa at Mon Repos, which he had not seen since 1922. Not even the old caretaker there recognized him. After Andrew told him who he was, the old man burst in tears and kissed his hands. The scene consciously evoked that in Homer's *Odyssey* where Odysseus finally returns to Ithaca and is recognized only by his old swineherd. When Andrew returned to the yacht, it was reported, he himself wept.

Even though the newspaper repeatedly emphasized that Andrew's visit was strictly incognito, in line with the official announcement, it had made its point. When Greek supporters heard that Andrew was in the country, many tried to meet him wherever the yacht called at. *Ellinikon Mellon* was careful not to urge its readers to actually go and meet Andrew but the sentimental tone in which it reported on his visit to Greece could hardly have had any other result. The Prince was described as weeping constantly and begging those supporters he met to keep his visit a secret. It was as if Andrew was visiting Greece as an outcast under the republic and fearing exposure and arrest! 'As was expected,' the report concluded, 'news of the popular prince's arrival in Greece moved to tears not only those close to him but all who honour his struggles and his comrades. Few, however, came in contact with him as he insisted on strict incognito. His Royal Highness was moved by his visit to the fatherland and told his close friends that his wish is to return to Greece for ever when conditions allow this'.[23]

What happened next was exactly what George and Metaxas wanted Andrew to avoid at all costs. On 21 May 1936 instead of going to Nafplion and then off to Turkey, Andrew stepped off the yacht *Davida* at Phaleron, where he was greeted by a large and frenzied crowd. This was some 'incognito'! The tumultuous welcome seems to have moved Andrew to cast all caution to the winds and plunge back into the political arena again. That same day George, Paul and Ioannis Metaxas were all away from Athens; George and Paul were in Corfu and Metaxas in his home island of Cephalonia to attend events marking the seventy-second anniversary of its cession to Greece from Britain. They would soon regret having left Andrew behind them unguarded. On the day of his arrival in Athens, Andrew, in the company of Menelaos Metaxas and various politicians of the right and the far right, delivered a rousing speech to a gathering of royalists in the leafy northern Athens suburb of Halandri. Once more he excoriated Venizelos and his supporters and praised his royalist friends' 'long and hard struggles' on behalf of the throne. It was certainly payback time for Andrew: he was now at home in Greece while Venizelists like Plastiras languished in exile in France, a spectacular reversal of roles. Andrew could not hide his glee in front of the cheering audience.

At Halandri the massed crowd of royalists called loudly on Andrew to stay in Greece and not leave them.[24] Xenophon Hatzisarantos, a lawyer and leader of the royalist Union of Constitutional Youth (Enosis Syntagmatikis Neolaias), who was there at Halandri handed the Prince a letter in which he was urged to live permanently in Greece to fulfil 'the wish of all Greek people'. Hatzisarantos, a fanatic monarchist who had written a number of newspaper articles in support of the cause, had published a book called *Why We Are Monarchists*. He considered himself as sharing the common struggle of overthrowing the republic. Andrew, he said, needed to remain in Greece and continue his fight against the lurking Venizelists. Andrew's brief reply to Hatzisarantos' letter, also in writing and leaked to the press, thanked him politely but avoided giving a clear answer about whether he would stay. But at the very end of his reply Andrew could no longer hold back his frustration, claiming that 'like everyone else, he [Andrew] also had to obey the King's orders'. That was as close as he could come to blaming his uncle for keeping him out of Greek affairs.[25]

The next day, on 22 May, *Ellinikon Mellon* printed details of Andrew's visit and speech at Halandri as its main news item. On the day after that, its front-page leader proclaimed: 'Kudos to the Prince! He Spoke the Language of Truth!' The editorial went so far as to assert that Andrew had said exactly what other 'more prestigious personalities' (a clear reference to King George and the Crown Prince Paul) should have said upon arriving in Greece. *Ellinikon Mellon* advised Venizelist supporters peremptorily to shut up and not have the temerity to consider themselves as equals of the monarchists, and that they should be grateful to King George's 'unjustified' clemency for letting them walk the streets. The newspaper then attacked the King's *rapprochement* policy as 'nonsense'. It was, of course, a thinly-veiled swipe at George himself, a point duly picked up by the Venizelist daily *Eleftheron Bima* on 24 May; the newspaper fingered Andrew as the main spokesman of the extremists. George must have felt some alarm. It was probably no accident that after 4 August 1936, when Metaxas established his dictatorship with the King's approval, Hatzisarantos, though always a loyal monarchist, was sent into exile along with various republicans and communists. (One wonders how they managed to get along.)[26]

If the 26 January 1936 general election had given the majority to the Populist Party, Andrew's involvement in politics would have been sidelined and eventually forgotten. However, the election gave a majority to no party and the government crisis continued unabated. Caretaker governments were put in place by George in order that future general elections might bring an end to the crisis. These caretaker governments were short lived, one of the prime ministers, Konstantinos Demertzis, dying in office in April.[27] Andrew's indiscretions during his brief visit of May and June fortunately had no lasting ill effects. However, the monarchist Ioannis Metaxas, who was (caretaker) prime minister at the time, had plans of his own. As we have seen, on 4 August 1936 he secured the King's agreement to suspend the constitution and rule by decree as dictator–prime minister. Metaxas, not the King, was now the boss, and ordered, rather than advised, Andrew to stay away.

Embittered, Andrew returned to the south of France which had been his home in previous years. His feelings can be imagined: for years he had fought hard to restore the Greek monarchy while his brothers, Princes George, Nicholas and Christopher, who had not by any means been as active in the cause, could freely return to Greece whenever they liked. (In fact, the last two died on their native soil within two years of each other in 1938 and 1940 and were buried there. Nicholas' last words were reputed to have been 'I am happy to die in my beloved country'. Both initially had not been allowed to return when George was restored but that decision had been quickly reversed in their case.) In contrast, Andrew had won his fight but could not claim the spoils and remained essentially an exile! In interviews to the international press he insisted it was his own decision not to return to Greece. However, in private, as early as the summer of 1936, his close friends at Monte Carlo noted that he missed living in Greece and that this saddened him.[28] Not surprisingly, the yacht *Davida* which he eventually bought from Townsend and became his permanent residence at Monte Carlo, flew the Greek flag. Andrew was not bitter about Greece and its people but about his own family, and especially King George.

On 30 October 1936, as a form of consolation, Andrew was commissioned back in the Greek Army as a general. Yet the commission proved to be only symbolic, as he would merely be an aide-de-camp to George II and hold no substantial officer's duty.[29] To add insult to injury, Princes Christopher and Nicholas, who did not particularly share Andrew's passion for their military profession and had barely lifted a finger for the cause, also got back their generals' stars. From now on, Andrew's rare and brief visits to Greece coincided with important functions which George had to attend as head of state, with the bemedalled Andrew at his side as ADC.[30]

The most important of these visits took place in November 1936 during the funerals of ex-King Constantine, his wife Sophia and his mother Olga, as it was during this visit that the future of his son Philip was first seriously discussed (see the following chapter). After that Andrew's visits became rarer; he would visit on his own, lying low and hiding from public view on his yacht, except on the rare occasions of family events, such as weddings or funerals, or whenever he accompanied George as his ADC at official functions. He would then sail off again to the south of France and Monte Carlo. It wasn't much different from regular exile, though he could return to Greece for short visits. And unlike in the years of the republic, when Andrew's actions and interviews were extensively covered by the Greek press and talked about by the people, after 1935 he became a virtual non-person, was seldom mentioned in the Greek newspapers except for a few lines on the back pages.

On 30 March 1937 Andrew sailed on the *Davida* to Egypt and visited the flourishing Greek community in Cairo.[31] There he gave a prepared speech in which he called his countrymen to put aside the divisions of the past and work together on behalf of the Greek government. Everything in the speech, in fact, was fully in line with the official policy of dictator Metaxas. Andrew's visit to Cairo was closely monitored by Greek diplomats, so he took no chances. Yet a few weeks later Andrew almost caused a diplomatic incident between Greece and Britain when he sailed on the *Davida* to Cyprus without asking the British authorities there for permission to land on the island. Cyprus was a British Crown Colony and only six years before had been roiled by a popular revolt demanding union with Greece. The uprising had been put down, but since then the British had been uneasy about the possibilities of Greek intervention.

Andrew disembarked at Larnaca and made a brief tour of the town. The Greek Cypriots were enthusiastic about the visit and mobbed him wherever he went. He met and talked with many local officials, to the unease of the British. Andrew made clear to the Greek Cypriots his hatred of republicanism by telling them that their problems had been the fault of the Venizelist Greek consul on the island who had stirred up the 1931 revolt. Andrew felt free again to revert to his favourite theme of Venizelist-bashing. News of his visit spread virally; when the yacht appeared off the harbour of Limassol, enthusiastic crowds lined the quay. But he appeared to be late in disembarking. Boats full of supporters approached the yacht to ask him when he would go ashore; he assured them he would, but in the end the yacht sailed off, leaving the people on the quayside dumbfounded.[32] The British officials on Cyprus breathed sighs of relief. Andrew's actions on Cyprus caused a small hiccup in Greek–British diplomatic relations. At Limassol did Andrew receive some subtle message it would be wiser to stay put on the yacht? Or was he just happy to needle the British, who after all were a major factor in George's decision not to allow him to live in Greece? In the end, nothing of any consequence happened and Andrew's Cyprus 'adventure' was kept out of the Greek press.

On his way home to the south of France and Monaco with the *Davida*, Andrew made a stop in Athens. There on 19 May 1937 British ambassador Waterlow marked the coronation of George VI by a special film show of the coronation at a central Athens cinema. King George, Prince Peter, Ioannis Metaxas, his cabinet ministers, and foreign diplomats in the Greek capital attended the event. As Andrew was in Athens, he also turned up. One imagines Waterlow to have been in an awkward position as he held Andrew in low esteem and the latter's recent visit to Cyprus had not improved matters. Andrew for his part had little love for the British ambassador who, he believed, had denied him his right to live in his own country. Nevertheless their meeting was uneventful and the day following the screening, Andrew left Athens on board the *Davida*.[33]

Andrew's break with Greece appeared to have become permanent in June 1937 when he sold Mon Repos to the King.[34] It was a clear signal that he had finished with the country for good. From then on he briefly visited Greece in spring and autumn (October being his favourite month for coming to the country) and his stays there lasted no more than two or three weeks: in some cases just a few days. Andrew spent three weeks in Greece in October 1937, mostly in the northern part of the country. On the 8th he was with King George observing war games.[35] Later in the month, on the 25th, he was in Thessaloniki for the twenty-fifth anniversary of the Greek annexation of the city during the First Balkan War – an event in which his brother Constantine I had played a prominent role.[36]

On 8 January 1938 Crown Prince Paul and Frederica were married in Athens, and Philip was one of the best men. Andrew came to Athens for the wedding along with Philip and left again after a few days. However, a month later Andrew stayed away from the funeral of his brother Prince Nicholas, the father of Marina, Duchess of Kent.[37] He did come to Greece in March and on the 21st accompanied George at the Zappeion Hall for the opening of an art exhibition.[38] The venue was evocative, as it was there that the infamous 'apology ceremony of the flag' had taken place in 1916, which Andrew considered Greece's greatest humiliation and laid at Venizelos' door. Andrew, as we have seen, had represented the defeated royalists at the ceremony. On 19 August 1938 Andrew's former aide, long-time friend and confidant, Menelaos Metaxas, died in Athens. Andrew was not at his funeral the following day and neither were any other members of the royal family. King George was represented by one of his aides, a colonel. The dictator Ioannis Metaxas did attend Menelaos' funeral but that was because he happened to be his cousin, something which the newspapers duly took note of.[39]

We find Andrew in Greece again in October 1938 for his annual long stay of two to three weeks. On the 9th he was present at the unveiling of a statue of his late brother Constantine at Athens' 'Field of Mars', a large park. Later in the month, he accompanied King George as ADC at a function at the Benaki Museum and a ceremony marking one hundred years since the founding of Athens Polytechnic University.[40] In 1939, Andrew's spring visit to Greece commenced on 19 April.[41] On the 26th he attended an official dinner at the Egyptian embassy in Athens.[42] On 3 May, just before leaving Greece, he accompanied George to a photographic exhibition at the Polish embassy.[43] He was again in Greece for three weeks in October and early November, accompanying George at army exercises, the annual celebration of the annexation of Thessaloniki and the graduation of Greek Air Force officers on 28 October.[44] On 8 November he attended the theatre along with George and other members of the royal family.[45] Andrew's last visit to Greece was in late January 1940, to see his dying brother Christopher, who passed away on the 21st of the month. According to press reports, Andrew came to Athens a few hours before his brother died.[46] It is clear that this trip had not been planned; Andrew and Christopher had always been close, especially during the republic when both were in exile.

The change in Andrew's circumstances after 1935 meant that though his financial worries were over as he was bankrolled by the Greek state as a royal and a general, he no longer had a real aim in life. Even with his generous income, Andrew lived well above his financial means. The sale of Mon Repos helped finance his lavish – some would say reckless – lifestyle. It is therefore not surprising that from early 1936 onwards he figures prominently in the society columns, at the gaming tables of Monte Carlo and at the galas of the rich and famous.[47] The casinos were, in fact, Andrew's favourite hangouts. During the same period he also developed a drinking problem.[48] According to newspaper reports, his best friends at Monte Carlo were David Townsend and Gilbert Beale, wealthy individuals whose yachts Andrew had made his home (as we have seen, he eventually bought Townsend's *Davida*, and lived on it); these same reports discreetly avoided any mention of his mistress, the young and beautiful French Countess, Andrée de la Bigne, even though their relationship was an open secret in Monte Carlo.[49]

But there was another, deeper reason for Andrew's inner distress: his realization that his irrevocable absence from Greece meant that his son Philip was now excluded from growing up in the country as a genuine Greek royal. The lingering trauma over his 1922 court martial and ensuing dislike of the Greeks who supported Venizelos was not the whole story; by 1935 he had pretty much put the trauma behind him to work tirelessly to restore the monarchy. The book he had written about his involvement in the Asia Minor campaign in 1921 had, in his eyes, set the record straight in that area, and indeed, his sentence of exile had been quashed in 1936. Andrew had every reason to consider himself a winner. If he had been encouraged to live in Greece after 1935, it is almost certain that his attitude would have been different. Andrew remained a fanatic Greek at heart, to the point of accusing his political enemies of not being as Greek as he considered himself to be! His wife Alice and their four daughters were also staunchly Greek patriots. Philip, however, because of the unusual circumstances of his youth did not grow up as a Greek. But in 1936 this could have changed, and as we will see, Alice tried hard as late as 1939 to persuade Philip to make Greece his permanent home.

The fact that Andrew did not want his son growing up in the country of his birth was directly attributable to the treatment he suffered from members of his own family after 1935, as the newly re-enthroned George II kept him on a tight leash. Andrew took his revenge by making sure that his son was kept away from Greece, thus preventing him from developing a personal relationship with the country and considering it his own. Andrew eventually was successful in this, but his seeking revenge through Philip would have serious repercussions on his own family in the long run, as it removed the only Greek royal who might have kept the whole family in place in future tribulations.

Chapter 9

Three Funerals, a Crown and a Boy

I n November 1936 a week-long ceremony took place in Athens, a
ceremony deemed to be of the highest importance for the Greek
state, but long since forgotten. From Tuesday 17 to Sunday 22
November, the funerals of ex-King Constantine I, his wife queen Sophia
and his mother Queen Olga were held. All three had died years before
their funerals: Constantine in 1923, Olga in 1926 and Sophia in 1932.
Constantine had barely lived past the banishment of the royal family in
1922 and the latter two passed away in the years of the republic. The Greek
governments of 1923 and 1932 rather pettily did not allow Constantine
and Sophia to be buried in Greece (though they had no problem with
Olga's 1926 funeral), apparently fearing that the traditional royal burial
ground at Tatoi might become a place of royalist pilgrimage. As a result
the caskets of the three royal deceased were placed in the crypt of the
Russian Orthodox Church of Florence to await the hoped-for time when
they could be moved to their proper place at Tatoi.

The governments' refusal to admit Constantine's remains for burial
rankled bitterly with Greek royalists, who mourned 'the great unburied
deceased' along with his mother and wife. This term had a strong
emotional value for many Greeks as it harked back to the last Byzantine
emperor, Constantine XI Palaiologos, who had died fighting the Turks
during the fall of Constantinople in 1453 and whose body was never
accounted for. According to a popular legend, Constantine XI's body
turned into a marble pillar, and his spirit would not find eternal peace
until Constantinople was reclaimed by the Greeks. And as we have seen,
Constantine I of Greece consciously viewed himself as the successor of
Palaiologos, unofficially adopting the title Constantine XII.

Thus a great deal of emotional and historical symbolism swirled
around the issue of the long-delayed royal funerals. It was also quite high
on the political agenda as another potential battleground for republicans

and royalists. The issue of 'the great unburied dead' emerged in 1933 at the height of economic depression. With the electoral victory of the Populist Party in March 1933 thousands of royalists signed a petition addressed to Prime Minister Tsaldaris to allow the funerals to be held in Athens. But Tsaldaris was in a tight spot; though a monarchist himself, in 1932 he had pledged in the parliament to support the republic. While privately sympathetic to the return of the deceased royals to Greece, he held off granting permission during his tenure of two and a half years, until October 1935. Tsaldaris also feared that if he gave permission, his own government might well be thrust into the shadow of a restored George II. Adding to his confusion and hesitation was the fact that many royalists in his own government and Populist Party were working secretly to undermine him. By May 1936 the petition had gathered more than two million signatures – something like one-third of the population of Greece at the time.[1]

In November 1935 when George II finally returned to the throne, his relatives still lay unburied in Florence. The way was open for them, too, to return to their native soil. The issue was not now the restoration of the monarchy; that was already accomplished. The royal funerals would be a demonstration of pomp and splendour on a scale never before seen. Preparations were begun as soon as George returned. The obsequies were scheduled to mark the first anniversary of the restoration and to send the message that the monarchy this time was in Greece to stay.

On 15 November 1936 the royal remains were lifted out of the crypt in the Russian Church of Florence and transported by special train to Brindisi, to be transferred to Greece's most iconic warship, the armoured cruiser *Averof*, for the journey home. Accompanying them were Prince Paul, Princess Irene (daughter of Constantine), Princess Maria and her husband, Admiral Pericles Ioannidis. A flotilla of nine Greek cruisers, two Italian battleships and five Italian cruisers flanked the *Averof*, which arrived at the port of Piraeus in the early hours of 17 November. While the *Averof* was still offshore, the caskets, along with the members of the royal family and cabinet ministers who had accompanied them from Italy, were moved to the Greek cruiser *Hydra*, which ferried them to the dockside. On board were George and the rest of the family. Ashore, seamen tied the caskets to gun carriages. The cortege then made its solemn way to the Piraeus railway station, escorted by a band playing sombre music and an honour guard of the Greek Navy and elite Evzone palace guards. Constant gun salutes accompanied the procession. Following the caskets were King George, on foot and alone, and behind him his brother (and heir) Prince Paul. Bringing up the rear of the foot procession were the cabinet, with Ioannis Metaxas at their head, along with senior military and civilian officials. The royal ladies followed behind in cars. At the station the caskets were put on a special train, which took them to Athens' Omonia Square station, from where they were driven to Athens Cathedral for the funeral service.

With all the streets and public buildings on the route draped with black bunting, thousands of Athenians watched in silence on the pavements or crowded on balconies. All the shops were closed as the state had declared an official day of mourning. Lining the route were soldiers standing at attention and presenting arms. For six days the caskets lay in state in Athens Cathedral, as thousands filed past to pay their respects. By official police order, for the first day all singing and playing music in public was prohibited. On 22 November, a Sunday, the deceased royals were finally interred in their home soil at Tatoi.[2]

After the event, foreign dignitaries commented about how well it had been organized, opining that Greece had never witnessed anything like it before. Almost all the members of the Greek royal family had been brought together. It was also Philip's first time back in Greece since he had left in such a hurry in an orange crate as an eighteen-month-old infant in 1922. Though his name was well known in the country, as the only son of Andrew, hardly any Greek had actually seen him in the flesh. So, when he appeared to the Athenians in November 1936 he cut an intriguing figure among the older, more familiar, royals. The toddler had grown into a dashing, handsome, and polite young man. He was noticed wherever he went in Athens.[3] What made Philip's presence even more noticeable was the fact that he belonged to the third generation of Greek male royals who comprised a rather small group of just four cousins, the others being George II himself, Prince Paul, and their cousin Prince Peter (the son of 'Big' George).[4] They were the sole insurance against the ever-present possibility that the royals could once again find themselves kicked out.[5]

Though in late 1936 George had been back on his throne for just a year, the question of his succession loomed. A clear-cut succession arrangement was required that would give the throne some extra foundation to avoid the tribulations of the previous two decades. George was divorced with no children, and by all accounts had no intention of re-marrying to secure an heir. His brother Paul thus served as official heir, but as he, too, was single and childless, speculation ran further afield, in the direction of Prince Peter and, of course, young Philip. George's immediate succession would not have been a problem, as Paul was there to step into George's place in the event of the unexpected. But Paul, as far as anyone knew then, might remain a bachelor; even if he married, there was no guarantee that he would produce the necessary male heir. So Princes Peter and Philip had sporting chances of succeeding to the Greek throne. Of the two, Philip in fact had the better prospects, for reasons that will become apparent (though Peter was older and had formal precedence). Thus Philip's attendance at the funerals of his grandmother, uncle and aunt in Athens was not simply a social event but one of considerable dynastic significance. He was already third in line to the throne. King George appeared to see the potential in the fifteen-year-old prince and considered him a possible future Greek king; but for this, Philip had to be brought closer to the country and its royal circle. None of this, it must be said, escaped the tightest secrecy of the royal environment and fortunately, the press had barely an inkling of what was going on in the King's mind.

Philip attended all the pageantry of the first day of the funerals and dutifully was part of the procession escorting the caskets from Piraeus to Omonia to Athens Cathedral. However, on 22 November when the caskets were taken back through the centre of Athens for burial at Tatoi, Philip was not in the procession accompanying them. He is not seen in the film footage (see below) and the newspapers did not mention him among the princes who walked behind the caskets. What had happened was revealed many years later by his cousin, Princess Alexandra. Philip and Alexandra were both fifteen at the time, with no other relatives close to them in age. As a result, they were together for most of the time during the ceremony. On the day of the obsequies in Athens Cathedral, the royals had lunch beforehand; in the cathedral later, Alexandra noticed that Philip was unwell. He groaned as he held his stomach and appeared to be about to be sick at any moment. The culprit seems to have been the tainted lobster he had for lunch. As a result, he decided not to walk in the procession with the other princes but follow in the same car with Alexandra. He eventually threw up in the car into his top hat; not knowing what to do next, he handed the top hat with its contents to an unsuspecting ADC who opened the car door of the car when it stopped outside the palace.[6] Philip's nausea, however, may also have been triggered by something of vital import that happened while he was in Athens; he had been faced with a momentous decision that might make or break the rest of his life: where should he belong – Britain or Greece? The choice, when it was made, was not Philip's but his father's, and would utterly change his life.

We have a very rare visual record of Philip during this most important time in his life, a record unknown for almost nine decades. The funerals of Constantine, Sophia and Olga were filmed and highlights were shown in cinema newsreels throughout Greece. Much of this footage is now lost, but a segment of approximately one and a half minutes has survived, showing the arrival of the royal caskets at Piraeus on 17 November and the procession from Omonia Square up Stadiou Street. There is also a shorter segment, lasting one minute and fifteen seconds, of the final stage of the funerals on 22 November showing the procession going down Stadiou Street to Omonia Square on the way to Tatoi. The elaborate pageantry of the ceremonies comes out vividly in the footage.

The first segment shows the cruiser *Hydra* arriving and docking at Piraeus, and George II boarding the ship with his three uncles, Andrew, Nicholas and Christopher, and three princesses, Maria, Irene and Catherine, dressed in black. The camera pans round to Metaxas and his cabinet standing at attention. After a gap, the footage resumes with Greek sailors carrying Constantine's casket from the cruiser to the gun carriage. Then there is a shot of senior Army officers standing at attention. Up to that point the film has obviously been edited to show highlights only. However, as the procession begins with the caskets in the front, escorted by sailors and evzones, there is a continuous segment of footage lasting twenty-five seconds, showing members of the royal family taking their positions behind the caskets, following the Royal Chamberlain, Merkatis, who leads the walk at a slow pace. A few steps behind comes George, followed by Andrew, Nicholas, and Christopher, dressed in general's uniforms, and Paul in naval uniform. Then comes a curious moment.

At one point in the footage Paul instinctively pauses to allow his three uncles to pass in front of him and follow George. But that was not in accordance with protocol as Paul was the heir and thus his place would have been immediately behind George. Why Paul did this is not known. Obviously, it could be taken as a show of respect for his uncles. Paul had accompanied the caskets back from Italy and it is likely that he was either not briefed on details of the procession or didn't care much for protocol. The filmed moment merits more analysis. As Paul stops, Prince Christopher takes two steps in front of him. Was Christopher absent-minded, or did he, too, not think much of protocol? However, less than a second after he passes in front of Paul, Christopher is stopped in his tracks by Andrew. With military precision Andrew taps Christopher on the elbow with his right hand, and motions to Paul with the same hand to move forward, which the heir to throne does at once. It is remarkable that this particular scene was not edited out. It indicates that Andrew, while no longer enjoying any influence on the political scene in Greece, still was a man to be reckoned with in the family.

Behind the senior royals, the next generation of male members of the family begin to appear in the film, walking from the *Hydra* to take their positions in the procession. They include Princes Peter and Philip and the German husbands of Greek princesses including two of Philip's German brothers-in-law: Gottfried, Prince of Hohenlohe-Langenburg (husband of Margaret), and Berthold, the Margrave of Baden (husband of Theodora). All are in civilian clothes except Gottfried who as an officer of the German Air Force is in uniform. Philip is the last to appear, looking much older than his fifteen years, which may be why he was not identified on this film until now. In his left hand he is holding the top hat into which he would be sick a few days later. Andrew is putting Christopher and Paul in their places, but Philip seems hardly to realize what his father is doing as he stares ahead. Philip takes his place on the far right of the line. Next to him is Gottfried in his German Army uniform. As the procession gets underway both appear to be absorbed in conversation while everyone else is silent; Philip's body language suggests that he is interested in what Gottfried has to say and is not just making small talk. Gottfried, twenty-five years Philip's senior, may have thought that all the pomp and ceremony might be stressful for someone as young as Philip who was not accustomed to such happenings. Was it an attempt to try and cheer up Philip? The Second World War was still three years away, and so Philip was friendly with all his German brothers-in-law, Nazis or not. He was, however, rather closer to Berthold, who had arranged for him to study under Kurt Hahn and incidentally never became a Nazi Party member. In the procession Berthold is seen standing at some distance from Philip, while the footage shows there was a good relationship between Philip and Gottfried.

This, the earliest known film footage of Philip, is clearly meant to show him acting as a member of the Greek royal family, in the same frames as his father. Though there exist photographs of a younger Philip with his father Andrew, this is the first time both together appear on film. Andrew does not seem to be interacting with his son, as according to protocol they were placed in different parts of the procession. It was a fact, however, that they were no longer close in real life, with Philip having to rely on other relatives for his well-being. The apparent presence of Gottfried as a father-figure of sorts in this event is somewhat poignant.

The royal funerals were not only filmed for newsreels but also received Greece's earliest live radio coverage. Though the country yet lacked a national radio broadcaster, many Greeks had radios that could receive special broadcasts via the Telecommunications Ministry. They could also receive broadcasts from Italian stations. A team of reporters with a microphone had been stationed at the start of the funeral procession at Piraeus, another at the centre of Omonoia Square, a third at Syntagma Square and a fourth outside Athens Cathedral.[7] When the newsreels were screened later in Greece's cinemas, the radio soundtrack was incorporated in the film. One of the first reporters at Piraeus was a famous actress and household name, Eleni Papadaki. Sadly, none of her live narration has survived, but we still have the gun salute as the *Hydra* docks at Piraeus and the last few bars of the Greek national anthem. Papadaki's microphone has also picked up background sounds such as the footsteps of the sailors escorting the caskets and then those of the royals. As soon as Gottfried and Philip appear in camera view, they are overheard talking to each other – not in low voices, as one might expect, but quite loudly. They are speaking in German, and though the words are not easily discernible, their voices are. Philip's has a fifteen-year-old high pitch, rising above the deeper tones of Gottfried. Philip appears to be replying to a question put to him. This, incidentally, is the earliest known recording of Philip speaking, besides the first time he is seen on film.

It is an irony of history that the earliest preserved video and audio recording of Philip is from a Greek royal event that has been all but forgotten. The royal funerals were meant to buttress the shaky restored monarchy in Greece, and to all intents and purposes Philip was viewed as vital to that effort. That week of November 1936, in fact, would prove to be crucial for Philip's future, as the family got together in Athens to discuss it.

Chapter 10

Whither 'Philippos'?

In November 1935, following the restoration of the monarchy in Greece, Philip, the boy without a country, again became 'His Royal Highness, Prince Philippos of Greece'. It would have been logical to assume that as a result of this fortunate change, Philip would have moved to Athens and assumed his role as a regular royal. However, as he was still a minor and therefore not yet free to decide his own future, the decision was solely that of Andrew; neither did his English relatives in Britain, maternal grandmother Victoria and uncles George and 'Dickie' Mountbatten, who at the time were acting as his guardians and looked after him in Britain, have any say in the matter. As we have seen, Andrew was dead against Philip's moving to Greece, as he himself was not allowed to.

However, besides the opposition of his father, there was also a practical matter that would have made such a move very difficult for Philip at the time. He did not have any personal knowledge of Greece and could not really speak much Greek, though he did have a limited understanding of it.[1] Philip thus would have had a hard time attending secondary school in Greece, even if he went to one of the elite private schools where English was also used in the classroom. Besides, in 1935 Andrew was already at Gordonstoun, Hahn's school with its unique programme to which no school in Greece could offer anything similar. Consequently, even King George II, who wanted cousin Philip to move one day to Greece, was of the opinion that he would first have to graduate from Gordonstoun. That, however, was nearly four years away, in 1939. Hence there would be plenty of time to talk again about Philip's Greek prospects when he was a more mature eighteen.

The question of young Philip becoming an active member of the Greek royal family as soon as possible was not just a consequence of the love and affection that his relatives undoubtedly had for him, but more importantly, it was linked directly to the family's future. In the year of his restoration George II had been divorced from Elizabeth of Romania for several years and seemed to have no subsequent life partner on the horizon.[2] The union had not been blessed with offspring, and it was obvious that an order of succession needed to be worked out in case something happened to the King. In such circumstances his designated heir was his brother Paul, thirty-five and still a bachelor. But would Paul marry and have children? Rather simplifying matters was the Greek equivalent of the Salic Law, entitling only males to become monarch. This meant that Paul not only had to get married and have children but he would also have to have a son who would succeed him after his own reign. If not, the succession would devolve on Constantine I's surviving brothers, of whom the eldest was Prince ('Big') George. But he, like all the brothers, by 1935 was getting on in years; even Christopher, the youngest one at forty-seven, was thirteen years older than Paul. It seemed more than likely that Paul or even George II would outlive their uncles.[3]

But as long as even one of Constantine's brothers lived long enough, he would have a direct claim to the throne after Paul. In fact, Prince Peter, the son of Prince George, was technically next in line for the throne. After him came Andrew's son, Philip, a mere fourteen in 1935. But Peter's case was troublesome. His father, Prince George, was openly gay with a lover in Denmark[4] – something Greek society was far from ready to accept in its royals. It was probably no accident that Prince George was the royal who had maintained the least contact with Greece; he had permanently settled in France, and rarely visited his homeland. His wife Princess Marie Bonaparte, a distant descendant of Napoleon I, had herself a complex psycho-sexual orientation and was seeking counselling about it from none other than Sigmund Freud, who had also been consulted about Princess Alice's mental perturbations. (Marie would eventually become a disciple of Freud and a capable psychoanalyst in her own right.) Their son Peter, while sexually normal, was heavily into psychology and cultural anthropology and developing ideas quite beyond the conservative ethos of a European royal family.

Peter was by far the most unconventional member of the Greek royal family. There is a story (uncorroborated) that one day in the 1930s he was riding in Germany's Black Forest with Princess Frederica of Hanover when she went up to a tree and carved a swastika on it. At that moment, the story goes, Peter at once broke off whatever relationship he had with the girl. It's possible that this tale was elaborated later to burnish Peter's democratic credentials. But there is no doubt that his political views were far from conservative. His mother Marie Bonaparte had in fact helped Freud escape Nazi-held Vienna and relocate in London. Peter, who adored his mother, underwent psychoanalysis before becoming seriously involved in anthropology. He came strongly under the influence of Hungarian psychoanalyst Geza Roheim, a pioneer in the field.

Prince Peter took a degree in law from the Sorbonne in the early 1930s, supplementing it with a postgraduate course in anthropology at the London School of Economics. He became keenly interested – unhealthily, some would say – in the sexual practices of Third World tribal societies.[5] He was a quite extraordinary royal in many senses, but at the same time this extraordinariness undermined his candidacy for the throne in one of Europe's most conservative societies. He was variously accused of having pro-Nazi or communist sympathies. Not that he particularly minded all the criticism. But a breaking point came in 1938 when he married a Belarusian divorceé named Irina Ovchinnikova, herself suspected of being a communist. This earned him the nickname 'Red Prince'. What was just as bad, he had not asked permission from the family, with the result that he was stricken off the Greek royal succession list by his own father.[6]

The result of this was that Philip automatically became second in line for the Greek succession behind Paul. But Greece was not finished with Prince Peter. On 28 October 1940 he was in Istanbul when he learned that Italy had just invaded Greece; he at once rushed to Athens to join the Army, being given the rank of captain and appointed liaison officer with the British staff officers advising the Greeks. When Greece fell to the Germans in April 1941 he joined King George in fleeing to Crete and then the Middle East. After the war he resumed his anthropological research and wanderings. Yet some in Greece remembered him saying that he dreamed of modernizing the Greek monarchy in order to help it survive in radically changing social and economic conditions, and continued to hope that someday he might occupy the throne. But too much was stacked against him.

Thus in 1935 and soon afterward, the way appeared unobstructed for Philip to be a realistic candidate for the Greek throne. The international press took note of this and highlighted the serious concerns George had about his own succession; one publication went so far as to assert as early as 1935 that the King was actively considering adopting Philip as his heir apparent.[7] As we will see, starting in 1938 Alice also overtly urged Philip in that direction, with the agreement of the King. Philip himself, away from Greece at the time and busy at Gordonstoun, must almost certainly have been aware of what was being mapped out for him.

It was in late 1936 that the issue of Philip's role in Greece was thrashed out, when almost the entire family gathered in Athens. In November of that year, Philip came to Greece for the first time since leaving as an infant. The occasion was, as we have seen, the official funerals of his grandmother Olga, uncle Constantine and aunt Sophia. Philip certainly would have had had no memory of Constantine, and perhaps the vaguest recollection of Olga, who died when he was five, and rather more of Sophia, whom he had met a few times before she died when he was ten. Thus Philip's first visit to Greece would have offered a good opportunity for him to assess his possible future role in the country. Unlike his father, Philip was too young to have local political skeletons in his cupboard, a great advantage for a Greek royal in the public spotlight. For two decades now the people had suffered from destructive divisions and misrule, and yearned for unity; the country was in dire need of a period of internal peace and tranquility. Moreover, in 1936 Europe was darkened with constant crisis, which made it even more important that the Greeks put aside their political divisions and work together for the progress of their country and to boost its resistance to any external threats likely to appear.

On 19 November 1936 all the members of the royal family who had gathered in Athens for the royal funerals, including Andrew and Philip, assembled to dine together at the sumptuous Pentelikon Hotel in the quiet and leafy northern suburb of Kifissia.[8] It was their first chance to meet and, so to speak, let their hair down in a relaxed atmosphere, away from the strictures of ceremony, protocol, and publicity. Very likely Philip's future was raised at this meeting. The King was known to favour an arrangement that would see Philip finishing Gordonstoun and then attending the Greek Naval Academy for commissioning into the Royal

Hellenic Navy.[9] That alone, of course, would not set Philip automatically on a fast track to the throne, but it would help matters along. All Greece's kings, including George, had undergone military training of some sort, which had entitled them to wear ceremonial uniform. Moreover, Louis Mountbatten's father had told George V that 'there [was] no more fitting preparation for a king than to have been trained in the Navy.'[10] For one, such a move would have helped Philip to adapt quickly to Greek society as a royal and get to know better the people he might one day reign over.

But as in 1936 Philip was still a minor, it was up to his father to decide. Andrew was thoroughly negative even to the mere idea of his son living in Greece. He informed his nephew the King in no uncertain terms that no son of his would ever attend a Greek military institute of any kind. We do not know what Andrew's reasons to the King were; Andrew did tell his mother-in-law he was certain that after Philip joined the Greek Navy he would be eventually kicked out, as he himself had been from the Army no fewer than three times.[11] Doubtless Andrew still suffered from the painful memories not only of his own humiliations at the hands of arrogant republican officers, but also those of Constantine I, Alexander, and George II. His own ordeal of the 1922 court martial and its verdict of perpetual banishment had stigmatized him. Almost every other royal had a similar story to tell. In all conscience, he could not let his son in for a similar tribulation and possibly disgrace in the form of expulsion. However, it is quite likely that Andrew's refusal to consider a royal role for Philip was in fact a way of getting back at George for not allowing him to stay in Greece without, however, appearing to give offence to his nephew.[12]

When Andrew left Athens on 28 November 1936, Philip remained behind with his relatives in Greece for another fortnight.[13] He departed in the company of his sisters Theodora and Margaret and their husbands on 12 December.[14] The implication is that for the remainder of his stay in Athens, Philip was no longer under the direct influence of his father. It would appear that the youngster was beginning to warm to the idea of living in sunny Greece, contrary to his father's wishes. Members of the Greek royal family claim that Philip was consciously thinking of following Gordonstoun with Greece. According to his cousin, Princess Alexandra, it was the pomp and ceremony of the royal funerals which he had attended that made him truly realize what royalty was all about.[15] The young boy who appears in the newsreels of the time as rather shy or even embarrassed was in fact impressed by what he saw around him.

When Philip arrived in Greece he still had no personal knowledge of the country. The belated funerals of the deceased royals had been organized in a spectacular manner and on a lavish scale never seen before in the country. Everyone, Greek or foreign, who attended never failed to be highly impressed, and the fifteen-year-old Philip was no exception. The event, in effect, formed his first serious impression of the country of his birth and drove home to him the potential importance of being a prince of Greece. During the years of the Greek republic Philip had been referred to by that title in the international press, but the title had precious little real value, as the monarchy in Greece had been abolished and his family was in exile. As we have seen, in those years Philip did attend British royal ceremonies. Though the British royals treated him kindly, they could not hide the uncomfortable fact that he was more of a 'poor relation' than a prince in his own right. This, however, did not apply to Athens, where Philip could see personally that he was respected and treated as someone of substance in the country. That alone could have done much to ignite his interest in living in Greece as one of its princes.

His cousin Princess Alexandra notes that during his first visit to Athens, Philip talked continuously with his older Greek relatives and asked them many questions; it was evident that he had taken a keen interest in the country and life there.[16] With his father away it would have been easier for Philip to talk to his relatives, especially the older ones of Andrew's generation. Almost certainly a number of uncles, aunts and cousins would have advised him to establish himself in Greece as a key member of its royal family. Besides Alexandra's references, Philip's sister Theodora said he confided to her that he 'wanted to join the Greek Navy'.[17] As will become apparent, there is plenty of evidence that after 1936, even though Philip was growing up in the United Kingdom and acquiring very British characteristics and traits, he continued to consider Greece as his own country where he would eventually settle once he completed his studies at Gordonstoun.

Exactly a year after Philip and Andrew attended the belated funerals of their relatives in Athens, they were called to another funeral in Germany

– this time of Cecile, one of Philip's elder sisters who on 16 November 1937 was killed in a plane crash in Belgium along with her husband, Prince George Donatus of Hesse Darmstadt, their two children and her mother-in-law. Cecile was pregnant at the time. The family had been flying to England to attend a wedding. At Gordonstoun, Hahn broke the news to sixteen-year-old Philip, who took it remarkably well. 'His sorrow was that of a man,' Hahn would recall later.[18] Andrew travelled to London to meet Philip and they went together to Darmstadt in Germany to attend the funerals. It was the first time that Philip saw his father after a year's separation, and this latest funeral was a traumatic experience for both. All sources agree that Cecile was Andrew's favourite daughter and her sudden loss hit him very hard. Philip would stay with Cecile and her family whenever he was in Germany, and indeed had done so just a few weeks before the tragedy.

The funeral was conducted with splendour and pomp, but it was also a tragically strange occasion as the event teemed with Nazis in uniforms, and swastika flags fluttered everywhere. As the cortege passed through the main streets of Darmstadt, bystanders on the pavements gave the Nazi salute. An existing photo of the Darmstadt funeral procession is particularly interesting when compared to film footage of the procession in Athens a year before.[19] In Darmstadt Philip is seen as walking, second on the left, in the front row behind the caskets, flanked on either side by his surviving brothers-in-law, all dressed in German military uniform. Andrew is seen on the far left of the row behind Philip.[20] (The previous year, in Athens, Philip walked behind his father.) In the photograph, both Philip and Andrew are visibly distraught, whereas in Athens they had been less so. In these circumstances it is unlikely that father and son this time would have talked much about the latter's future.

However, both met again less than two months later, this time for a joyous event in Athens. On 9 January 1938 Prince Paul and Princess Frederica of Hanover were married, with Philip acting as best man along with his cousins King Michael of Romania and Prince Peter. This was the only occasion between December 1936 and his graduation from Gordonstoun in March 1939 that Philip visited Greece. He had received special permission from the school to travel, going first to Rome where he met up with his father and sisters Theodora and Margaret to go on by ship to Greece. A few days before the wedding in Athens, the international press had reported that Andrew would not attend as he was mourning the loss of Cecile and her family.[21] It is likely that this was what Andrew himself had told the journalists. But in the end he did go to Athens; what caused him to change his mind, if indeed he did, is unknown. Quite likely Andrew planned on being with Philip in Athens for some reason.

The marriage of Paul and Frederica was a big step forward in clarifying the issue of the Greek succession. In 1936 Paul had become engaged to nineteen-year-old Princess Frederica, the same Frederica who, according to widely circulated story, had carved a swastika into a tree and earned the ire of Prince Peter (she had indeed belonged to the Nazi Youth, almost compulsory for high-born young people). They had met (not for the first time) in Florence, where Frederica was studying art; at a chance meeting in the home of Paul's sister, Queen Helen of Romania, Frederica recalled that she 'lost [her] mind and heart' to the prince with the generous toothy smile.[22] At the Berlin Olympic Games of 1936 he proposed and she accepted. As a granddaughter of Kaiser Wilhelm II and thus a great-great-granddaughter of Britain's Queen Victoria (which incidentally placed her thirty-fourth in line of succession to the British throne), she had all the pedigree necessary for a solid royal marriage. The marriage was planned for 9 January 1938 and Frederica had to make the trip from Germany by train, which for a time was held up by snow in Yugoslavia. Paul waited for her at the Yugoslav border and boarded the train for the rest of the journey, to receive an official welcome by the King and crowds of well-wishers at Athens' Larissis Station.

Paul's political convictions were unlike those of most royals. He despised Metaxas and his dictatorship from the outset, a feeling that was mutual. His views were quite impeccably democratic, leaning towards a centrist position on most issues, a position he was to maintain, not without controversy, after he became king in 1947. At the same time he adhered strictly to the Orthodox faith, a sure mark of popularity with the people. The marriage was not only a love-match; it also raised hopes of an heir. On 2 November 1939 Princess Sophia was born. At least it was a start, but by Greece's succession law the heir, of course, had to be a boy.

The marriage of Paul and Frederica seems not to have affected the ambitions of Princess Alice, who in that same year, 1938, began planning a future for her son Philip in Greece; in short, she visualized him as eventual king. Since late 1936 Alice had been slowly and steadily overcoming what had been diagnosed as a form of mental illness (for lack of any other description). She was allowed furloughs from the clinics where she had been continuously hospitalized over the past six years. In the spring of 1937 she met Philip for the first time since last seeing him in the summer of 1932.[23] The tragic loss of her pregnant daughter Cecile, her son-in-law and two grandchildren seems to have acted as a form of shock treatment, enabling her to resume normal activity and overcome her mental condition.[24] From then on Alice to all intents and purposes became mentally quite healthy; never thereafter did she succumb to any psychological illness and was never subsequently hospitalized. After her recovery, Alice spent some time with her remaining daughters in Germany and her mother in England. In 1938 she decided to move permanently to Athens and dedicate herself to humanitarian work, desperately needed in the country as the result of years of economic and political crises exasperated by the 1930s world financial depression and the unceasing problems of assimilating the millions of Asia Minor refugees going back to 1922.

After marrying Andrew in 1903 Alice, as we have seen, had become a thoroughgoing patriotic Greek. Throughout all the subsequent vicissitudes she never lost her love for the country and its people, even during the long exile of her family between 1922 and 1935. It would appear that Alice's religious experience and conversion to Orthodoxy brought her even closer to the Greek people's heart. While she was confined to hospital, Alice's new-found Orthodox zeal could not really manifest itself; but after she had settled in Athens it blossomed. Alice was a genuine believer; her conversion had no ulterior or worldly motive. Her own Mountbatten family was not particularly religious, but when Victoria told Alice's brothers that she had converted to Orthodoxy, they replied that if she believed that this could be good for her they would not have minded even if she had taken up 'the Shinto religion'.[25] Of the Greek royal family, Ellen (Princess Nicholas) was considered as its most devout member. Being Russian, she was already Orthodox when she married, and did not need to convert. Ellen regularly attended church services and maintained contacts with the clergy, helping fund many churches and their organizations.

However, whereas Ellen's religiosity was pretty much confined to rarefied spiritual issues, that of Alice took on a much more practical aspect. For Alice, charitable works were the essence of her Orthodox faith. Here she followed in the footsteps of her late aunt Ella, the Grand Duchess Elizabeta Feodorovna of Russia, who had become a nun and founded a religious order. Alice had witnessed Elizabeta's charitable work during a visit to Russia in 1908 and had the idea of doing the same in Greece.[26] However much Alice admired Elizabeta's work, she had not yet converted to Orthodoxy and probably did not think in overtly religious terms. More than three decades later, however, when Alice decided to commit to charitable work in Greece, she drew inspiration from her own experience of having suffered mental anguish for years. And she had by now acquired a religious outlook which gave her added strength for her good works for those in need. In this context, if Alice wanted Philip to be with her in Athens as a prince and possibly a future monarch, it was not only out of the natural love of a mother for her son, but also her belief that he would ultimately be good for Greece and the monarchy, over and above any philanthropic work she did herself. However, it appears that Alice may have wished that a member of her own family could one day ascend to the throne of Greece. As we saw, three decades earlier the Austrian ambassador had reported to his government that after the 1909 military coup Alice planned to use the opportunity to have Andrew declared regent in the place of his father, George I, who was expected to abdicate; perhaps this would have opened the way for Andrew to become the future king of Greece instead of his eldest brother, Crown Prince Constantine. During the 1920s Alice had also concocted bizarre plans of Andrew ascending to the throne by first becoming President of the Republic. Her letter to Dickie while she was pregnant with Philip in early 1921 about her child – if it were a boy – becoming one day king of Greece shows that Alice had also Philip in her mind as a potential monarch of his country.

In early 1938 a serious attack of influenza in London nearly proved fatal for Alice, but by the early summer she had largely recovered. In June she consulted Menelaos Metaxas, who was visiting London at the time, about her idea of returning to Greece.[27] Alice finally put her plan into action in early October, when she arrived in Athens ostensibly to be present at the unveiling ceremony of a statue of Constantine I, her late brother-in-law.[28] It was the first time she set foot on the soil of the country she considered as her own after having had to leave in 1922 with Andrew and the rest of the family.[29] As we have seen, Andrew was also there, and for the first time in sixteen years the couple attended a public event in Greece together. It would, however, be the last, even though Alice would remain in Athens and Andrew would visit a few more times until his own final trip in January 1940.

Alice was resolved to live permanently in Athens and in November 1938, a month after her arrival, bought a small apartment at number 8 Koumbari Street in the central upscale Kolonaki district, within sight of both the Parliament building and the city palace. Initially Alice had hoped that Andrew would come and live with her in the flat; however, when Andrew did visit Athens he would stay at the palace as official ADC to King George. In fact there were several occasions between November 1938 and January 1940 when they could have attended the same public functions, but they were never seen together. It was as if they were avoiding each other in public. Though they did not actually divorce, Andrew and Alice were now living entirely separate lives and did not even keep up the pretence of having any real relationship at all. Nevertheless, in letters written to Philip and his sisters she continued to refer to Andrew in affectionate terms, going as far as to praise (in a letter to Philip) Andrew's French mistress as 'the friendly woman who looked after him'![30] Andrew, for his part, continued to see Alice's mother Victoria whenever he was in London and told her that he thought Alice's move to Athens a good idea.

After Alice settled in Greece she kept a very low profile, shunning public appearances and venues and appearing only at the most important royal ones. She was never mentioned in the Greek press as having attended galas and receptions – in contrast to other female royals, especially Alice's sister-in-law Ellen, who relished such social events and whose name was rarely absent from the society columns of the newspapers (where Alice's never appeared).[31]

Soon after settling in Athens, on 5 December 1938 Alice wrote to Philip telling him that as soon as he finished Gordonstoun he ought to come and live with her:

I have taken a small flat just for you and me. Two bedrooms, each with a bathroom and two sitting rooms, a little kitchen and pantry. I found some furniture stored away in various places in the Old Palace, which I had not seen again since 1917, a most agreeable surprise and the family here are giving me things to complete it (...) Dickie tells me there is a chance of you having a long holiday in Spring so I am looking forward to your living in our flat.[32]

Alice's plan for her son was not simply for him to have a home in Greece where he could stay with her during his holidays, but to give him a start in the important role of Greek prince.[33] It would be a leg up for him, possibly, to eventually become king. There was a subtle tug-of-war here: Alice, who was Greek by marriage, and whose British family the Mountbattens were in charge of Philip in Britain, did everything she could to lure him to Greece, while Philip's actual Greek father wanted him to live in Britain and stay away from his country of birth.

From Philip's standpoint the key development was that as Alice now had her own flat in Kolonaki, he could at last have somewhere to call home, after almost a decade of living pillar-to-post with relatives when he was not at school. Philip himself in 1944, in what is likely to have been his only interview published in a British newspaper during the Second World War, seemed to acknowledge that fact as he is quoted as saying that since 1941 he had not seen 'my home in Athens'.[34]

In early March 1939 the eighteen-year-old Philip graduated from Gordonstoun. Following the advice of his mother, just after his graduation he left for Greece. His visit lasted almost two months and had little to do with recreation. It was more of a test for a future, more permanent, move to Greece. Hahn noted disapprovingly that Philip was keen to move to Athens.[35] Alice herself, in a letter to her brother Dickie Mountbatten dated 12 March 1939, described in a positive light how Philip was getting along in Athens. Dickie had taken over as Philip's guardian in Britain from his brother Georgie, who had passed away in April 1938, and was to prove instrumental in Philip's acceptance at Dartmouth for training as a Royal Navy officer.

On 19 March 1939 Philip and Alice were reported in the Greek press as being among the dignitaries, including George II, greeting Paul and

Frederica at the Athens railway station. During the previous week the couple had taken a tour of the Greek provinces so that Frederica could start getting to know her new country.[36] One month later, on 13 April 1939, Philip was still in Athens and was a guest at a society wedding at which Paul and Frederica were the *koumbaroi*.[37] A *koumbaros* becomes a symbolic relative of the married couple, which in Greece still entails a strong social tie with all the obligations that it entails (it is more important than the equivalent of best man in an Anglo-Saxon wedding). Royal family members and prominent politicians sought the *koumbaros* connection with other influential people to strengthen their support base. Young Philip was drawn into this networking game as, after acting as *koumbaros* for Paul and Frederica at the beginning of 1938, he took on the role again on 24 December 1938 at the wedding of Helene Foufounis and one W.N. Kirby.[38] Foufounis' royalist family had been exiled from Greece and lived at Saint-Cloud near Paris where Andrew and Alice lived in the 1920s. Philip and Helene had grown up together and were friends from childhood. When she and Kirby were married in the Greek Orthodox Cathedral in London, Philip agreed to be the all-important *koumbaros*.

On 14 April 1939 Philip accompanied Paul and Frederica to a tennis tournament of Mediterranean countries hosted by Athens. The next day some Greek newspapers ran photographs of the three arriving to watch one of the matches.[39] More importantly, ten days later, Philip attended a Te Deum at Athens Cathedral in honour of King George's name day (23 April). One of the photographs shows Philip walking behind the King as they exit the cathedral.[40] This was Philip's last official venue he attended in Greece, as two days later he left for Britain to sit the entrance examinations for the Royal Naval College at Dartmouth. Dickie Mountbatten had arranged for a tutor to help Philip with the material, showing an active interest in his nephew's welfare. Philip passed the exams and in May began his training as a naval cadet.[41] This did not entail any problems for Philip in travelling to Greece, as he retained his Greek citizenship and was not a British subject. Philip would be trained in the Royal Navy, but it was assumed that after his commissioning he would transfer to the Greek Navy. An Admiralty memo to the Foreign Office dated 18 April 1939 (when Philip was in Athens) confirms this, saying that after Philip attained the rank of acting sub-lieutenant he would no longer be part of the Royal Navy.[42]

The Foreign Office would certainly have taken an interest in Philip starting his training at Dartmouth, not only because he was a foreigner but also because he was a prince of another country and a candidate for its throne. The possibility that he might end up serving in the Royal Navy could have had serious diplomatic repercussions in relations between Britain and Greece. The Admiralty memo is signed by a 'Mr Mountain', who was almost certainly Dickie Mountbatten himself, who is known to have used that pseudonym on other occasions.[43] Even George VI intervened so that there would be no problem about Philip being trained in the Royal Navy.[44] On 3 May King George and Queen Elizabeth dined with Philip and his grandmother Victoria at Buckingham Palace.[45] During the dinner Philip talked with the King and Queen about his forthcoming training at Dartmouth. George VI had also been an officer in the Royal Navy and may have shared some of his experiences with Philip, who after all happened to be a relative. One assumes also that Philip was asked about his visit to Greece and for news of George II and other members of the Greek royal family.

After Philip left Athens in late April 1939, Alice became lonely. It is likely she had qualms about her son entering Dartmouth instead of the Hellenic Naval Academy. Possibly to seek solace and spiritual enlightenment, Alice decided to go to the Holy Land for the first time in her life. This visit, hitherto unknown, began on 2 May when Alice arrived at Haifa on a Romanian vessel and travelled on to Jerusalem that same day. She stayed at the King David Hotel for a day until the Greek Orthodox Patriarch of Jerusalem made arrangements for her to move to a cell in the facilities of the Patriarchate.[46] Alice remained in Jerusalem for a fortnight and visited all the sites linked to Christ's life and suffering. Her pilgrimage was done in strict secrecy from the prying eyes of the press. One may speculate that its effects played an important role in the decisions she was to take about her future and that of Philip; her visit to the Orthodox Patriarchate of Jerusalem had far-reaching consequences for the rest of her life. It strengthened her determination to found her own Orthodox convent, and she would eventually choose Jerusalem to be her final resting place.

Andrew arrived in Athens on 19 April but there is no record of his meeting Alice; when she returned from the Holy Land, he had already left for Monte Carlo. Alice decided on a visit to Britain to see Philip. But another family tragedy forestalled her. When Cecile and her family boarded the fatal aircraft to fly to Britain in 1937, they had to leave behind their youngest child, one-year-old Johanna, as she was too young to travel. In the spring of 1939 Johanna became gravely ill with meningitis; Alice rushed to Germany in June, but the child died shortly afterwards. In this moment of grief Alice found the strength to write to Philip that she took some comfort from the fact that at least Andrew was not there to see his grandchild die, as it would have broken his heart; Johanna, Alice wrote, looked exactly as Cecile had at that age.[47] We have seen that at no point did Alice ever betray any hostility to Andrew, in word or in deed, and never belaboured him in her letters to her children. Some authorities claim she was still quite in love with Andrew despite everything. What is certain is that she was psychologically quite robust in order to cope with little Johanna's loss coming soon after the loss of Cecile and her family. The conclusion must be that her dedication to religion had fortified her against the evils of life.

In August 1939, on Philip's first holiday break from Dartmouth, Alice lost no time in arranging for him to return to Athens, arriving there together by boat from Italy on the nineteenth.[48] On 30 August Philip, in the company of Paul and Frederica, visited the posh northern suburb of Kifissia, where they were the guests of honour at the opening of the local sporting club.[49] On these occasions, of course, Philip acted out his role as a prince of the Greek royal family, getting to know the country and its people better. Not only Alice but also other family members were grooming him for this. References of the time show that Philip went along with it all willingly, and there was a distinct possibility of his living in Greece permanently after Dartmouth.

While in Athens, Philip usually attended public functions in the company of Paul and Frederica. As someone who hardly spoke Greek, it was essential he be with Paul, whose mother tongue *was* Greek, as much as possible. Besides, he was in the company of the official heir to the throne, and if that heir was still childless, he had a high position in the succession list. Philip's position was further strengthened in 1939 when his cousin Prince Peter, as we have seen, was excluded from the succession. (Peter at the time was no longer in Greece and stayed out of the public spotlight.)

It is scarcely surprising, then, that Philip's visits to Greece acquired a semi-official character and were carefully monitored by the press which recorded them in detail. His attendance at public venues was announced in palace news bulletins. The authoritarian Metaxas government also kept a protective eye on him. A naval captain, Nikolaos (Nicky) Merlin, was seconded to act as Philip's chaperone wherever he went. Merlin was a cosmopolitan Greek who had grown up in France and lived in Athens after joining the Greek Navy.[50] Fluent in English and French, Merlin acted as an interpreter for Philip and showed him around in Athens. Alice noted that Merlin 'kept a paternal eye' on Philip.[51] Presumably the two men would have sampled Athens' best night clubs and bars, something which Philip would have been unable to do in the company of his mother or his prestigious cousin, Prince Paul. Alice wrote to Dickie Mountbatten that she had made the arrangements for Captain Merlin to accompany her son; therefore we can conclude that it was Merlin's official duty and not something he did in his spare time. But was it Alice's decision? Even though she was a princess and aunt of the King, she would not have had the authority. More likely it was arranged on an official level, probably by King George in consultation with the government.

A curious pattern emerges here. Both Andrew and Philip made visits to Athens, but their paths apparently never crossed as far the Greek people knew. When Andrew arrived in Athens for a brief visit on 19 April 1939, Philip was still there. However, there is not a single reference in the Greek press to them attending the same venues together (the last event they jointly attended had been the 1938 wedding of Paul and Frederica). Of course, they may well have met in private. However, there seems to have been an attempt to dissociate Philip from his father in the eyes of the public. As all announcements concerning the attendance by royals at various functions emanated from the palace, it could be that this policy originated from the King himself.

When the Second World War broke out on 1 September 1939, Philip was still in Greece. Two days later Great Britain entered the war. This could have presented Philip with a serious problem, as the country in which he was being trained to become a naval officer was now in a state of war, while his own country, Greece, was neutral. For all he knew, Dartmouth might well decide to terminate his training, as the Royal Navy now would need men to send into battle rather than a high-profile foreigner whose country was neutral and who would hence be kept out of any war zone. Philip's English grandmother Victoria told her son Dickie Mountbatten that in her opinion it might be better for Philip to stay in Greece 'where he belonged' and not return to England.[52]

Philip had the alternative of continuing his training at the Greek Naval Academy. He appears to have accepted that possibility, so Alice seized the opportunity, writing to Dickie on 14 September:

'[Philip] naturally would like best to go on training in England especially as he knows the language and the people. But he feels quite rightly that as he is such an utter stranger to the people and language here, if he does not now try & re-establish contact with the people, it will be still more difficult for him to do so later on. This effort to try and feel at home here and know and understand everything in the country is more important even than his naval career, which will be modest in such a small navy'.[53]

This letter indicates that Alice believed she was winning the battle and that her son would finally stay in Greece and take up his rightful position as one of the country's princes. It also shows that Philip himself more or less had accepted that. The reasoning was for Philip to remain in Greece and transfer to the Hellenic Naval Academy. As he had already finished a term at Dartmouth, he would be ahead of his classmates, as the Hellenic Academy's curriculum and training were similar to those of Dartmouth (the organization and training of the Greek Navy at the time was based to a great degree on those of the Royal Navy). Besides, English was the main foreign language taught in the academy, which itself was something of a rarity at a time when almost all Greece's higher education institutions preferred French for that role.

And then, out of the blue, George II told Philip that it would be better for him to return to England and finish his training in the Royal Navy rather than stay in Greece.[54] It came as a surprise to Philip and Alice, as until then the King had been the most prominent advocate for Philip's entering the Hellenic Naval Academy.[55] The reason for George's apparent u-turn is not known. The reasonable assumption is that he came to the conclusion that as Philip had already completed a term at Dartmouth, it would be better for him to take the risk to return to Britain, a country at war, and complete his remaining three terms of Royal Navy training, the last two of which would be on a training cruiser. Thus Philip would have had the opportunity to undergo a standard of training far superior to whatever the Hellenic Naval Academy could offer. This, however, did not mean that George was giving up on Philip as a Greek prince or even as a possible future successor of his. Philip was still a foreigner in the Royal Navy and nothing had apparently altered the understanding that he would eventually serve in the navy of his own country where he could put to good use the skills and experience he had acquired at Dartmouth. Did George have assurances – possibly from his cousin George VI – that Philip would be able to finish his course, and more importantly, be kept away from the war?

There is another, rather less likely, explanation why George agreed that Philip return to Britain. In late July 1939 at the end of his first term at Dartmouth and a month before he arrived in Greece, Philip met Princess Elizabeth when she paid a visit to his college with her parents, George VI and Queen Elizabeth, and her sister, Princess Margaret. Philip appears to have been the cadet who spent the most time with the royals, especially Elizabeth, during the visit. It is believed that Dickie Mountbatten engineered the contacts between his nephew and the British royal family, as a means of encouraging Philip as a potential suitor. If this was Mountbatten's intention, it manifestly succeeded, as this was the earliest occasion on which there is evidence that Elizabeth not only took notice of Philip but could have developed distinct feelings for him.[56] Philip, however, is unlikely to have felt the same for the then thirteen-year-old princess, and besides at that time he was infatuated with an American girl of his own age (see following chapter). In 1941, while he was at sea with the Royal Navy, Philip began a correspondence with Elizabeth. Early that year members of the Greek royal family in Athens were talking openly about the two eventually getting married and mooting this possibility as a way of impressing British friends.[57] So it may be not that far-fetched that George II knew early on, in the summer of 1939, that his cousin Philip had a good chance of marrying the future Queen of Great Britain.

He may therefore have considered such a match a far better prospect for Philip, as well as the wider Greek royalty, than being just one more Greek prince – not to mention the strong bond such a marriage would forge between two nations.

On 21 September 1939 Philip left neutral Greece for Britain that was already in its third week of war against Nazi Germany. Alice's true feelings at this period are hard to fathom. She wrote to him in December 1939 with the news that Prince Peter had been booted off the succession roster because of his 'undesirable' marriage to Irina Ovchinnikova. In the same letter she added that Paul and Frederica were expecting a new baby, and hoped it would be a boy and thus a direct heir.[58] But was the 'hope' a genuine one, or did she secretly wish for another girl (their first child, Princess Sophia, was now a year old) so that her son would still have a sporting chance for the throne?

From October 1939 to April 1940, the period dubbed the 'Phoney War' by the British media, Alice felt secure enough to travel to Britain for a quiet Christmas with Philip and her relatives. She returned to Athens in late January 1940, missing Prince Christopher's funeral by a few days. It was another case of Alice and Andrew just missing each other at an Athens state function; in this case Andrew did attend his brother's funeral – but it was the last time he would visit his homeland. As Alice was close to Christopher, it is tempting to assume that she just didn't care to run into Andrew. The war, and France's capitulation to the Germans in June 1940, cut off Andrew in France, where he died in 1944. But the truth remains that Alice missed the opportunity to see for the last time the man with whom she had been together for almost forty years – many of them happy ones – and with whom she had five children. However, by a strange twist, the war also unexpectedly brought Philip back to Athens in early 1941.

In January and February 1941, for the only time in Greek history, a Greek prince was seen in his own capital strolling around in the uniform of a British midshipman serving in the Mediterranean fleet of the Royal Navy. One wonders whether people like Captain 'Nicky" Merlin, his onetime chaperone, would have been confronted with the dilemma of either saluting or being saluted by Prince Philip of Greece, Midshipman RN! There was apparently no difficulty of that sort. After getting off his ship, HMS *Valiant*, at Piraeus Philip made his way to the Grande Bretagne Hotel in central Athens, where the Greek General Staff was headquartered; Italian forces had invaded from the northwest on 28 October 1940, and the Greek Army was fully occupied in an epic battle to drive the Italians back into Albania, a campaign that so far had scored remarkable successes.

A British Army and Royal Air Force military mission was in Athens advising the Greek command, whose liaison officer with the British was none other than Captain Prince Peter. On occasion Peter had been irked by the bossiness of some of the British brass, and when a Royal Navy officer marched into his office his first reaction was, 'Oh, another pushy Brit. What does this one want?' Then he relaxed as he saw it was Philip. After the initial greetings, Philip asked Peter what he was doing behind a desk and not at the front in Albania. Peter replied that he believed himself more useful in the liaison role. At the moment he had been drawing up a report for the Greek commander-in-chief, Lieutenant General Alexandros Papagos, and according to Peter's later memoir, Philip helped him with it – indicating that, contrary to what was generally maintained, Philip knew enough Greek at the time, as such memos were always couched in complex officialese. After Philip left, Peter began wondering: what indeed *was* he doing pushing papers in Athens? He would get the chance to see action soon enough.[59]

Chapter 11

A Prince in Love and War

We may now backtrack a little from the critical days of 1939 when Philip's potential course towards the Greek throne appears to have been derailed. There was another cause of his attention being turned elsewhere. When Gordonstoun broke up for the summer of 1938, Philip was given the opportunity to holiday outside Britain. In August and September he was in Venice, invited by his aunt Aspasia, the widow of King Alexander of Greece, who was living permanently in the city with her daughter Alexandra.[1] While accompanying his aunt and cousin to various functions in Venice Philip met Cobina Wright, a glamorous American socialite, aspiring actress and singer, and seventeen years old like himself.[2] Her mother, also named Cobina Wright, had married a wealthy American industrialist and with her daughter was able to live the high life. Mother and daughter were in Venice visiting the Countess Castelbarco, the daughter of celebrated conductor Arturo Toscanini.[3]

According to what Cobina told her friends in later years, Philip introduced himself to her as 'Philip Prince of Greece'. Cobina, intrigued, asked him what his surname was. Philip simply replied that princes didn't have surnames, only the name of their country.[4] This American girl who had never before met a real prince was no doubt impressed; even more impressed was her mother, who was with her and virtually pushed her into Philip's arms![5] A romantic relationship was duly formed between Philip and the younger Cobina, and over the next three weeks they were seen together in Venice on gondolas, in bars and at the seaside. Philip's infatuation for Cobina was such that he told society columnist Paul Maury, with whom he was close at the time, that Venice 'was his favourite place in the whole world'.[6] This, then, was no brief summer romance – at least on the part of Philip, who followed Cobina to London after she left Venice. In London the romance continued for another week until Cobina and her mother left for America. The night before their departure Philip gave the girl a gold bracelet inscribed with the words 'I Love You' next to a Greek flag.[7] It may have been a small detail, but the inscription shows that in the autumn of 1938 Philip still saw himself as a Greek and did not hesitate to show it in his first serious romantic relationship.

Rumours flew that the couple were about to marry and that Cobina was prepared to give up a career in the entertainment business in favour of becoming a Greek princess, and someday, even perhaps Queen of Greece. Andrew and Alice would certainly have heard about Philip's love interest and neither would have considered Cobina a proper match for their royal son; yet neither seemed to be in a position to do anything about it. Philip, having been thrown upon his own resources for most of his young life, was flexing his muscles of independence and was not about to knuckle under to his parents. He insisted on his feelings for Cobina. When in 1939, a few months before the outbreak of the Second World War, Prince Philip entered Dartmouth Royal Naval College as a cadet, it sounded the death knell of his relationship with Cobina; his military status was probably not something she could accept as an aspiring show business personality. Therefore, she in all likelihood ended the affair. Moreover, for her Philip was merely one in a string of affairs, far from a classic Prince Charming.

Though at the time the relationship was never mentioned in the British or Greek press, it was avidly followed by American reporters. The fact that a prince was pursuing an American girl reminded the American public of the Edward VIII and Wallis Simpson affair, albeit on a smaller scale. What particularly fascinated them was the fact that the wholesome American girl was no pushover for this very handsome prince and was keeping him at a distance. On 21 July 1939 Cobina had to make it clear in an interview that though Philip was a 'good friend' she was not in love with him, and he was certainly not coming to the United States to marry her as 'conditions in Europe are so uncertain that he cannot get away right now'. Some media love-interest was kept up, however, as she said in the same interview that she and Philip continued to correspond.[8] On 29 July the *Minneapolis Star* ran a story by Leonard Lyons according to which 'Crown [sic] Prince Philip of Greece, who now is in the British navy, wrote to friends here that the British government won't permit him to travel anywhere in Europe now except to Holland, Belgium and the North of France'. This information may well have come from letters Philip wrote to Cobina.

There is evidence that Philip did in fact want to go to America and find Cobina but his joining the Royal Navy and the imminent war stopped him. The society columnist Nancy Randolph wrote in January 1940, in 'U.S. Lad Beats Prince to Cobina Jr.'s. Heart'[9] that Philip had by then lost any chance of conquering his sweetheart. According to this article, Philip at the time was still writing love letters to her, but she didn't bother to reply to them. The reason was that Cobina had moved on to another relationship, this time with actor Bobby Stack and had ceased caring for Midshipman RN Prince Philip of Greece. According to the columnist, Cobina's rejection so upset the Prince that he even wrote to her mother asking why her daughter was not answering his letters![10] Mother Cobina certainly had every interest in getting her daughter to marry Philip and become a princess, and must have done what she could to turn her daughter's mind that way, but apparently to no avail.

Society columnist Paul Maury claimed that Philip was still in love with Cobina even as late as December 1940:

Prince Philip of Greece, who has just signed up as a midshipman in the British Navy, is, by far, the best looking of all the Athens princelings. Only a few summers back, tall, young and blond Philip was happily summering at the Italian Lido, across from Venice, and his closest friends were culled from the titled Italian set 'beachcombing' by the Adriatic. Now he is to take his place with the British Mediterranean fleet and assist in the bombing of the one city he, himself, told me was his favorite place of the whole world – Venice. New Yorkers will remember Prince Philip of Greece as the young royal who fell so madly in love that same summer with Cobina Wright Jr., who was among the U.S.A. vacationists at the Lido. Prince Philip not only yearned to make the beauteous Cobina his Princess – he pleaded with her to elope, in the good old American fashion.'[11]

Though such details mentioned in the American newspapers might appear typical gossip-column fodder, more fanciful than not (especially the bit about the British planning to bombard Venice!), the essence appears to have been corroborated by interviews given by Cobina, her friends or even (former) friends of Philip at the time, years later.[12] These agree with more sober coverage in the American press during 1939 and 1940 that Philip was madly in love with Cobina and wrote her passionate letters asking her to marry him. All this was presumably leaked to the press by Cobina, her mother and her friends, very likely in an attempt to enhance her image in pursuit of a career in Hollywood.

As we have seen, during August and September 1939 Philip was in Greece. There is not a single reference to Cobina in the Greek press, though it is certain that their relationship would have been known in the more exalted circles of society who read American newspapers. Ioannis Metaxas, Greece's dictator at the time, had made it clear to the press that he would not tolerate any embarrassing stories about the royals and that probably put a damper on the reports. Perhaps it was lucky for Philip that he did not end up with Cobina in Greece; by an accident of linguistics, her name sounds identical to the Greek word *kombina*, meaning a shady deal. Even under Metaxas' strict censorship journalists would have had found ways of making jokes out of the similarity, to the embarrassment of the prince who wished to marry her.

Cobina eventually followed in the footsteps of her namesake mother, wed a wealthy industrialist and put aside any artistic aspirations. So on Sunday, 7 December 1941, the day of the attack on Pearl Harbor, the *Tampa Bay Times* ran an article by Ursula Petrie about Cobina's wedding to the man she finally chose, Palmer Beaudette, entitled 'A glamour bride's mother: Now it's my turn for love'. The main theme of the story is Cobina's mother's claim that as her daughter had got married it was now her turn to do the same. Prince Philip rates a mention as just one of the many rich and famous chaps who at one point had a liaison with the daughter: 'Her swains have been legion – American Legion with an Overseas Division'. What is interesting about this story is that it includes the only known photograph of Philip together with Cobina. They are shown seated next to each other having drinks; opposite them is Sir Robert Peel, Sixth Baronet, a fellow cadet of Philip at the Royal Naval College, Dartmouth, and one year older than him. Philip and Peel are in navy uniform, showing that the photograph was taken around the summer of 1939. The fact that Robert Peel is in the company of Philip and Cobina would suggest that he may have been a good friend of Philip's at Dartmouth. Shortly after this photograph was taken, the Second World War broke out.

This photograph is evidence that Cobina was in Britain in 1939 and that she met up with Philip after their love affair a year before.[13] She had already long made it clear that she did not love him but wanted to stay good friends. Was the picture taken during their final meeting? Cobina is smiling with her eyes closed and is obviously enjoying the moment. In contrast, Philip appears surprised by the photographer and has an embarrassed expression. This makes it likely that the photograph may have been taken by a *paparazzo* who used a flash, which could be why Cobina closed her eyes as the picture was snapped.

The affair with Cobina was one of the first of Philip's many fabled encounters with the press. It would have been an unsettling experience for the eighteen-year-old prince brought up with the ideals of truth, honesty and nobility. The issue of the American newspaper with the photo happened to circulate on the day of Pearl Harbor, and so it is unlikely that much reader attention was paid to it. Only four months later, Sir Robert Peel, the third person in the photograph, was killed in action. When war broke out in September 1939, Peel had decided not to complete his officer's course at Dartmouth and enlisted as an ordinary seaman so that he could be in active service as soon as possible. On 5 April 1942 his ship, the destroyer HMS *Tenedos*, was attacked by Japanese bombers and sunk in Colombo Harbour, Ceylon (now Sri Lanka), after receiving a direct hit from a 500-pound bomb. Ordinary Seaman Sir Robert Peel was killed along with other crew members who had volunteered to carry ammunition from below decks to the stern guns of the *Tenedos*.[14]

In late September 1939 Philip returned to England from Greece and resumed his training as a naval cadet at Dartmouth. Four months later he graduated at the top of his class, winning the King's Dirk as best all-round cadet of the year. That was the kind of distinction that his father had failed to achieve four decades before at the Military Academy in his own country. Philip also won the Eardley-Howard-Crocket Prize which was awarded to the best cadet at Dartmouth and on graduation he became a midshipman; Dickie Mountbatten arranged to have him posted to the battleship HMS *Ramillies* which was based at Colombo. As Greece was still neutral at the time and Philip a Greek citizen, it was deemed important that he be kept away from anything resembling a war zone. Philip would get his training at sea on the *Ramillies* in the Far East where there were no German naval forces and Japan was not yet in the war.

The duty of the *Ramillies* was to escort troopships ferrying Australian soldiers to Britain across the Indian Ocean stretch. In early April 1940 when the battleship arrived at Australia with Philip on board, the Greek consul in Sydney, Aimilios Vrysakis, was asked to 'look after' the Prince and help make sure his first visit to Australia should be as incognito as it could get. But the ever-irrepressible Philip decided to make a surprise appearance in a Sunday mass at the Greek Orthodox Cathedral of Saint Sophia in Sydney to greet his fellow Greeks. The rumour spread rapidly that Prince Philip was in town on leave from his ship, which galvanized local reporters into trying to chase him down in the Sydney clubs. One reporter managed to do it and asked Philip if he really was the Prince. Philip denied it, claiming a case of mistaken identity. The next day a photograph of Philip appeared in the local *Daily Telegraph*; the caption referred to him as a 'mystery man' and asked readers to help 'trace him', rather in the manner of a wanted criminal:

Mystery Man In Sydney. Have you seen this man in the city? He is Prince Philip of Greece, at present incognito somewhere in Sydney. His address is unknown. His future plans in Australia are a mystery. He blandly denied he was Prince Philip when questioned in a fashionable night club in the city. 'My dear fellow, I am afraid it is a case of mistaken identity', he said. It was reported last night that he would attend the 11 o'clock service in the Greek Cathedral this morning....[15]

But the cat was out of the bag. After the Australian press essentially revealed his presence in Sydney there was no longer any real reason for him to continue incognito. When he attended the service at the Saint Sophia Greek Orthodox Cathedral, almost the whole Greek community of Sydney as well as a host of ordinary Australians crammed into the church to see him. Archbishop Timotheos, the Greek primate of Australia, delivered a speech of welcome after the service.[16]

Philip spent much of his remaining time on shore leave at Romano's, the swankiest club in Sydney. The *Australian Women's Weekly* caught him on camera there, with the caption:

> Photographed at last...camera-shy Prince Philip of Greece shows remarkable resemblance to [the] Duke of Kent. He is applauding [the] orchestra at Romano's where he frequently dances incognito.[17]

In this photograph nineteen-year-old Philip bears a striking resemblance to his grandson Prince William at the same age. The news that he frequented this club drew a number of attractive Australian girls to him. The attention of the press, however, seems to have irritated him as he left Sydney for a few days to visit a sheep station in the countryside.[18] Philip seems to have fallen in love with Australia and its people during his visit there in 1940. Many more visits would follow, enabling him to establish a close relationship with that country which he has retained throughout his long life.

In May 1940 Philip was transferred to the heavy cruiser HMS *Kent* operating between India, Ceylon and South Africa – still safely far from the actual fighting. It was while he was serving on the *Kent* that an event more than 4,000 miles away in Greece would have a major impact on his life. On 2 June 1940 a 101-gun salute from the artillery garrison on Lykavittos Hill boomed over Athens to announce the birth of a boy to Paul and Frederica – the future King Constantine II. Metaxas conveyed his congratulations in the form of a miniature uniform of the National Youth Organization – which Paul at once consigned to the fireplace.[19] The birth of Constantine had the effect of pushing Philip decisively away from any realistic prospect of assuming the Greek throne, even though Princess Alice never ceased to harbour her secret hopes that Philip would continue to be a Greek prince. In fact, Greece had not yet finished with Philip.

Greece was slowly being pushed into the Second World War on the side of the Allies even though Ioannis Metaxas, who ruled the country as a fascist-type dictator, might have been expected to favour the Axis.

Metaxas, however, was always quite clear whose side he would be on in the event of war – the side of Great Britain, the mistress of the Mediterranean. Nonetheless, Germany loomed large in Greek affairs in the 1930s. Metaxas himself had first-hand experience of the Germans and their military methods, having graduated top of his class in the Berlin Kriegsacademie, or Staff College. He admired them, yet knew what they were capable of. In 1935 Germany was Greece's biggest trading partner; in return for olives, raisins, fruit and minerals Greece received armaments and heavy industrial equipment such as locomotives. The livelihoods of many thousands of Greeks thus depended on the German economy. Metaxas' tightrope act was to keep out of the Germans' political clutches while retaining good commercial ties with them. His character and that of the King proved to be up to that task.

Opinion in Britain, however, was uncertain. There was a powerful streak of anti-Metaxas sentiment, especially in left-wing and liberal circles; British conservative supporters tended to mute their opinions for fear of being tainted by a 'fascist' brush. That was one reason why there was no trade agreement between Britain and Greece until 1940 and why Germany rushed to fill the vacuum. But King George had lost none of his admiration for the British and their constitutional propriety; and he and Metaxas remained steadfast in their support for Great Britain in the gathering storm over Europe.

At the end it was Mussolini's Italy and not Nazi Germany which dragged Greece into the Second World War. After a series of provocations, following the Italian conquest of Albania in April 1939, the most blatant being the torpedoing of the Greek light cruiser *Elli* on 15 August 1940 (see Appendix 1), on 28 October Mussolini sent his forces over the northwest border from Albania. He wanted to copy his partner Hitler, who during the previous spring and early summer had subdued most western European countries and in early October had added Romania to his conquests. This turned out to be Metaxas' finest hour; he had been awakened in the early hours of the 28th by the Italian minister, Emanuele Grazzi, with Mussolini's ultimatum that Greece allow the passage of Italian troops through its territory. This was supposed to be a 'guarantee' that Greece would not back Britain. Metaxas' defiant reply, *'Alors, c'est la guerre'* ('Well then, it's war'), has gone down in history condensed into the single word *'Ochi!* ' ('No!'). Greece's mobilization found the entire nation, in one of the very rare cases in its history, united. The old rift between royalists and Venizelists evaporated as if by magic; even hard-line communists jailed by Metaxas joined up. Compton Mackenzie, that redoubtable British admirer of Venizelos and foe of the royalist Metaxas, when he heard the news 'never wanted to shake any man so warmly by the hand.'[20]

It was a war effort that at first resounded with glory. Within days the Greek divisions under General Alexandros Papagos, the commander in chief of the Greek Army, had driven the attacking Italians out of northwest Greece and into the inhospitable crags of Albania. Bells rang in Greek churches as one by one ethnic Greek towns in southern Albania were wrested from the Italians. Then the bitter Albanian winter set in, and both armies suffered desperately from the excessive cold and logistical problems in the mountains. In January 1941 the Greek advance had ground to a standstill in the ice and snowdrifts, with hopes that a new advance could take place in the spring. But on 29 January, after a brief illness, Metaxas died. The passing of this undoubted architect of Greek triumphs dealt the nation a severe blow. And it fell to the taciturn George II to assume the role of effective national leader and standard-bearer. A desperate Italian counter-offensive that began on 9 March butted itself to pieces, but by the time that three-week battle ended, the Germans were on the point of bursting into Greece from Bulgaria.

On the day Italy attacked Greece, Philip ceased being a neutral and became an ally of Britain. Two days later, on 31 October 1940, the *Manchester Guardian* ran the following item revealing details about the Greek prince serving the Royal Navy who was soon to take part in the fighting:[21] Headlined 'A Greek Prince in the Navy', it read:

A member of the Greek royal house has been serving in the Royal Navy since the outbreak of war and has been at sea since January. He has seen active service in the last few months.[22] This is Prince Philip of Greece, cousin of King George of Greece and close in succession [*sic*] to the throne. He is a cousin of our own King George too; his mother is daughter of Prince Louis of Battenberg, who was our First Sea Lord in 1914, and the elder sister of Lord Louis Mountbatten, also on active service as a captain RN. Prince Philip, who is in his teens, is a midshipman in a ship now in waters not unimportant to his own country. He was destined for the Greek Navy but came to this country to learn his trade. He went to Gordonstoun, the Scottish preparatory school, and to Dartmouth, where he won the King's Dirk – the Navy's equivalent of Sandhurst's Sword of Honour, awarded to the best all-round cadet of his year. Prince Philip is an athlete in the Greek tradition; he won the javelin-throwing at a recent interport sports meeting.

The story then went on to discuss how Philip, a foreigner, could become a commissioned officer in the Royal Navy while retaining his nationality, something not permitted in peacetime but accepted in time of war:

As a midshipman Prince Philip does not hold a King's commission. He does not receive that until he is confirmed in rank as a sub-lieutenant. Now that we are at war he may receive a commission and retain his nationality, as, for instance, French and Polish officers have done in the Navy and Americans in the Air Force; in peace-time only a British subject may be commissioned. That is why the Spanish prince who served with the Navy some few years ago became the Service's senior acting sub-lieutenant but was never confirmed in his rank.[23]

In mid-December 1940 it was announced that Philip would be transferred 'around Christmas' to a Royal Navy ship of the Mediterranean Fleet.[24] This meant that he would soon be fighting in an important war zone against the Italians. On 1 January 1941 Philip was posted to the battleship HMS *Valiant* based at Alexandria; three days later he was in his first battle when his ship supported General Archibald Wavell's advance into Cyrenaica against the Italians. The *Valiant* took part in the bombardment of the city of Bardia. As we have seen, Philip's father, uncles and cousins had all been officers in the Greek Army. They had participated in the various conflicts Greece was involved in during the first quarter of the twentieth century. However, none had fought on any front line, and thus Philip was the first and only Greek royal to do so. Though he was not in the Greek Navy he was fighting the same foe his Greek compatriots were also fighting at the time in Albania, across the Mediterranean littoral from Libya.

A week after he had taken part in his first combat action, in mid-January 1941, Philip took leave from Alexandria and went to Athens, staying there for five weeks until late February. King George II wrote to Philip's grandmother Victoria on 20 January informing her that Philip was in Athens.[25] Yet five weeks seems like a long time for shore leave, especially as the *Valiant* was stationed at Alexandria. Some British newspapers in early April 1941 quoted Philip as saying he took his leave because so far it was 'a dull war' and there was 'no shooting'.[26] This seems to be a surprising stance for a very junior officer to take, even if he was a foreign prince; a mere midshipman could not saunter away on leave from his battleship simply when he felt like it, or because he was bored with a war where, in his view, there was 'no shooting'.

One possible explanation is that Philip was sent to Athens on a special mission under cover of regular leave, to act as a liaison between Greek officers and their British advisers. In January and February 1941 the talks centred on what kind of military aid Britain could send embattled Greece in the event of a German invasion. Such an invasion was expected in the spring as Hitler wanted to help his ally Mussolini whose forces had suffered a series of humiliating defeats in Albania. The Anglo-Greek talks took place at the highest level, with the participation of George II, Metaxas and, following the latter's death, the new prime minister Alexandros Koryzis, plus General Papagos, the Greek commander-in-chief. In the later phases of the talks the British were represented by Anthony Eden, recently appointed foreign secretary, and General Wavell, the commander of the British troops in North Africa. At the same time Greek and British staff officers cooperated in assessing the various needs of the Greeks in their ongoing fight against the Italians. As a Greek who had been trained in the Royal Navy, Philip was likely to be useful in this liaison programme. If this was indeed the case, he would have been privy to sensitive military information which he would not have been able to divulge even to his royal relatives in Greece.

Philip's cousin Princess Alexandra writes that while he was in Athens he used to visit her at her house on the slopes of Lykavittos, the conical hill that rises up abruptly out of the city centre overlooking the Kolonaki district where Alice's flat was located. However, Alexandra makes the point that Philip always turned up unexpected; she never knew when his next visit would occur.[27] Philip Eade, the leading biographer of the young Prince Philip, thinks that he may have been trying to avoid meeting Alexandra too often, using his naval duties in Athens as an excuse.[28] This may be so, but it does indicate that Philip during his time on leave in Athens was occupied with tasks linked to the war effort – far from lounging around as one might expect of a young low-ranking officer on leave. Philip's cousin Prince Peter strongly implied that Philip was involved in important work in Athens. We have already seen how Captain Prince Peter, who acted as the chief Greek liaison officer with the British, had an unexpected visit from Philip, who asked him (in his typically blunt way) why he was stuck in an office and not up at the front. The report to General Papagos that Philip helped Peter to draft could well have contained classified information, and the fact that Peter entrusted Philip with such a task shows that he may have had clearance from the highest level. That report was probably Prince Philip's only contribution to the Greek war effort in early 1941 that we know of. Philip was in Athens on 29 January, the day of Metaxas' death, and attended the funeral two days later. [29] According to an announcement from the palace, Philip was at the funeral along with King George and their cousins, Princes Peter and Paul.[30]

During his five-week sojourn in Athens, Philip stayed at his mother's flat at Kolonaki. However, they saw little of each other as Alice was very busy with her voluntary work helping families of Greek soldiers fighting on the Albanian front. When war broke out Alice had not had the chance to form the kind of philanthropic organization with a Christian character that she had envisaged since returning to Greece in 1938. Instead, she became the head of an association named Proodos (Progress) that was under the aegis of the Parnassos Literary Society. Parnassos, the oldest and most prestigious literary society in Greece, had been an official non-profit organization since 1875. Alice headed up a group of female volunteers who donated parcels of food and clothing to the families of the absent soldiers.

Contrary to what she had done three decades before during the First Balkan War, Alice did not go to the front as a nurse, but remained in Athens. She set up the headquarters of her association in her summer house at 10 Pefkon Street in the northern Athens suburb of Neon Herakleion.[31] As this was more than 15 kilometres from the city centre, Alice was able to be in her flat at Kolonaki only three or two days a week. King George, in his letter to Victoria informing her of Philip's arrival in Athens, also mentions that Alice was so busy with helping the soldiers' families that the rest of the royal family could see her only on Sundays. At the same time the birth of Constantine to Paul and Frederica a few months before, which had bumped Philip quite a way down the succession line, must have been a disappointment to her. But she figured that as a prince of Greece, her son would continue to play that role after the war. She would stick to that belief during the subsequent Axis occupation of Greece, which Alice lived through in Athens, as evidenced in letters she managed to send to Dickie Mountbatten and Philip via her sister Louise in neutral Sweden.

In late February 1941 Philip was back on the *Valiant* in Alexandria. The Mediterranean Fleet now had the task of escorting the British expeditionary force that would land in Greece as soon as the green light was given. On 1 March the German Wehrmacht began crossing the Danube into Bulgaria – the clearest sign yet that Greece was next on the list. Koryzis, who succeeded Metaxas as prime minister, had told the British that if the Germans crossed the Danube he would accept any assistance the British could offer to Greece. But there was a catch. Koryzis, like Metaxas before him, had feared that any British military intervention would be used by Hitler as an excuse to attack Greece – a forecast that came devastatingly true. The ferrying of the British expeditionary force from Egypt to Greece, Operation Lustre, began on 2 March; the port of disembarkation for the troops with all their equipment and supplies was Piraeus. One of the British warships escorting the convoys was the *Valiant*. But did this mean that Philip would be able to return to Athens only a few days after he had left? Unfortunately not. The *Valiant* was based in Alexandria, and that is where the ship returned after each voyage. (In fact Philip would not see Athens again until almost a decade later, in 1950, during a brief visit with his wife, the then Princess Elizabeth.)[32]

On 27 March the Italians tried to intercept a large convoy with parts of the British expeditionary force by sending their most powerful warships to intercept the shipping lane between Alexandria and Piraeus. The British had been forewarned about this movement from intercepted Italian radio messages. The Mediterranean Fleet under Admiral Sir John Cunningham encountered the Italian fleet off Cape Matapan in the southern Peloponnese and battered it to shreds. After the battle the Italian Navy ceased to be a real threat to the British in the Mediterranean, and it was only the timely intervention of the Germans in the area a week later that increased the combat activity in that theatre. Not yet twenty years old, Philip played a crucial part in the naval action at Matapan. His *Valiant* had a key role in sending two Italian cruisers, the *Zara* and the *Fiume*, to the bottom of the sea within the space of five minutes. The *Valiant's* task, according to fleet tactical orders, was to light up the enemy ships when they entered radar range; Midshipman Prince Philip headed a section of the searchlight control. As his beams penetrated the night the *Valiant* pumped more than thirty shells into the *Zara* and *Fiume*; three-quarters were direct hits. For this Philip was mentioned in despatches by Cunningham and awarded the Greek War Cross by his own country. He deserved the accolades. Cape Matapan made Philip into a hardened veteran, and even though he was to see more action for the duration of the war, this could well have been his finest hour.

Philip's actions at the Battle of Cape Matapan were covered extensively in the British press which made much of the fact that he was a Greek prince serving as a midshipman in the Royal Navy. At the time Greece was Britain's only active ally. With Philip in the front rank of fighting, the message was that he symbolized two countries fighting the Axis side-by-side in the name of the ideals of humanity they shared. Some press reports quoted the 'blond, blue-eyed, handsome 19-year-old' prince on the action he saw. For example:

Prince Philip, who was serving as a midshipman aboard the battleship *Valiant*, said: 'It was as near murder as anything could be in war time, just smashing the cruisers *Fiume* and *Zara* and seeing them burst into tremendous sheets of flame. I hate to think how much worse it might have been for the Italian warships if we had met them by day instead of in a night action'. The entire action, he said, was 'magnificent'.[33]

Philip's words to the newspapers show not only the sheer scale of the destruction of the Italian warships, but also, interestingly, his feelings of pity for their crews. It reveals a deep compassion for humanity, even for one's enemies, which accords well with his mother's character and beliefs (Alice would have been proud of her son's statement). This also ties in with Princess Alexandra's assertion that after the action Philip scoured the surface of the sea with his searchlights for Italian survivors.[34] Alexandra could well have heard it from Philip himself in Alexandria four weeks later, after she had been evacuated there from Athens with the other members of the Greek royal family.

The defeats of the Italians by both land and sea during March 1941 probably accelerated the German attack on Greece which began on 6 April, smashing through the resolute and heroic Greek defences on the Greek-Bulgarian frontier at Forts Istibey and Rupel and sweeping aside the paltry British force sent to shore up the Greeks. Within three weeks it was all over. Athens was occupied and the swastika fluttered on the Acropolis of Athens. King George had many trying periods in his life, but this would turn out to be by far the most trying of all. In the closing months of 1940, when Greece was earning British admiration for beating an Axis aggressor, German agents had attempted to gain influence with the Greek royal family. The most obvious target was Paul's wife Frederica, ex-Kaiser Wilhelm II's granddaughter. One day Frederica received a letter from her father, Prince Ernst August III of Hanover, strongly suggesting that she might influence the Greek government to cooperate with the Third Reich. But there were certain coded signals in the letter that caused Frederica to suspect that her father had written it under duress. Notifying her husband, King George and Metaxas, she arranged a telephone call between her and Prince Ernst August which she suspected would be tapped by the Germans.

'Daddy, I received your letter,' Frederica said.

'What letter?'

'The one where you give me lots of advice.'

'Oh, that. But you always were a wilful and disobedient girl, right?'

That clinched it. Prince Ernst August was actually giving her the opposite advice to what his letter on the surface stated. From then on there was never the slightest thought of collaborating with Nazi Germany in anything, regardless of any blood ties with old Kaiser Wilhelm.[35]

Ex-King Constantine II today firmly rejects suggestions, often raised by anti-monarchists in Greece and elsewhere, that Frederica harboured pro-Nazi sympathies. They cite the story, never confirmed, of her carving a swastika on a tree in the Black Forest, causing Prince Peter to break a supposed courtship. But her marriage to Paul, who by no means had any far-right proclivities and was a determined foe of all authoritarianism, contradicts that theory. True, she was of a stern Teutonic character that would rub many the wrong way, but her devotion to her easy-going liberal husband never wavered. Moreover, her noble Hanover family in Germany detested crude Nazism. Frederica herself wrote to the ex-Kaiser with the request that if he could at all influence affairs, to see that none of his grandchildren – her siblings – should be sent to fight Greeks when war would inevitably break out. Wilhelm got the German authorities to agree – but instead they sent the grandsons to the far worse Russian front.

On 26 March 1941 – when the last Italian counter-offensive in Albania had failed and the Germans were poised to invade Greece – Frederica sent a letter to her father by way of a German visitor to Athens (the regular post being highly irregular and untrustworthy at that time). She wrote:

Why should the fascists be helped? Their help is useless, they're finished for good. But if Germany for all that were to invade Greece, then for Greece that would be the greatest glory conceivable.

In the same letter she rubbished the official German line that the Führer had nothing personally against the Greeks, that it was Britain that was the main foe, and hence Greece needed to be occupied to deprive the British of naval bases. 'Of course,' Frederica wrote, 'it's easier for the Germans to come here rather than go to Britain.' For a long time German diplomats had been wheedling the Greek government to form part of the Führer's planned 'European community' where no petty notions of national independence would come to mar the grand pattern of European (i.e. German) law and order. If that should happen, Frederica warned, German soldiers would be standing guard at the palace. And instead of ceremonial processions to Athens Cathedral, the royals would be taken to 'film premieres about Bismarck and other such people.'

The letter reveals above all that she did not want her German kinfolk to regard Greece as just another Balkan backwater. The country's history and heritage were too great for that. Did not the Führer himself admire the ancient Greeks as some of the first true 'Aryans'? Frederica saw at first hand how the Greeks 'fight at the front like lions and come home like children, so gentle and polite.' Above all, she could not believe that the country of her birth could sneak up like a thief on the country of her adoption as a royal. 'My German blood rebels at such pettiness.'[36]

Hitler's panzer divisions and Luftwaffe squadrons overran Greece in short order. The British expeditionary force retreated in chaos to ports in southern Greece to be evacuated to Crete or Egypt. But King George had no intention of allowing himself to be seized. On 22 April Frederica, her infant son Constantine and his elder sister Sophia were bundled into a Royal Air Force Short Sunderland flying boat for the flight to as-yet-unoccupied Crete. At any moment the lumbering aircraft could have been shot down by the Luftwaffe patrolling the skies of the Aegean Sea. The Luftwaffe command had, in fact, been informed that high-level royalty were in the Sunderland, and dive-bombed the Souda naval base in Crete, forcing Frederica and her children to shelter in a slit trench by the officers' mess.[37]

The following day the Sunderland picked up King George, Crown Prince Paul, senior Greek civil and military officials and the remnants of the British forces staffs and flew them to Crete. Before leaving, the King issued a stirring message of hope for his subjugated people. 'Do not be discouraged at this painful moment of history,' the message said. 'We will always be with you... Be of good courage. The good days will return.' Staying in Athens until the last moment were Captain Prince Peter and General Sir Henry Maitland Wilson, the commander of the British expeditionary force. On the eve of the German entry into Athens they made a perilous journey by car to Argos. There they hid in the olive groves for a day or so as German aircraft strafed and bombed the area, until an overloaded Sunderland evacuated them from Nafplion bay on 29 April.

Group Captain Arthur Gould Lee was one of the very last to get away. His task was to safely evacuate about 2,000 Royal Air Force men, who had been left behind languishing in Argos, to Kalamata on the south coast of Greece, where they were successfully taken off by the Royal Navy. Gould Lee made his own escape in a fishing boat crammed with a couple of dozen British and Greek troops. As he sailed off he saw 'the dust of a German motor patrol' about to enter the village they had just embarked from. After an all-night journey they hid in a cove on the island of Kythera for a day and arrived at Chania, Crete, on 30 April. He was the last RAF man to leave mainland Greece.[38]

Gould Lee hardly had time to rest, as at two in the morning of 1 May he was shaken awake and led with several others to a flying boat lying in Souda Bay. It was a civilian BOAC Sunderland operated by volunteer crew, blacked out and invisible in the gloom. It was hard to see where the wooden jetty ended and the sea began. As the dim figures shuffled about, Gould Lee heard 'a most unexpected noise' – a crying baby, and then the soothing voice of the mother. The baby's crying presently stopped, which was just as well because the party on the jetty had to wait a long time in the cold before a launch arrived to take them out to the Sunderland, visible only by 'a weak gleam from the carefully shielded door.' It was only inside the plane that Gould-Lee saw that the baby was Prince Constantine, in the arms of Frederica. Paul was also there, as well as Princess Sophia, clutching her mother's hand.

By some miracle, as the pilot had no shore lights to guide him, the heavily-laden Sunderland took off – and just in time, as minutes later the Luftwaffe screamed down on the base. As the big aircraft droned southwards, dawn slowly peeped through the cabin curtains; few of the passengers were in any mood for talk, and it was a good chance to doze and catch up on lost sleep. The problem for Gould Lee was that Constantine's crying, and sometimes that of Sophia, would periodically drag him back awake. After the plane landed in Alexandria harbour Frederica discovered why her children had been crying so much: their little bodies were covered in red bedbug bites. It took Constantine a week to recover. But the family was safe.

King George had ordered Paul and his family to take refuge in Egypt while he himself stayed on in Crete, intending at first to stay and fight in the only free Greek territory left. It was not to be. The initial plan was for the Greek government to re-establish itself on Crete, but there wasn't enough time for that. The Luftwaffe commenced a ceaseless bombing of the island and its Greek, British and Commonwealth defenders. Like a fugitive the King scuttled from house to house, accompanied only by his entourage and Prince Peter. He understandably refused a suggestion by General Sir Bernard Freyberg, the commander of the New Zealand division, that George move into his headquarters that was being bombed several times a day. Freyberg appeared to think that a dead king was better than a captured one. 'It can't be helped if the King is killed,' he said as the bombs rained down death and destruction. 'What we have to avoid is his being taken prisoner.'

George laughed when Prince Peter told him what Freyberg had said. 'If I can avoid being killed, I much prefer it, thank you very much,' he deadpanned. The King preferred to hide out in the house of a former Venizelist guerrilla chieftain who now was only too glad to shelter the son of his arch-foe. In the morning of 20 May a lone German aircraft circled the house and dropped bombs nearby. The King had just risen and was shaving. Then there was a shout from Colonel Jasper Blunt, the British military attaché who was staying in the adjacent room. 'I can see thousands of them!' What he saw through his binoculars was a sky full of German aircraft, dive-bombing and strafing, with lumbering gliders disgorging hundreds of parachutists. The war's first successful airborne landing on a hostile shore was underway.

George, Peter, Blunt and a New Zealand platoon scrambled up a mountain path as squadrons of bombers roared overhead, their rear gunners perfectly visible. Two groups of parachutists floated down and opened fire. The New Zealanders returned the fire, Prince Peter potting away with an old Cretan rifle. The return fire deterred the Germans momentarily, enabling George and his group to dash to the Greek lines a short distance to the west. But the Greeks mistook them for Germans and loosed off at them. Prince Peter called out that they were allied personnel, but the shouted reply was that Greek-speaking Germans in Greek uniforms were about and no chances could be taken. Eventually the Greek troops got the word that their King was there and ceased fire, though one gendarme was wounded in the ankle.

From the Greek lines the party watched as Freyberg's New Zealanders mowed down the German parachutists as they floated to earth and after they landed. Freyberg advised the King to keep moving. George and his party mounted mules and trekked to Therisos, where they slept fitfully, tortured by fleas. The following day they received instructions from Freyberg to move down to the south coast of Crete. The trek over rocky and bushy terrain was exhausting; boots split open and there seemed no hope for any real rest, shelter or food. Prince Peter was depressed also by the complete absence of the RAF from the Luftwaffe-infested sky. The King, he recalled, 'was calm, but seemed dispirited and didn't talk.' During an argument over which route to take, George 'sat quietly on an outjutting rock, seemingly almost ill with fatigue.'

That night, shivering in the snow-covered White Mountains, Prince Peter heard the welcome sound of Bristol Hercules aero engines droning overhead; he figured they belonged to RAF Vickers Wellington bombers based in Egypt sent to bomb the Germans in north Crete. At daybreak the party marvelled at the superb view for hundreds of miles around. The prince wrote later:

We saw tiny warships moving in slow curves, and firing what looked like rockets against wasp-like planes that turned and dived and produced bright explosions beneath them.

What they witnessed was the Luftwaffe attack on a Royal Navy squadron which had just sunk fifty-two German invasion boats. That morning the party resumed its hike southwards. On the way a messenger brought a message to Blunt to the effect that Freyberg had been driven out of his corner of northwest Crete. The message was from the head of the British Military Mission who was in the southern fishing port of Sphakia waiting to evacuate the King and those with him that night. George and the others bedded down in the sand to await a British vessel they were told would come for them. In the middle of the night Harold Caccia, the British embassy first secretary who was in the party, saw torch signals out at sea. Taking some risk, Caccia embarked on a motorboat to investigate, returning with the welcome news that the destroyer HMS *Decoy* was out there waiting. It took several trips in the small motorboat to get them all to the ship. Soon the exhausted King and his party were sleeping on the floor of the ship's wardroom. The next morning they went onto the bridge to see the battleships HMS *Valiant,* on which Philip was still serving, and HMS *Queen Elizabeth* steaming ahead as escort.[39]

Philip's escorting of his royal cousin to safety in Egypt was probably his last action in the Mediterranean theatre, as a month later he was sent back to Britain for promotion. The troopship on which he travelled called at Cape Town, where King George, Prince Paul and Frederica were by now safely installed. During the Battle of Crete, Dickie Mountbatten's ship, HMS *Kelly,* was sunk by a Ju-87 Stuka dive-bomber. Dickie was pulled out of the water to safety by another British warship and taken to Alexandria. Shortly after disembarking there he was surprised to come across Philip whose own ship happened to be docked there.

But at the time not even Alexandria and the rest of Egypt was safe. As the Afrika Korps of General Erwin Rommel drew near to Alexandria it had become clear that the King and his entourage had to move yet again. (In the occupied Netherlands the elderly and ailing ex-Kaiser was anxious to know how his granddaughter and her family were faring. On 4 June he was finally told that they had managed to leave Crete, whereupon he rose from his sick bed, said 'Thank God!' and breathed his last.[40]) George set sail from Port Said, joining the rest of the royal family at Cape Town; Paul and Frederica and their children had already gone on ahead with the Bank of Greece's gold reserves that had luckily escaped the Germans' clutches.

Paul's family were the guests of the South African prime minister, General Jan Smuts, who regaled young Constantine with endless tales of adventure in the African jungles. Soon after their arrival Princess Irene was born. Paul and Frederica embarked on a fund-raising drive for those Greek forces that had escaped to the Middle East and were now fighting in North Africa under British command. King George, after a few weeks' rest, and his prime minister, Emmanuel Tsouderos, went to London, where he was given a hero's welcome by King George VI. The London *Times* of 23 September 1941 praised George as 'the outstanding leader of his country in its time of peril.' Wrote the *Daily Telegraph* on the same date: 'How much Greece herself owes to the devoted leadership of her King.' Other British newspapers joined in the praise.[41] The British government conferred upon George the Distinguished Service Order for his actions in Crete – the only reigning foreign sovereign to earn that decoration. In London, though it was badly scarred by the recent Blitz, the King and his government-in-exile could enjoy the stability and safety they needed to serve as a beacon of hope for their oppressed people.

Alice and her sister-in-law Ellen were the only members of the Greek royal family who refused to leave Greece just before Athens fell to the Germans on 27 April 1941. Alice wanted to stay and continue her philanthropic work that she knew now would be more vital than ever. Ellen told the rest of the family she would stay because her husband was buried at Tatoi. Two days earlier, on 25 April 1941, most of the Athens press published an open letter from Alice addressed to the ladies who had voluntarily worked with her in providing aid to the soldiers' families over the previous six months and thanking them for their contribution.[42] Alice's letter was written and published in Greece's darkest hour, when King and government had just left and the Germans were at the gates of Athens. It was a gesture of direct defiance to the Germans at a time when there seemed to be no other resistance against them. The British expeditionary force was hastily evacuating mainland Greece from ports in the south, while the Greek Army, which had been victorious against the Italians for almost six months, was forced to capitulate on 21 April after the Germans surrounded it in the northwest and cut off all chance of withdrawal southwards.

After Greece was overrun by the Axis, the German and Italian occupation forces ran the country while the Bulgarians occupied parts of the north. The greater part of the country was controlled by the Italians, who jointly controlled Athens with the Germans; the latter also administered the northern city of Thessaloniki, plus Crete and some Aegean islands. A puppet Greek government was installed by the occupiers, who tried to win over the Greeks through propaganda in the media and the creation of local pro-Nazi organizations funded and run by German secret services. All these attempts had little success as the great majority of Greeks never wavered in their opposition to the Axis and its puppet administration.

The occupiers resorted to forced labour, persecution, arrests and executions in retaliation for the first acts of resistance. The country's infrastructure was almost completely destroyed. Greece was forced to bear the huge costs of the occupation; much of its domestic produce, raw materials and wealth were confiscated and sent to Germany to fund the war. The direct result was a fearful famine that killed thousands of Greeks. Yet the Nazi atrocities in Greece only added fuel to the fire of resistance, which began soon after the country was subjugated. During the German invasion of April and May 1941 about 8,000 Allied soldiers were captured, and transported to Athens on their way to prisoner of war camps in Germany. Ordinary Greeks gave messages of encouragement to the prisoners as they passed through. Some prisoners managed to escape and were hidden by Greeks in their homes, acts which triggered savage reprisals. As we will see, Alice in Athens not only endured three and a half years of the Axis occupation nightmare but her philanthropic work helped sustain many Greek children who would have otherwise perished because of the famine. Alice, also, in direct defiance of the Nazis, saved the lives of the members of a Greek-Jewish family. (See Appendix 1).

On the night of 30 May 1941 two students, Apostolos Santas and Manolis Glezos, scaled the rocky east face of the Acropolis and tore down the swastika flag from the parapet. This is generally taken as the first overt act of Greek resistance. It was not long before large-scale demonstrations broke out in Athens; civil servants went on strike, the first such case in occupied Europe. At the same time, many Greeks escaped to the Middle East to join the Free Greeks fighting alongside the Allies in North Africa. Starting in the summer of 1942, the first guerrilla resistance groups appeared in the Greek mountains and began harassing the occupation forces. Following the Italian capitulation in September 1943, and for the last year of the occupation, the Germans took over most of Greece. Their oppression became harsher and even Alice fell under their suspicion. This was at the time when her German sons-in-law were showing signs of disillusionment with Hitler and dropping out of official favour; it was also clear to all but the most the fanatic Nazis that Germany was on the way to losing the war. After untold hardships Greece was liberated from the Axis in October 1944, but not after an estimated ten per cent of the population had perished as the result of famine, disease and executions;

the great majority of Greek Jews, who had played an important role in the economic and cultural life of Thessaloniki, disappeared into the Nazi death camps.

In June 1941 Prince Philip returned to Britain from the Mediterranean and was assigned to the Royal Navy's Home Station at Rosyth, where he stayed for two years. His vessel was an old 1918-vintage destroyer, HMS *Wallace*, on which he was commissioned sub-lieutenant in February 1942. For the next five months he did East coast convoy duty, after which he was promoted to lieutenant and re-assigned to the *Wallace*, rising to become its second-in-command and executive officer, still just twenty-one years old, the youngest Royal Navy officer to hold such a post. And he still wasn't even British!

Under the German occupation Alice was able to communicate with Philip through letters via her sister Louise in Sweden. Though these letters were not frequent, Alice was able to get regular news of her son through them. She was also able to learn what was going on with the war generally, despite the occupation authorities' savage censorship. Greeks had their radios altered so that they could receive only Axis stations; many of those who listened clandestinely to stations such as the BBC risked execution if discovered. In 1942 the Greek navy, fighting on the Allied side outside Greece, received a number of destroyers from the United States. Alice, well-informed and up to date on Allied developments, hoped that Philip might be transferred to one of those new ships. Few Greek naval officers had experience of such destroyers, and Philip was one of those few. But she was surprised, and told him so, to see that he was still serving in the Royal Navy and had not switched over to the Greek Navy.[43] Even during this dark period Alice was still expecting that Philip would take up again his role as one of the country's princes, serving abroad in its own navy.

In London in June 1942 Philip met New Zealand-born Australian journalist Frederick (Eric) Ehrenfried Baume.[44] Philip appears to have previously struck up a friendship with Baume, most probably a year before in the Middle East, and agreed to give him an interview for the Australian newspaper *The Truth*. This interview, hitherto neglected by Philip's biographers, is the first complete one involving the Prince ever to be published. Philip talks at length about the Australians who had fought in Greece in April and May 1941 trying in vain to stem the German advance, and asserts that Greeks and Australians shared the same temperament. Philip's keen sense of humour emerges in the interview, as well as a certain *joie de vivre*. Interestingly enough, it shows that not only does he know the Greek people intimately, but speaks as one of them. He did not tell Baume much about his visit to Australia in 1940, except for a humorous event that happened to the crew of HMS *Ramillies* while the battleship was docked in Sydney harbour. Philip often told that story, around then and later.[45] Here is an excerpt from the interview:

> Prince Philip: Back in town [London] is young Prince Philip of Greece, a sub-lieutenant in the Royal Navy. He called in to remind me how the Australians in Greece last year, and later in Egypt, won the Greeks' admiration by their speed in picking up the Greek language. 'As a matter of fact' said Prince Philip, 'they not only learned the Greek swear words with lightning speed, but the accompanying gestures seemed to come to them almost naturally. One of the gestures is so terrifying to a very orthodox Greek that he invariably crosses himself if it's used'.[46] Young Prince Philip is a great friend of Beatrice Lillie, the popular London actress, and Fred Emney. He is usually to be seen during his rare leave listening for hours to Fred, who is London's fattest and probably, cleverest comedian today. Philip still tells me a story of when he was in Sydney on a famous battleship.[47] One Sunday an 18-footer overturned near the ship, whereupon a boat was lowered and the 18-footer was recovered. The crew were taken to the wardroom and given plenty of good whisky. 'It may have been a coincidence', said Prince Philip, 'but within the next half-hour six boats overturned'.

HMS *Wallace* was pulled from North Sea convoy duty in May 1943 and sent into the Mediterranean to take part in the invasion of Sicily. By July the ship was at Malta, from where it sailed to support the Canadian landings on Sicily; a violent storm buffeted the ship on the night voyage, a seemingly sinister omen, but in the morning the storm cleared and the Canadians were able to land on Sicily unopposed. Prince Philip appears to have been hoping for a spot of action, and fretted until three

German dive-bombers screamed down on the *Wallace*; their aim was poor, however, and no bombs hit. Philip is credited with coming up with the idea of a burning decoy ship to deceive the attackers.[48] This appeared to have confused the attacking German pilots and may well have saved the *Wallace* and its crew. For the next ten days the destroyer patrolled the Sicilian waters, returning to Britain in September 1943.

In February 1944 Philip, thanks to his record on the *Wallace*, was appointed second-in-command of a newly-built destroyer, HMS *Whelp*, that was commissioned in May. During this period he was stationed in Northern England and did essential maintenance on his ship, working at the dockyards. The secret about his presence in Newcastle was leaked to the editor of the *Newcastle Journal and North Mail*. He thought that this would make a great story as each morning the prince took the same bus to work as all the other shipyard labourers. His reporter, Olga Franklin, a pretty, sexy and dynamic thirty-three-year-old, discovered the hotel Philip was staying at and went there to interview him. Philip until then had avoided giving interviews to the press, having made the sole exception for an Australian newspaper, as we have seen. But Olga Franklin must have made quite an impression on Philip, as she visited him at his hotel[49] and he agreed to give her his only interview for a British newspaper during the Second World War, headlined 'Greek Prince says he likes the North'.[50] Olga Franklin knew only that Philip was a Greek prince, and was therefore surprised when she saw that he looked more Scandinavian than Greek. He took the trouble to outline his ancestry to her, including how his grandfather George I became King of Greece. The reporter asked Philip if he found the Geordie accent hard to understand, to which he replied that on the contrary, he understood the locals perfectly, and was actually enjoying his stay in the North. (It would not have posed a problem to Philip who had lived for five years in Scotland!) At the end, Franklin thanked Philip 'for the good-humoured and kindly way he had accepted "exposure"'.

A few months later after a shakedown, HMS *Whelp* sailed via Portsmouth, Algiers, Malta and Suez to Ceylon (Sri Lanka), joining the 27th Flotilla of the Eastern Fleet. Soon his uncle, Lord Louis Mountbatten, would be the Supreme Allied Commander, South-East Asia. HMS *Whelp* supported the American siege of Okinawa, and Philip witnessed several

Japanese *kamikaze* suicide attacks (which were mostly aimed at the larger ships). February 1945 saw the ship in Melbourne for a refit, from where it escorted HMS *Duke of York* to Guam. In June 1945 Philip, on leave in Sydney, gave another interview to an Australian newspaper. The interview reveals him in not the best of moods, and it is clear that his service in the Pacific theatre was taking its toll psychologically. It is possible that he was reluctant to speak to the press, but some enterprising reporter may have ferreted him out and surprised him with questions. In order to get rid of the reporter he was quite blunt, without taking the trouble to pretend that all was fine and dandy. What stands out is his self-description as 'a discredited Balkan Prince'![51] Was this a reaction to some affront thrown at him in Sydney? However, this is exactly how he described himself to Cobina almost five years earlier, suggesting that it was a self-deprecating sarcasm he used often on himself at the time.[52]

PRINCE PHILIP HAS HARD TIME AT SEA, SYDNEY, Monday: Prince Philip of Greece, in an interview today appeared in a Royal Navy uniform. He said he wanted nothing written about himself because 'he had had a hard time at sea and wanted to enjoy himself incognito'. He described himself as 'a discredited Balkan Prince'. Prince Philip, who is not married, is second in command of a British destroyer and is a permanent member of the Royal Navy. While on HMS *Valiant* he took part in the evacuation of Crete and was later in action at Matapan.[53]

It was in Sydney that he learned of the atomic bomb on Hiroshima. Whereupon the *Whelp* escorted the *Duke of York* and USS *Missouri* on which Japan formally surrendered on 2 September. Prince Philip attended the actual signing of the Japanese surrender in Tokyo Bay on the US flagship.[54] In Greece when the Second World War broke out, six years later Philip was one of the few witnesses of its official end. From Japan the *Whelp* returned to Australia to take on supplies to Britain.

Late at night on 4 December, after a farewell party on the ship in Sydney harbour, a group of officers decided to hit the town for one last time. They felt they deserved it: they had survived a long war, they would not have to take part in an invasion of Japan which could have been horrendously costly, and above all they were going home. Already well lubricated on the *Whelp*, the officers ended up in a fairground and played about with childlike abandon. One of the fairground's features was a revolving barrel called 'the Spider' where they took turns tumbling about, not at all difficult in their state of inebriation. They did not notice photographers present. The next day several Australian newspapers ran photographs showing the officers of the *Whelp* hugely enjoying themselves in the revolving barrel; in the foreground a laughing Philip has fallen helplessly on his back. A reporter of the Sydney *Daily Telegraph* found the opportunity to interview Philip, whose mood this time was completely different to that of six months before when he was interviewed by the same newspaper. The interview ran in the 9 December 1945 edition of the newspaper, two days after the *Whelp* had sailed for Britain:

PRINCE TAKES AUSTRALIAN COSMETICS TO ENGLAND
Prince Philip of Greece, first lieutenant of the Royal Navy destroyer HMS *Whelp*, is taking back from Australia to England cosmetics to give his cousin, Princess Marina, the Duchess of Kent. Prince Philip is a cousin of King George of Greece. HMS *Whelp* left Sydney on Friday carrying 20 tons of food for Britain. Prince Philip said: 'I'm taking the cosmetics back for Christmas presents. Princess Marina will get some of them. I've got lipsticks, powder, lotions, and foundation what-nots. I really wouldn't know what brands. A girl bought them for another lieutenant and myself. We'll split them up on the ship. I'm also taking back some food, sugar, cheese, and chocolate. They are pretty short of most things in England.

'I don't think I'm taking anything else back. I'm a bad souvenir-hunter and a bad sightseer'. Commenting on his visit to [the fairground], Prince Philip said: 'I put on a bit of an act and smoked a cigar going round in the Spider. I was a bit weak in the knees when I got off. We went on just about everything'.

'On my visit to Australia, I enjoyed the week in Tasmania best. I liked the country, the people, and the food. I've enjoyed my stay in Sydney immensely. I've eaten so much that I can't get my clothes on. I would have liked to go to the country again in Australia. I stayed on a sheep station when I was here in 1940 on the *Ramillies.*'

The *Whelp* returned to Portsmouth in January 1946, with Prince Philip in command for the ship's final two months in commission. All before he was twenty-six.

Meanwhile, events in Greece were threatening the very foundations of Philip's wider family. While George II was in exile, powerful forces both in his own country and his allies were consciously working against him. By early 1942 the first armed resistance forces took shape in occupied Greece; very soon, however, most of them fell under the control of the Communist Party (KKE) which vowed to eradicate all traces of monarchy from Greece and thoroughly sovietize the country after the war. This was the former Venizelism in a new and more extreme guise. The main resistance army, the National Resistance Front (known by its Greek acronym EAM) was armed, funded and operationally organized by the British, even though its communist inclinations were well-known. Indeed, much left-wing and liberal press opinion (and not a few political figures) in Britain and the United States actively backed EAM as the only effective anti-Nazi force in Greece. Meanwhile, the EAM engineered mutinies in the Greek land, sea and air forces in the Middle East to ensure, in its words, that 'George would not again be fastened on our backs.' These tendencies would bear bitter fruit soon enough.

In South Africa, Prince Paul chafed at not being allowed to take a more active part in the war against the Axis; but as he was the Crown Prince, he had to be kept away from potential danger as much as possible. He was able to travel periodically to London and Cairo, where Prince Peter kept him *au courant* with the situation. Peter meanwhile had been promoted to major as the King's personal representative in the region. On a visit to London he was named a Commander of the Bath by George VI. Paul toyed with the idea of returning to Greece to join the resistance, but the King firmly scotched that idea: rather than helping the partisans, he might well be their victim. As the war raged on, Greece's royals became slowly aware that when hostilities ceased, as they were sure someday to do, their return to their homeland would not exactly be a walkover. Forces had been unleashed for which they were scarcely prepared.

By 1943 the Germans were losing the war and their withdrawal from Greece was only a matter of time. In an attempt to secure power after Greece was liberated, EAM started attacking other resistance organizations, the most important of which was EDES (National Republican Greek League). A civil war had thus begun even before the occupation had ended. Following the Italian capitulation in September 1943, EAM further strengthened its position through acquiring large amounts of weaponry from the Italians. EDES and other resistance organizations were led by former Venizelists who remained fiercely anti-royalist. Though they had recognized the exiled Greek government in Cairo, they openly opposed the return of George II to Greece after the war.[55] However, by early 1944, as a reaction to the communist-controlled EAM, they had dropped their opposition to the King's return.

There were attempts by the British and the exiled Greek government to put an end to this civil war by arranging a truce between EAM and EDES. They managed to broker a deal for an interim government of national unity under Georgios Papandreou, a leading Venizelist politician, which would assume power in Greece as soon as the Germans left the country. In return for EAM recognizing the Papandreou government, on 2 September 1944 it was offered six ministerial posts in the cabinet. It was also agreed that the question of the monarchy would be settled by a plebiscite after the political situation in Greece had become stable.

In September 1944 the retreating Germans pulled out of the Peloponnese and on 12 October the last of them left Athens. Six days later Papandreou returned to newly freed Athens accompanied by British troops under the command of General Ronald Scobie and was installed as prime minister of an interim national unity government. Thousands of Athenians who had suffered hugely under the Axis occupation celebrated ecstatically in the streets. British troops were welcomed with cheers, placards and Union Jacks. But the euphoria lasted just a few weeks. In a dispute over how to punish collaborationists, the EAM resigned from the government. The following day, 3 December, the police fired on a large demonstration in central Athens, killing 33 people and wounding 148. The incident triggered a month of armed clashes in Athens between armed members of EAM and security forces backed by British troops (23rd Armoured Brigade). The fighting was intense, claiming by some estimates up to 14,000 dead and destroying many buildings. At the end EAM was defeated by the superior firepower of the 23rd Armoured, backed up by the Royal Air Force. On Christmas

Day 1944 Winston Churchill paid a surprise visit to Athens and helped negotiate a truce with the communist insurgents at a meeting in Athens' smartest hotel, the Grand Bretagne, which had just spent several years serving as a headquarters for the Greek, British and German armies. The fighting officially ended on 12 February 1945 with the so-called Varkiza Agreement, named after the seaside suburb where it was signed.

The result of this brief but bloody civil war was that the Greeks were again polarized, in a reprise of the right-left rifts that had plagued the country before the war. Many former Venizelists who had supported the republic in the past, now out of fear of a communist takeover sided with the monarchists to support the return of George II. These included die-hard anti-monarchists such as Prince Andrew's former fellow cadet at the Military Academy and rival, Theodoros Pangalos, but also the very same Nikolaos Plastiras, who as a colonel had been under the command of Andrew in 1921 in the Asia Minor Campaign and one year later had taken over Greece by revolutionary decree and was chiefly responsible for Andrew's court martial and banishment.[56] It is an irony of history that Athens suffered the greatest destruction and loss of life during the Second World War not as the result of fighting between the Allies and the Axis but between the British and nationalists on the one side and left-wing Greeks on the other. Something very similar had occurred three decades previously; in 1916 Athens had been bombarded by the Allies and saw intense fighting between them and the Greeks, even though Greece was never allied to the Central Powers and she did eventually side with the Entente.

As for Alice, the thirty-three days of bitter fighting in December 1944 and January 1945 were undoubtedly the worst days of her life, coming as they did right after more than three years of nightmarish Axis Occupation. The 3 December 1944 demonstration took place in front of Prince George's mansion, where Alice was living at the time. Some demonstrators were shot dead a few dozen metres from her doorstep. Alice's biographer Hugo Vickers does not mention where Alice was at the time of the demonstration; neither is there any reference of this event in her letters to Philip, Dickie Mountbatten or Victoria. If she had witnessed such gruesome events she would probably have avoided talking about them in later years. Her philanthropic work, of course, was no guarantee for her safety as many civilians were killed in the crossfire. Civilian casualties were in fact higher than military casualties at the time. Alice may have been relatively safe as her area was controlled by British troops and the headquarters of General Scobie was located in the Grand Bretagne across the road. The main danger was from the continuous sniper fire against anyone incautious enough to move about. Even Churchill, as he was entering the British Embassy less than half a mile from Syntagma Square, narrowly escaped an EAM sniper's bullet that whizzed a few centimetres from his head.[57]

Princess Ellen also stayed in Athens during the occupation and had taken care to cultivate relations with the Germans; after the liberation, however, that taint of collaborationism placed her in grave danger. Unlike Alice, Ellen lived at Psychiko, a handsome suburb away from the city centre which came under EAM control.[58] So she moved with Alice into Prince George's mansion until the fighting ended and it was safe for her to return home.

On the day the disturbances broke out in Athens, Andrew died in the south of France. Alice received the news at just the same time as the fighting outside her door reached its climax. She had never stopped loving Andrew, and though they had not been together for many years and he had his French mistress, for Alice in the epicentre of war-torn Athens this sad event would only have added to her tribulations.

The Varkiza Agreement did not last long. Right-wing paramilitaries used the opportunity to launch attacks against disarmed communists and former supporters of the disbanded EAM. Tensions soared again, and a new round of fighting between the communists and government forces was in the works. In May 1945 the General Secretary of the Greek Communist Party (KKE), Nikos Zachariadis, was freed from the Dachau concentration camp. It was a historical irony that one of his fellow inmates was General Alexandros Papagos, who had commanded the Greek troops that repulsed the Italians in 1940–41; the Germans arrested him in 1942 along with four other ex-generals and packed them off to Germany. Zachariadis ordered the KKE to abstain from the general election of 31 March 1946, the first election in Greece for ten years. The winner was the right-wing monarchist party led by Constantinos Tsaldaris, who formed a government. Abstaining from that election was a serious error by the communists as it strengthened the new government and dealt a serious blow to their own power base. All those who had not voted in the March 1946 elections were suspected to be communists or sympathizers, and many were rounded up by the security forces. The KKE declared armed opposition to the new government, triggering a new civil war.

On 1 September 1946 the long-awaited plebiscite on the question of the return of George II was held. The result was expected to be positive for him as the government openly supported his return and so did many former republican-Venizelist politicians. In fact, 68.4 per cent of the voters endorsed the King's return. Most interestingly, before the plebiscite a persistent rumour went around in Athens that if George did not win, Philip would take his place as king of Greece![59] Though such a plan was never officially revealed, it was deemed important enough to be mentioned in the international press. It shows that Philip was a popular figure in Greece at the time, and that the rumour appears to have been started by a source within the Greek royal family. Even if the plebiscite had gone against the reinstatement of George, it is highly unlikely that Philip would have been used as an alternative candidate for the throne, as by this stage his marriage to Elizabeth was a certainty. The announcement of his engagement to the heiress of the British throne was in fact delayed until after the plebiscite so that it would not be used as a political issue in war-torn Greece.[60] George returned to Greece with Crown Prince Paul and Frederica at the end of September 1946, to be greeted by his two aunts, Alice and Ellen, the only royals who had remained in the country since 1941 at the start of the Axis occupation.

As for Philip, as we have seen, other, quite unwarlike considerations were pulling him towards Britain ever more strongly.

Chapter 12

The Elizabethan Solution

O n 18 December 1943 Philip was one of the guests at the annual Christmas pantomime of Princesses Elizabeth and Margaret.[1] Elizabeth played the part of Aladdin and Margaret that of Princess Roxanne. With them in the play were forty other children in supporting roles. At the start of the play Elizabeth popped out of a laundry basket, and the two princesses tap-danced and told jokes they had written themselves. More than four hundred people attended, with George VI and Queen Elizabeth in the front row along with the Duchess of Kent, Prince Philip, Princess Maria Louise and Princess Helena Victoria.

In retrospect this Christmas pantomime was important in cementing the attraction between the seventeen-year-old Elizabeth and Philip. It is well documented that immediately after the show Elizabeth made it known to some people close to her that she was in love with the handsome naval lieutenant seated next to her parents in the front row.[2] As we have seen, Elizabeth had first shown an interest in Philip back in 1939 when they had met at Dartmouth, where Philip was a naval cadet. After that Elizabeth and Philip corresponded while the latter was fighting at sea, and they did meet a few times between 1939 and 1943 when Philip happened to be in London and was invited to Buckingham Palace to dine with the Royal Family. The very few people aware of what was going on talked of a budding romance; indeed, as we have seen, as early as 1940 some members of the Greek royal family had suspected that one day Philip would marry Elizabeth.

One detail of this particular show indicates that Elizabeth was indeed already in love with Philip and used this opportunity of telling this in public but without giving anything away! No one watching the show had the slightest idea about this, with the exception of Philip himself and possibly Elizabeth's parents. It was a coded message to Philip that she was interested in him and which apparently has been overlooked in all later accounts about their relationship.

During the show Elizabeth and Margaret not only acted, danced, and told jokes; they also each sang a song. Margaret's was *Three Little Maids from School* from Gilbert and Sullivan's *The Mikado*, backed up by two other girls and getting an enthusiastic response. Elizabeth's song, however, was *In My Arms*, recorded in 1943 by Dick Haymes.[3] It is an erotic song, slightly melancholic but at the same time also humorous in line with the atmosphere of the event in which Elizabeth sang it. The song is also relatively long with lyrics stretching to fifty-two lines. Why did Elizabeth choose to perform this song in the pantomime show of 1943 out of hundreds available? It seems that it was the lyrics which attracted her to it which by sheer coincidence all applied to Philip in 1943! The song is the lament of a sailor who is 'sailing off' to the 'very thick of the fighting'. His relatives are all female. He has a cousin who sent him a sweater, a sister who sent him a letter and a grandmother who gave him candy. However he wants to have a girl friend with him before he leaves for the war at dawn. He gets bundles of letters but he wants to have a girl in his arms (hence the title of the song). In 1943 Philip's relatives were all female (with the exception of his father). In England with him were two members of the extended British Royal Family, his grandmother Victoria, Marchioness of Milford Haven and his cousin Marina Duchess of Kent (who was with him at the play as he had accompanied her there). Even the bundle of letters (Elizabeth's letters) has a meaning for Philip. By singing this song, Elizabeth was very likely showing Philip her interest in him and actually gently teasing him. Was this Princess Elizabeth's love call to Philip seated in the front row? We imagine that she would have exchanged glances with him as she was singing. The unspoken message was obvious: when the lonely sailor returned from the fighting after the end of the war, this time he would have in his arms a girl that had been waiting for him.

The war dragged on for another two years, and Philip witnessed its end with the official Japanese surrender on 2 September 1945 in Tokyo Bay. Philip returned to Britain on board his ship, the HMS *Whelp*, in January 1946. That same year, on 9 July, Buckingham Palace held its first official post-war garden fête. Some 7,000 high-born guests thronged the grounds, and despite the austerity, the event was a resounding success. One of the guests, Prince Philip, was especially favoured. By now he most likely had forgotten all about Cobina Wright and asked Princess Elizabeth, daughter and heiress presumptive of George VI, to marry him. And she, attracted to him ever since she was a young teenager, said yes. According to reports in *The Times* his naturalization as a British citizen, thanks to his wartime service in the Royal Navy, was just a matter of time.[4]

But not everyone in Britain was impressed. Some were spooked by the prince's sisters' German/Nazi links. Courtiers in the palace were irked by his air of aggressive independence. Even after Elizabeth II's coronation at least one old-school officer sniffed at having 'some bloody Greek' as the Queen's consort and successfully blocked him from being appointed Colonel of the Grenadier Guards.[5] But the King himself seemed to like him enough. The wedding of Elizabeth and Philip in 1947 eclipsed any such negativity. It was the first global media event involving royalty (though Philip's surviving sisters were notably not invited). The new young royal couple symbolized Britain's emergence from war and suffering into a new modernity. Philip himself was happy to walk to his job at the Admiralty across St. James's Park with no personal security whatsoever. He was now fully British, in position and character as well as by naturalization.

By the same token, however, he appeared to have finally turned his back on his Greek royal origins. The reasons are complex, as indeed, he was always a complex individual. It has been endlessly reiterated, in Greece as well as Britain, that the Greek royal family never had any real Greek 'blood,' being essentially Danish-German. But the 'blood' argument proves inadequate when it comes to political realities. For that matter, only a small fraction of Elizabeth II's 'blood' is Anglo-Saxon; most is German anyway. The Swedish royal house derives directly from a French Napoleonic officer, Count Bernadotte. Yet in neither country has there been any significant complaint along those lines, strong enough to shake a throne – if we except George V's hurried adoption of the Windsor surname in 1917. The ancient Greek orator Isokrates defined a Greek even then as someone who is educated in the Greek way, and that can apply to any nationality today.

Greece in 1947 was a precarious place. George II had returned, but on 1 April he died, worn out in body and spirit. The country was in the throes of a brutal civil war. Britain had had to relinquish its protection duties to the United States, which from that year on became the guarantor of Greece's independence and democratic liberties, but also treated the country as a protectorate. Generous amounts of American aid got the country back on its feet in time for King Paul to reign in the spirit of hope and rising prosperity that characterized the 1950s. Until then, however, Philip may well have often thanked the good luck that had driven him to Britain instead of a career in the Royal Hellenic Navy or even the throne as King Philippos. On that throne, we know now, he would not have lasted one-quarter as long as he as lasted as Duke of Edinburgh.

When Princess Elizabeth received the news of her father's death in February 1952, she and Prince Philip were staying at a guesthouse in Kenya. Philip in fact had received the news first from his equerry, Mike Parker. According to an eyewitness, Philip covered his face with a newspaper he had been reading and said, 'This will be such a shock'. His conduct towards Elizabeth in this tragic moment was by all accounts admirable, but that didn't seem to cut much ice with Churchill, who was again prime minister, and who did not hesitate to express his distrust of a foreign-born prince with, as he claimed, no money.

'Philip was superb,' said Lady Pamela Hicks, the daughter of Lord Louis Mountbatten, recalling the occasion sixty-seven years later. With his wife's elevation to the throne his Royal Navy prospects were suddenly in tatters; no more could he hope to become First Sea Lord. As Lady Hicks said:

> He gives up his career. He's always going to be walking three paces behind his wife, and the whole court and aristocracy are against him. For months he had no job. The Queen thinks of several jobs for him but Churchill says no – [he's] Greek, not a well-born Scotsman.[6]

Philip of course knew all about this undercurrent of ethnicist prejudice against him, and it must have rankled. He could either have let it poison his inner life or build up a hard carapace to flatten his critics who imagined themselves somehow superior. He could out-Brit the Brits, in a way. Commendably, he appears to have chosen the latter. A large part of his vigorous no-nonsense approach to life and disdain of political correctness must come from this rejection he felt earlier in his life. The petty snobbery shown to this Greek prince of Danish-German blood would be flung back in his critics' faces. Three paces behind his wife he would always be fated to walk, but nothing would stay his sharp damn-the-torpedoes-full-speed-ahead tongue.

Chapter 13

Meanwhile, Back at the Ranch

In the years and decades following Prince Philip's marriage to Princess Elizabeth and his later elevation to Duke of Edinburgh when she became Queen, he would have ample and repeated chances to thank history for derailing his chance of becoming a sovereign of Greece. King Paul began his reign amidst the darkness and uncertainty of civil war. In April 1947 it was by no means clear that he and his pro-Western government would survive the constant attacks by communist-led rebels who held large sections of the countryside. In December 1944 Athens itself had been barely saved by a heroic defence by national troops and gendarmes, backed up by British forces. But two and a half years later Britain could no longer handle the task alone, and fortunately American President Harry Truman had stepped in with his country's infinitely greater resources. Greece's predicament had been taken very seriously in Washington DC. Truman's secretary of state, Dean Acheson, fretted that Greece 'was in the position of a semi-conscious patient on the critical list'.[1] That semi-conscious patient on 3 March 1947 – a month before George II's death – begged Washington for aid, as British forces were scheduled to pull out precipitately.

Paul was generally known as a frank and honest man, a genuine democrat and genial personality. But in July 1948, while the civil war was still raging, his forthrightness got Greece into a spot of diplomatic trouble. Interviewed by the *New York Times,* he went on record as saying that it was high time Cyprus was released from Britain's colonial clutches and united with Greece. The statement shocked the government, which had its hands full suppressing a bloody insurrection and could ill afford to alienate Britain which, in the final analysis, had helped liberate Greece from Axis occupation. Of course the King had not the slightest power to act personally. But it was precisely that which somehow made him feel he needed to make some gesture to satisfy patriotic Greeks of whatever political stripe. Scandinavian-type royal figurehead roles were not for him; as Greece's number one citizen he felt fully entitled to express an opinion, like it or lump it. The issue quickly faded from the headlines, but it undoubtedly raised his popularity.[2] In 1949 the Civil War ended with the victory of the government forces.

Throughout the 1950s Paul represented a country that made great strides in post-war recovery; it joined Nato in 1952 and for the next twenty or so years was to receive vast amounts of American military and financial aid. As the only Balkan country not behind the Iron Curtain, Greece was cemented firmly into the Western camp, which no doubt kept it democratic and its people enjoying a rising standard of living. Of course, there was a measure of domestic opposition stemming mostly from remnants of the failed communist insurrection of the 1940s. Greece's left-wingers never accepted the monarchy; others were disturbed at the active role the crown took in political affairs in contrast to those of Britain and the Scandinavian countries. And it was this role, unwisely kept up, that would prove to be the downfall of the Glücksburg dynasty.

One man who sought to curb the powers of the palace was Konstantinos Karamanlis, a bluff conservative ex-lawyer from the north who, as prime minister between 1955 and 1963, and then again from 1974 to 1980, led Greece through some of its most peaceful and prosperous years. Though a man of the right, Karamanlis saw early the potential dangers of an independent monarchy and tried to head them off. This brought him into direct conflict with Queen Frederica and complicated his relations with Paul. In a memo to the latter Karamanlis demanded that the palace cut back its visible luxuries and taxpayer-funded foreign jaunts, that royal speeches henceforth be vetted by the government, and that there be a senior liaison official to coordinate the actions of both parties.[3] In Britain such matters would be blindingly obvious, and considering that large areas of Greece were still dirt-poor and lacked roads and electricity, they were eminently reasonable.

But it attests to the bubble that the Greek monarchy was living in that Karamanlis' memo was taken as a direct attack on the throne. Paul himself understood the thinking behind the memo, but insisted on interpreting the role of king as a force for keeping the country on the proper democratic road. He also had a lingering distrust of the right-wing governments of the 1950s and early 1960s as too ready to adopt authoritarian policies to keep the left out of the picture. When on 16 February 1964 a centrist government was elected for the first time, Paul was only too happy to swear it in. But by then he was already gravely ill with stomach cancer; on 6 March he died, to be succeeded by his son, twenty-four-year old Constantine II. From the outset, the young new king was faced by one political crisis after another.

By the mid-sixties Greek politics had once again become seriously polarized. On the one side were the conservatives, the crown, big business, much of the peasantry and the Americans; and on the other an amorphous mixture of urban intellectuals and workers, students and left-wing carryovers from the Civil War bearing long-standing grudges against the right, backed covertly by the Soviet Union. Enter Frederica, who after her husband's death felt she had to be the dynasty's pillar of strength. She had very much a mind of her own; in 1963, disregarding sage advice from her prime minister Karamanlis (whom she despised), she travelled to London only to be heckled in the street by Greek leftists and British sympathizers. The incident triggered a wholly unnecessary diplomatic crisis. Stories of Frederica's authoritarian character were legion, magnified of course by her family connection to the late Kaiser. The result was that though a majority of Greeks wanted to keep their king, as the twentieth century progressed the throne's popular support began to erode. If Paul had lived for another ten or twenty years he may well have maintained the crown's popularity; his tragedy is that he died too soon to leave a lasting legacy in that department.

When Constantine II began his reign he still bore the scars of wartime when, at one point, his mother Frederica slept on the floor outside his room in Alexandria to protect him from assassination plots that she had heard were afoot. He owed his mother a great deal, and hence was susceptible to her autocratic tutelage; he naturally sought her advice in the troubled decade of the 1960s. That advice was for him to stand firm against any centrist or leftist politicians, even if elected by the popular will, as they could never quite be trusted not to bring in communism by the back door, as it were. The powerful United States diplomatic establishment in Athens fully backed this stand.

The year 1965, however, was one in which a stark choice faced the Greek monarchy. Either it could slide peacefully into a purely figurehead role, as in Britain and other northern European countries, or insist on having a say in how the country was run. In that year during a meeting of the Crown Council, Constantine opted for the latter course. His rationale (perhaps influenced by Frederica's strong personality) was that as a monarch filled a key position in the state mechanism, he should retain some powers. A powerless king was no king at all. In an address to political leaders he said he considered the crown and democracy one and the same, indivisible: 'Here we are all royalists, all democrats... I do not recognize that anyone is more of a democrat than anyone else.'[4] The sentiment was nobly uttered, but the choice proved to be a most unfortunate one, as it turned the great bulk of liberal opinion against him. 'The King reigns but does not rule' was to be a potent opposition rallying cry that would doom the Greek monarchy in short order.

Constantine's activist stance was put to a test in the summer of 1965 when he unwisely dismissed the newly-elected centrist leader, Georgios Papandreou, triggering riots in the streets of Athens. The King thus put his first foot wrong but seems not to have realized it, as he was famously blindsided by the colonels' coup of April 1967. An inept attempt to seize back power and boot out the colonels fizzled in December of that year and Constantine and his family were forced to flee to Rome in a lumbering Greek Air Force C-47 transport. Six years later the coup strongman, Colonel George Papadopoulos, declared the King deposed and proclaimed a republic, the second in modern Greek history, with himself as president. After the junta's collapse in July 1974 the Greek people in December were given the choice of either bringing back the deposed Constantine or confirming the republic. Encouraged by politicians of the right and left who feared an independent power centre in the form of the King, they chose the latter course by a two-thirds majority.

Greek royalists have since claimed that the 1974 plebiscite had serious procedural flaws; indeed it did, but not so much as to affect the outcome. As early as 1968 the noted Hellenist C.M. Woodhouse wrote that the Greek monarchy, 'and the powers it had enjoyed since 1864, had unmistakably had its day'.[5] For many years Greece's political establishment, right and left, and an obedient media, spurned the exiled Constantine as a non-person. He was allowed back briefly just once, in February 1981, to attend Frederica's funeral at the Tatoi palace. When he alighted from the chartered Olympic Airways Boeing 737 at Tatoi air base, he knelt to kiss the ground, his face streaked with tears. During the 1980s a socialist government stripped him and his family of all their property assets in Greece as well as their Greek citizenship, a move widely condemned as petty and illegal. In 1993 he was again allowed to cruise the Greek islands as a simple tourist, and it would take several more years for him and his children – Alexia (born 1965), Paul (1967), Nicholas (1969), Theodora (1983) and Philip (1986) – to be able to spend time in their own country again without fear of harassment. So again there is a Prince Philip in the Greek royal family.

Chapter 14

What If...?

L ooking at the tribulations of the Greek royals over the decades, especially since the late 1940s, leads inevitably to wondering how a King Philippos of Greece would have fared under the same or similar circumstances. We need to tread carefully here, as we approach the treacherously thin ice of counterfactual history. What would Greece have been like if King Philippos, instead of marrying Britain's Elizabeth, had moved into the palace in the centre of Athens? Considering that he at one point had been a credible candidate to succeed George II, the question is not an idle one. One sub-question is whether as King of Greece, rather than the Duke of Edinburgh, he would have smoothed out the often-rocky course of British-Greek post-war relations that have always had geostrategic implications in the Mediterranean area.

Geographically, Greece was highly important for British interests until the latter half of the twentieth century. It lay athwart the key imperial route to India. Its long and convoluted coastline and island archipelagos could prove priceless for any sea power with a major presence in the Mediterranean – first Britain and then the United States. In 1947 the Truman Doctrine, in which the United States took over responsibility for Greece and Turkey as bulwarks of the West in the Cold War, saw British influence in Greece evaporate almost overnight. American rather than British warships henceforth were to call at Greek ports, American bases to sprout on Greek soil. King Paul, in whose reign this development took place, had no choice but to accept American suzerainty, even to the choice of who would be his prime minister.

If there was one issue that bedevilled British-Greek relations in the post-war decades, that was Cyprus. This is not the place to untangle the complex history of the problem or to apportion any blame among Greece, Cyprus, Turkey and Great Britain, whose attempts to regularize the status of Cyprus worked at cross purposes. On 1 April 1955 an armed independence movement, the National Organization of Cypriot Combatants (known by its Greek acronym EOKA), raised the standard of revolt. The British colonial administration hit back hard, earning the enmity of many Greeks who yearned for Cyprus' union with Greece but placing successive Greek governments in a very difficult position, as Greece and Britain were, and are, key Nato allies. Thanks largely to the insurrection, Cyprus became independent in 1960, as Britain, Greece and Turkey agreed to be 'guarantor powers.'

The emptiness of that concept became evident very quickly, as no-one knew quite what a 'guarantor power' was supposed to do. The Turkish-Cypriot minority felt slighted by the Greek-Cypriot majority, and throughout the 1960s the two communities engaged in sporadic violence. Britain's interest was to keep its two large sovereign air bases on the island – deemed vital for a military presence close to the Middle East – and hope the internal problem somehow would go away. Which of course it didn't. In July 1974 a Greek-inspired attempted coup that aimed to forcibly annex Cyprus to Greece fizzled; the twin results were a full-scale Turkish military invasion of the island and the fall of the discredited junta in Greece (that had planned and executed the coup), followed by the restoration of democratic rule. In 1983 the Turkish portion declared itself the 'Turkish Republic of Northern Cyprus' but only Turkey gave it diplomatic recognition.

The importance of the subject here is how it impacted on the reputation of Prince Philip in his homeland. In the 1950s the British government's response to Greek agitation was, in Woodhouse's words, 'coldly rational,' which only served to infuriate Greek public opinion. Many Greeks nursed dark suspicions that Britain favoured Turkey in this issue; it was not true, but neither could it be disproved. In Britain, relatives of British servicemen killed by EOKA guerrillas added their voices against Greece. Many marriages between British men and Greek women were severely strained, and some broke up over the issue. And Greeks and Greek-Cypriots in Britain wondered angrily why Prince Philip was remaining silent and not throwing his weight behind the Greek cause. Many Greeks who had fought with the Allies during the Second World War and had been awarded British medals sent them back as a sign of protest over Cyprus.

Of course, Prince Philip could do nothing of the kind. In Buckingham Palace he did not have the kind of authority of King Paul who, as we have seen, did not hesitate to sound off about Cyprus in the *New York Times*. That indiscretion had earned Paul a rap on the knuckles from Washington and London, and Philip was not about to risk the same ire. Until 1960 Cyprus was a British Crown Colony whose head of state was his wife the Queen. Anything Philip said or did would have been interpreted variously by Greece, Turkey or Cyprus as interference. But was he happy to remain silent? What was his real attitude to Greek nationalist aspirations? His father Prince Andrew, we must not forget, almost lost his life over a reckless Greek gamble into Asia Minor. Cyprus, more than 200 miles from the nearest Greek island, was indefensible in case of war, as the Turkish invasion of 1974 showed. All these considerations probably played a part in Philip's staying out of the whole thing.

In March 1963, in Sydney, Australia, a young boy asked Philip if he was Greek, and Philip replied, 'No, I was born in Greece but I am not Greek.' In the following days, MPs in the Greek parliament and leading Greek newspapers severely criticized Philip for his statement; the Athenian daily *Ethnos* in an editorial of 6 March 1963 told Philip that if he thought that he was not Greek he should then remove the country's flag from his coat of arms.[1] On 12 March the centrist daily *Eleftheria* ran a story on its front page about Philip selling the flat on Patriarchou Ioakeim Street in Athens that Alice had bought in 1949 and passed on to Philip a year later. *Eleftheria* included details of the sales agreement which allegedly showed that he had paid no tax on the deal as a law of 1949 exempted members of the Greek royal family from paying tax on property sales. As Philip had sold the apartment on 23 June 1953, it was apparent that he used his status as a Greek royal to avoid paying tax. In 1963 that was hard to reconcile with Philip's statement in Sydney that he was 'not Greek'.

When the Cyprus crisis intensified in 1956 and the British authorities on the island began executing captured members of the EOKA militant independence movement, Philip almost overnight changed from a favourite son of sorts to a target of ballooning anti-British sentiment. This was manifested in numerous press articles in Greece but culminated in a little-known event which took place in Athens in May 1956. When Philip and Elizabeth were married in 1947 the residents of the working-class district Nikaia near Piraeus decided to honour Philip and Elizabeth by building a church dedicated to their namesake saints. Many locals, among them impoverished refugees from the Asia Minor collapse of 1922, supported the public subscription. In fact, Nikaia was (and still is) a left-wing stronghold, often referred to as 'Kokkinia', or Red Town. Nevertheless, such was the popularity of Philip as a future consort of a British queen that local politics were set aside for this occasion. The foundation stone for the church of Saints Philip and Elizabeth at Nikaia was laid on the day of the royal wedding in London, and the church was ready in 1949. When Philip and Elizabeth visited Greece in 1950 they called at 'their church' and each planted a tree next to it. By coincidence, two intact ancient Greek vases had been found while the foundations were being dug; they were given as a present to the couple. Philip and Elizabeth in their turn dedicated to the church a holy icon depicting their namesake saints. The visit was considered an important event in the annals of Nikaia.[2] A large marble plaque commemorating the connection was placed above the entrance to the church.

However, six years later, in 1956, the entire Athens City Council, led by its mayor, ex-General Pausanias Katsotas, marched to the church and took turns in smashing the plaque with a sledgehammer. (This was reminiscent of the *damnatio memoriae* ritual of ancient Rome, when after the decision of the Senate portraits of and inscriptions with the names of undesirable emperors were destroyed.) Katsotas was a monarchist and during World War Two had fought side by side with the British in North Africa as commander of the Greek Brigade at El Alamein. During the civil strife of December 1944 Katsotas was the military commander of Athens and one of the commanders of the government troops fighting alongside the British forces against EAM. (Today at the church of Saints Philip and Elizabeth there is no record of its link to the British royals, though the two trees planted by Philip and Elizabeth are still there.)

Also in 1956, there were reports in the international press that Philip was on an EOKA hit list. Two members of the organization were said to have been sent to Britain to assassinate him as a 'traitor'; as a result, his security was tightened and the number of his bodyguards tripled. This was most likely why there was no attempt against his life at the end.[3] Relations between Britain and Greece were normalized again in 1960 after Cyprus became independent. But after 1950 Elizabeth never visited Greece again; Philip, however, was a frequent visitor to the country during the 1960s. This renewed relationship with his country of birth came to an abrupt end in 1967 when the colonels' regime took power in Greece.

Many of the Greek monarchy's problems in the 1950s and 1960s were its own fault – the events of 1965 and 1967 come to mind. For too long the Greek royals had lived in a bubble of their own making, through which they viewed Greek society's problems as through a distorting lens. Frederica's lack of understanding of Greek society's problems and Constantine II's lack of judgement at crucial moments were direct results of such distortion, and were to have disastrous consequences for the family and played a significant role in the subsequent abolition of the Greek monarchy,

On the contrary a King Philippos, it would seem, would not have been plagued by either a domineering mother or wayward judgement. Alice in her day had been the most popular member of the Greek royal family. During the Balkan Wars, through her initiatives for the soldiers fighting on the front and also their families back home, she established a close connection with ordinary Greeks, including many who were opponents of the monarchy. Even during the thirteen years when the royal family was in exile and Greece a republic Alice was still remembered with fondness by the people. It is worth noting that at the time when the Venizelist newspapers were attacking Andrew about his interference in Greek politics they were careful not to implicate Alice. When the English edition of Andrew's book came out in 1930 with Alice's introduction, the articles in the republican newspapers blasted Andrew but treated Alice with kid gloves, merely pointing out that she had included mistakes in her text in a desperate attempt to defend her husband's actions. When the monarchy was re-established in 1935, Alice made a point of abstaining from the pomp and ceremony of the palace and also avoided high society functions. This did not go unnoticed by most Greeks who at the same time read in their newspapers about other princesses – Alice's in-laws and nieces – who attended such venues to show off their precious jewellery and expensive outfits at a time when the country was going through hard times and a new world war was on the horizon.

The Greeks' respect for Alice was further enhanced in the years that followed as a result of her stance during the Second World War and especially during the devastating Axis occupation of their country. Alice had aided thousands of famished children and their families on her own initiative, enabling provisions to enter the country and working in soup kitchens. Alice was compared favourably with the rest of the royal family, who had left as the Germans advanced. Even the fact that Alice had converted to Orthodoxy endeared her to the Greeks, as her conversion was seen as part of her commitment to serve Greeks in need. No doubt Alice would have been a considerable asset for a King Philippos.

Considering the way in which Philip has flawlessly carried out his strictly apolitical duties in Britain, it is reasonable to assume that on the Greek throne he would not have made Constantine II's mistake of insisting on a degree of palace activism in the face of overwhelming public sentiment. This, as we have seen, led directly to the abolition of the monarchy in the early 1970s. Philip's character and his schooling at Gordonstoun would have helped him to avoid going against the will of the people. If confronted with the temptation to act unconstitutionally, it is unlikely that Philip would have taken that path. His respect for democratic values owes a lot to his schooling at Gordonstoun. This does not, however, mean that Philip would have been a passive observer and a pawn of any government. His character was forged from his exceptional childhood and unconventional growing-up process. Nothing was given to him for free, despite his title of 'Prince Philip of Greece'. Even as a young boy he had to use his brains and wits in order to achieve his goals. Philip thus had acquired great experience in dealing with people, something that would have come in handy if he had to confront the notoriously wily and fractious Greek politicians as their monarch.

Philip's outgoing character, the way he relates to people from all walks of life – even the so-called 'gaffes' beloved of the mass media – might well have endeared him to the Greeks who have an innate aversion to strait-laced convention. His grandfather George I had a similar character which had won over the people of his adopted country and helped him to rule them for fifty years; anecdotes and quips connected to George are remembered to this day. That had not applied to George's successors, who were much more regal; for example, George II's otherwise-admirable reserve and dignity did not earn him many popularity points.

If Philip had served in the Greek Navy instead of the British, he would still have fought during the Second World War from 1940 onwards. He would most likely have survived as well, as wartime casualties in the former were much less than in the latter. As a prince and potential heir to the throne, he would almost certainly have been kept out of harm's way as much as possible, such as serving on warships escorting convoys. However, he would have seen active service and in 1945 Philip would have been a 'front line' war hero, a unique feature for a Greek royal. Though almost all male members of the family of the generation of Philip and that of his father had been trained in the Greek military none had actually been on the front line, apart from Andrew in 1921 in Asia Minor and Philip's uncle, Constantine I, during the Balkan Wars. Philip's front-line war service would have been a great asset as a future king, as Greeks hold in high respect those who have put their lives on the line for their country.

To continue this brief excursion into counterfactual history, if back in 1936 Philip's father had decided differently about his son's future, would Philip have fulfilled his potential (and destiny) as a leader? We have mentioned some positive assumptions along those lines, but there are also negative ones. For example, almost certainly some segment of Greek public opinion would have tainted him a 'foreigner' – most ironically, as some in Britain had looked sideways at 'the Greek'! Would he have taken as many pains to appear fully Greek to his compatriots as he took to appear completely British at the side of Britain's Queen? Would he have been able to address the Parliament, for example, in flawless Greek as all the kings going back at least to Constantine I had done? Perhaps only he can answer these questions.

As of this writing, Prince Philip, the Duke of Edinburgh, is about to hit his century. As such, he has had far more royal experiences than any comparable figure. He may not show it off too much, but a core of Greece remains inside him; it is a spiritual rather than an ethno-nationalist core, as evidenced in his regular visits to Mount Athos, the 'Holy Mountain' of the Greek Orthodox Church that proved such a pillar of strength to his mother in her extremely difficult times. It was the faith of his Russian grandmother Olga which she carefully passed down to her descendants. Part of Philip's 'core of steel' is probably an inner knowledge that the things of this world will all pass away, and that the superficial obsessions and shibboleths of a materialistic society ultimately have little value when compared to the inner world – that world which undoubtedly has kept him safe and unscathed for so long.

Appendix I

Alice – Away From The Spotlight

A s we have seen, when the Germans invaded Greece in 1941 Princess Alice elected to stay in Athens and help its suffering people. Her privileged position may have shielded her from the worst fate, of starving to death or being tortured by the Gestapo, but she did suffer to the point of losing 26 kilos in a few months during the fearful winter of 1941–42 when foodstuffs in Greece had all but disappeared.[1] However, for Alice these hardships made her even more determined to continue helping the Greek people as she had done from the time she first came to their country. This was by far the most trying period she had ever lived through, for not only the poor who desperately needed her help, but also the great majority of people who before the war had good jobs in the public and private sectors but were now destitute. Only those who collaborated with the occupiers managed to maintain some decent standard of living; some amassed considerable wealth through the black market, racketeering and extortion, and from paid services to the Germans and Italians.

Thanks to the help of her sister Louise, the wife of Crown Prince Gustav Adolf (the future King Gustav VI Adolf) of neutral Sweden, Alice was able to bring vital foodstuffs and medicines from that country. Gustav Adolf was a good friend of the Greek people as before the war he had carried out amateur archaeology in Greece and knew the country well. Besides seeing to the importation of essentials, Alice laboured alongside other women in the soup kitchens for poor families and their children. She also helped run two hospices for orphans. A photograph of ladies distributing soup to children in Athens reportedly shows Alice on the far right wearing the uniform of a nurse. Haggard and undernourished, she is hardly recognizable. (After the war, when Alice visited England, her relatives were surprised to see how much older she looked). She is known to have distributed even the foods that Dickie Mountbatten had found a way of sending her through the Red Cross for her personal use.[2] In a letter to him Alice wrote that every day she helped feed some 17,000 children between the ages of one and six. Though this number for Athens alone might appear to be excessive, it probably includes all the children who were surviving on the supplies which Alice had brought to Greece.

In order to secure funds for her philanthropic work Alice sold her flat in Koumbari Street, which she had bought in the first place so that Philip could have a place to stay in Athens. Now, however, knowing that the war would keep her son away for a long time, she moved to the vacant mansion of her brother-in-law, Prince George, in Akademias Street. At this time Alice drew closer to her sister-in-law Ellen than ever before. They worked together to distribute food to needy children. They differed, however, in that Alice shunned social contacts with the Germans other than the strictly official ones of applying for permits for her work or visas to go to Sweden and Germany to bring back supplies. Alice's biographer Hugo Vickers records that at the beginning of the occupation she was visited by a German general to inform her that if she wanted anything she need only ask him. Alice replied that the only thing she wanted was for his army to get out of her country![3] And while she lost 26 kilos sharing the hardships of the Greeks, Ellen by contrast entertained high-ranking German officers in her home; these officers were flattered to be the guests of one who after all was the mother-in-law of the Duke of Kent, brother of George VI! Well-supplied Ellen certainly was in no danger of starvation.

Though Alice may have annoyed the Germans, they tolerated her, as by feeding a large number of Greeks she had assumed a responsibility that according to international law belonged to the occupation forces. Therefore the Axis occupation authorities did not interfere with Alice's work and helped her when she requested permission to travel to Germany and Sweden. Yet she must have been something of a complex puzzle to the Germans. First, she was born a German princess but was married to a Greek prince. Second, her own family had become British subjects but she had not (if she had been a British subject she would have been incarcerated as an enemy alien). Third, her four daughters had all married German nobles, mostly sympathetic to Nazism; Sophie's husband, Prince Christian of Hesse, was actually a high-ranking SS official. Fourth, she was a cousin of Prince Viktor Erbach-Schönberg, who was the German ambassador to Greece at the time the country was invaded. And fifth, her son was an active officer in Britain's Royal Navy.

The Germans very likely concluded that Alice was either at heart pro-German or at least someone who would not actively oppose them. She is not known to have taken part in any of the Resistance actions against the Axis. (But even if she had, she would not have advertised it after the war.) Her task was to feed the children. In this she followed her Christian beliefs – that it was better to save lives than take them, even if the lives were enemy Nazi ones. In fact, in 1944 while Greece was still under German occupation, Alice went to Germany and was happy to meet her sons-in-law even though they were serving in the German Army – which meant that if they happened to encounter her beloved son Philip they were duty bound to try and kill him! This is exactly what Philip's sister Sophie told British journalist Clifford Webb who came across her in April 1945 shortly after the Allies had occupied her city of Kronberg. In June 1943 Sophie's SS husband was stationed in Sicily as part of the defence against the Allied landings of that month; one of the Allied vessels was HMS *Wallace*, on which Philip was serving at the time. Webb published his interview with Sophie under the headline: 'Husband (Fought For Nazis): Brother (For The Allies)'.[4] Prince Christian of Hesse would be killed in a place crash in November 1943.

In 1944 Alice was questioned by the Gestapo in her house.[5] The Athens daily *Bradini,* in a series of articles published in 1979 about the Axis occupation, quoted an Athenian who had been arrested by the Germans as saying that he saw a woman being interrogated at the Gestapo headquarters as a suspected resistance fighter. He said that it could have been Princess Alice, though he was not certain.[6] Alice, however, is known to have committed an act of distinct resistance. This was not planned and she did not give a second thought about doing it. From 1943 onwards, the German occupation forces rounded up Greek Jews and sent them to Auschwitz and almost certain death. One family, the Cohens, sought shelter with Alice at Prince George's mansion. Alice thus placed herself at great risk.[7] Fortunately, the Germans never found out that Alice was harbouring the Cohens, who thus survived the war. For this reason posthumously in 1993 Alice was declared by the Yad Vashem, the World Holocaust Remembrance Centre in Israel, as 'Righteous Among the

Nations' for having saved Jews during the Second World War.[8] After
the liberation of Greece from the Nazi occupation and the end of the
Second World War, Alice remained in Athens: she resumed her travels
to England, seeing her relatives there, and in 1947 attended the royal
wedding of her son in London.

The year 1948 marked a watershed in Alice's life, as she decided to
move out of Athens and live permanently on the island of Tinos in the
Cyclades. Tinos, perhaps not as well-known touristically as other Cycladic
islands, nonetheless holds great importance for the Greek Orthodox as it
is the location of the monastery of the Dormition of the Virgin Mary. The
ornate hilltop monastery was founded in 1823 when a holy icon of the
Virgin was discovered on the site. To this day the icon is believed to have
miraculous properties, and an elaborate religious festival is celebrated
on the island every 15 August, the feast day of the Dormition (called
the Assumption by Catholics). Tinos holds the same sacred significance
for the Greeks that, for example, Lourdes has for the French. As the
monastery was founded during the War of Independence (1821–1829) it
became linked to Greek patriotism. This was further reinforced when on
15 August 1940, during the festival of the Dormition, an Italian submarine
torpedoed and sank the Greek light cruiser *Elli* which was in the harbour
of Tinos as part of the celebrations. It was the most blatant act of hostility
by the Italians while Greece was still neutral. The Metaxas government
had evidence of the submarine's nationality but, trying to stay out of war,
kept it secret. Two months later, when Italy attacked Greece and dragged
it into the war, the slogan 'Revenge for the *Elli*' became the battle-cry of
the Greek soldiers fighting on the Albanian front. Alice's choice of place
for her organization's head office therefore was linked not only to Greek
religion but also to patriotism.

At Tinos, Alice adhered to the austere life of a nun, and from this time
onwards until her death twenty years later she wore her characteristic
nun's attire. But she never took the vows of a nun and was therefore not
ordained. Her purpose was to establish on Tinos her charitable Christian
organization, the Sisterhood of Martha and Mary, and associate it with
the local monastery. This organization would train volunteer nurses who
would offer their services for free to the poor and needy. She may have
wished to emulate her aunt Ella's religious-charitable organization in

Tsarist Russia, but Ella had been an ordained nun and her organization was an actual convent, the trained nurses also being nuns. This would not apply to the Sisterhood of Martha and Mary, which was to be religious in name only as it was not associated with the Greek Orthodox Church and the trainees were ordinary women. In fact, an organization with nurses caring for poor elderly and sick people within a religious establishment was something unusual for Greece and quite different to the various charitable foundations which the Church operated.

The fact that Alice was aiming to set up a charitable foundation was seen in a positive light by the majority of Greeks, but it was also somewhat confusing to them as this would be her own personal institution which she ran in the best way she thought right, without following any established rules. There was a general, but erroneous, impression that Alice was aiming to found an Orthodox convent with her as mother superior and nuns working as nurses. Though Alice never claimed to be a nun, all Greeks looking at her simple and austere attire were certain that she was, referring to her in private as the 'Princess-Nun'.[9] Most saw this positively, as it reminded them of the many Byzantine princesses and empresses who had ended their lives in convents. Prominent among these was the mother of the last Emperor, Constantine XI, Helena Dragasi, who like Alice was a foreign princess (from Serbia) and, a few years before her son's heroic death defending doomed Constantinople, had became mother superior of a Greek monastery near Corinth under the name 'Ypomoni' (Patience); after her death she was beatified by the Orthodox Church.

Even though Alice's plans were well received at Tinos, they in the end did not materialize because of a lack of funds for building the facilities and meeting the exorbitant costs of shipping the building materials to the island. For the next decade Alice worked hard to attract the funding. She decided that it would be better to base the organization in Athens, where she could use her summer home in the suburb of Neon Herakleion as the headquarters, thus saving considerable building costs. Having the organization in Athens would also attract a larger number of trainee girls than it would on a small island. So in 1949 Alice moved back to Athens where she bought a flat on Patriarchou Ioakeim Street in the Kolonaki district not far from her previous flat on Koumbari Street.[10] However, she spent most of her time at her villa in Neon Herakleion which was now the headquarters of the Christian Sisterhood of Martha and Mary.

Alice's timing for establishing her charitable organization in Athens was fortunate, as 1949 saw the end of the Greek Civil War. That bitter conflict had left a poisonous legacy of right-left enmity; the leftist and communist losers of the Civil War were jailed and persecuted. But, as we have seen, the advent of King Paul to the throne did much to calm the political waters and the 1950s ushered in a new period of peace and development after a decade of war and extreme hardship for the Greek people. As soon as she returned to Athens, Alice began travelling abroad to raise funds for the Sisterhood of Martha and Mary. In 1950 she visited the United States at the invitation of the Greek-American chairman of Twentieth Century Fox, Spyros Skouras, who covered all her expenses. Skouras, a fierce Greek patriot, had been chairman of the American Relief Fund for Greece during the Second World War and had organized many high-profile events that had brought in millions of dollars to aid the Greeks. Skouras helped Alice collect financial aid mainly from the Greek-American community and also his American friends. Afterwards Alice travelled to England and happened to be with her mother Victoria when the latter died in 1950.

While Alice was in the USA she appears to have been impressed by the way charitable organizations there held fundraisers through galas attended by the rich and famous. Skouras was an experienced and capable organizer of such events, and Alice is likely to have received advice from him. When she returned to Athens she planned to hold a big gala event for the wealthy Greeks in order to get funds for her organization. She briefed Virginia Simopoulos, her longtime lady-in-waiting and friend, about her plan and assigned her to work out the details in organizing the gala, which was held on 15 November 1951 in the Grande Bretagne Hotel and included a bridge contest and an exhibition of the latest designs of women's evening dresses by Greek fashion designers. The dresses were donated to Alice's charity fund and sold off in a lottery. All proceeds from these events went to building a church in the grounds of Alice's villa at Neon Herakleion where the trainee nurses could have a place of worship.[11] The event was a great success and Alice decided to repeat the fund raiser every November at the Grande Bretagne.

Alice was invited back to America by Skouras in 1952 and was there when Britain's George VI passed away. This meant that her daughter in law, Elizabeth, would become Queen and Philip the Royal Consort. The result was that her presence in the United States was spotlighted by the local media. Alice's next trip outside Greece was to London for Elizabeth's coronation in 1953. She attended the ceremony at Westminster Cathedral dressed in her nun-like attire and made a great impression on all who watched the ceremony in the cathedral or on television, as she walked in front of the official procession. Alice herself admitted in interviews to the press that she basically attended the coronation in the hope of acquiring funds for her Athens-based organization. The most important of these interviews took place in Athens shortly before flying to London for Elizabeth's coronation. Among other things she told the dumbfounded reporter that her greatest sorrow was that as Philip had given up his Orthodox faith so that he could marry Elizabeth, 'he will have to face life without protection and help' from the old faith. According to the story, Alice believed that even if Philip became a good Anglican, it was only as an Orthodox that he could be a true Christian.[12] This shows how devoted to Orthodoxy Alice had become by this time.

As Alice was now the Queen's mother-in-law, her Sisterhood of Martha and Mary received more publicity. The November fund-raising galas at the Grande Bretagne figured prominently in the social calendar of the Greek high and diplomatic society.[13] That is, until January 1955, when Virginia Simopoulos died. She had been in charge of organizing the fundraisers. Her place as lady-in-waiting to Alice was taken up by Kitty Valaoriti, a neighbour of hers in Kolonaki. That year also saw the last gala of the Sisterhood of Martha and Mary at Grande Bretagne; it was a mere shadow of the previous ones, essentially limited to a lottery of various items.[14] These had been gifts to Alice from various sources. It was clear that the death of Virginia had dealt a severe blow to Alice's attempt to attract funds. Eventually, Alice had to give up her philanthropic activities, and in 1959 the Sisterhood of Martha and Mary had to be wound up. This was not only the result of a lack of funds, but also because most of the girls who were trained as volunteer nurses usually left the organization shortly afterwards, and ended up getting married or being employed elsewhere with a salary.

Interestingly enough, Philip himself has attributed the failure of the Sisterhood of Martha and Mary to Alice's lack of the organizational skills necessary for such an undertaking.[15] He implies that Alice should have appointed a manager to handle practical matters rather than arranging everything herself. Yet, as we have seen, Alice through her life had displayed some organizational abilities; in her younger years she had run the Embroidery School in Athens with great success, training hundreds of girls as seamstresses. After her family's exile in 1922, Alice at one time ran a high street shop in the centre of Paris. It may be that in later life her religious fervour took centre stage in her thinking rather than the practical day-to-day issues of management. Hugo Vickers in his biography of Alice makes it clear that on several occasions during this period she appeared not to have an instinct for the value of money, as she spent much more than she could afford. Even after the Sisterhood of Martha and Mary ceased to function, Alice arranged that the facilities at her villa at Neon Herakleion continued to be used in philanthropy; they were turned into a day care centre for the elderly but without any religious association.

The failure of her organization gave Alice free time that she could use in various ways. She travelled abroad, mostly to Britain and Sweden, spending time with her sister Louise, who by now was the Swedish Queen (she was with her in 1965 shortly before Louise's death). She also visited India and Bahrain intending to do philanthropic work in those countries, but the attempts did not bear fruit. In 1961 Philip visited her in Athens with his children, Charles and Anne, but she saw more of her grandchildren whenever she visited England. Alice pampered them as a typical Greek grandmother would, though in a strict religious spirit. She taught them to call her *yiayia*, which is Greek for grandma. She was particularly happy when Philip's third son, Prince Andrew, was named after his grandfather (in Greece it is standard for the names of grandparents to be given to the grandchildren).

Alice also had time now to be with the other members of the Greek royal family. And here there arose a problem. Alice had a good relationship with King Paul, who like her was a fervent Orthodox Christian and liked the simple life. However, she did not see eye to eye with Frederica. (In fact, not many people did.) The dislike was mutual and during the 1950s Frederica snubbed Alice on several occasions by not inviting her to family functions. Alice most likely disapproved of Frederica's rather ostentatious love of display and her meddling in politics which was eroding the monarchy's popularity.[16] In January 1964 Paul died and was succeeded by his 24-year-old son, Constantine II. Soon afterwards, in 1965, as we have seen, the King became embroiled in a serious political crisis with his prime minister, Georgios Papandreou. This crisis indirectly led to the 21 April 1967 Colonels' coup and the establishment of a military junta in Greece for the next seven years.

As a consequence of the coup, Philip and Elizabeth arranged for Alice in May 1967 to come and live with them in Britain for her own protection. The junta's intentions for the monarchy were then inscrutable; though it had seized power in Constantine's name and its members were staunch monarchists, the feeling was not mutual. In fact the junta strongmen were fully aware that Constantine at some point would stage a countercoup. He did, on 13 December 1967, and failed miserably; Constantine fled the country with his family.

Alice was then eighty-two years old and in failing health. In fact she was the last surviving member of her generation of the royal family. If she had been in Athens at the time, it is unlikely that she would have joined Constantine and the remaining members of the family in their desperate flight to Rome. She almost certainly would have elected to remain alone in Athens, come what may. The colonels' regime would not have harmed her or made her life difficult in any way. On the contrary, the fact that she was the mother-in-law of the British Queen could have tempted the regime to use her presence in Athens as propaganda that all was well and normal in Greece. Interestingly, after Alice moved to London, the Greek embassy made it known that she was free to return to Greece whenever she wished.

When Alice left Athens she donated her villa at Neon Herakleion to the Greek Red Cross to be used as a day care centre for elderly people. Today it belongs to the municipality of Neon Herakleion and continues to function in the way that Princess Alice had wanted. A sign at the entrance informs the visitor about Alice and the history of the villa.[17] Alice spent her last two years with Philip, Elizabeth and her grandchildren, and died on 5 December 1969 in Buckingham Palace, aged eighty-four. She had requested to be buried in Jerusalem in the crypt of Russian Orthodox

Convent of Mary Magdalene where her aunt Ella, her inspiration in life, is also buried. Yet her wish was not fulfilled until 1988 when her coffin was finally moved from Windsor Castle to Jerusalem. In her final resting place Alice makes it known that she considered herself a Greek. Her funerary inscription is in English: 'Alice Princess Andrew of Greece. Princess of Battenberg 25 February 1885 – 5 December 1969'. But beneath is the Greek phrase 'ΓΕΝΗΘΗΤΩ ΤΟ ΘΕΛΗΜΑ ΣΟΥ' (Thy Will Be Done) from the Lord's Prayer. And Alice's coffin in the crypt is permanently draped by a Greek flag.[18]

Princess Elizabeth's Song in the 1943 Windsor Pantomime Show

In My Arms
(Ted Grouya / Frank Loesser)

As sung by Dick Haymes (with The Song Spinners), 1943
(Also recorded by Eddie Cantor and Ina Ray Hutton)

His cousin had sent him a sweater
And his sister wrote a letter
But he wanted something much better
This boy who was sailing away
For his buddies were with their sweethearts
All around him with their sweethearts
Now he'd never had any sweethearts
And over and over he'd say

In my arms, in my arms
Ain't I never gonna have a girl in my arms
In my arms, in my arms
Ain't I never gonna get a bundle of charms
Comes the dawn, I'll be gone
I just gotta have a honey holdin' me tight
You can keep your knittin' and purlin'
If I'm gonna go to Berlin
Gimme a girl in my arms tonight

His grandma had sent him some candy
And as he chewed on the candy
He said my morale is just dandy
And still there's a tear in my eye

For his buddies were there with their sweethearts
Kissing bye–bye with their sweethearts
Now he'd never had any sweethearts
And over and over he'd cry

In my arms, in my arms
Ain't I never gonna have a girl in my arms
In my arms, in my arms
Ain't I never gonna get a bundle of charms
Comes the dawn, I'll be gone
And I thank you for the many letters you'll write
As for something nice and cute and female
I'll never get it in the V-mail
Gimme a girl in my arms tonight

In my arms, in my arms
Ain't I never gonna have a girl in my arms
In my arms, in my arms
Ain't I never gonna get a bundle of charms
Comes the dawn, I'll be gone
I'll be headin' for the very thick of the fight
You can wine and dine and cigarette me
But if you really wanna get me
Gimme a girl in my arms tonight

In my arms, in my arms
Ain't I never gonna have a girl in my arms
In my arms, in my arms
Ain't I never gonna get a bundle of charms
Comes the dawn, I'll be gone
Now does anyone wanna please treat me right
You can keep your shavin' cream and lotion
If I'm a-gonna cross the ocean
Give me a girl in my arms tonight

In My Arms from Lyrics.com. STANDS4 LLC, 2020. Web. 28 Aug. 2020. <https://www.lyrics.com/lyric/1216672/Dick+Haymes>.

Notes

Chapter 1: 1921
1. Gould-Lee, p. 31.

Chapter 2: The Making of the Greek Dynasty
1. Gould-Lee, p. 23.
2. Ploumidis in *Istoria* 618, p. 28.
3. Petropulos, in Couloumbis *et al*, p. 68.
4. Ibid.
5. Kambanis, in TRD 11.
6. The assailants were caught and guillotined. The site, on Syngrou Avenue, is today marked by the Church of Saint Saviour (*Aghios Sostis*), built to commemorate the occasion
7. Gould-Lee, pp. 28–9
8. Veremis, T., 'The National Society', in *Kathimerini*, 11 May 1997
9. Pikros, I. 'The Course of the War', in *Kathimerini*, 11May 1997
10. Couloumbis *et al*, 31
11. In Sabatakaki, p. 202
12. Ibid, p. 22
13. Const. I, pp. 29–30
14. Gould-Lee, p. 34
15. Polykratis, p. 45
16. Pipinelis, pp. 77–80

Chapter 3: Andrew and Alice
1. Xanthakis, p. 7
2. After Andrew, the youngest of the sons of George I, Prince Christopher, would also attend the Military Academy. Their other brother, George was also an officer but in the Navy and had studied at the Danish Naval Academy at Copenhagen which his namesake father also attended before he became King of Greece.
3. Nikolaos Zorbas was one of the ablest Greek officers of his time and commandant of the Military Academy between 1899–1906.
4. Tsichlis, p. 70.
5. ELIA Archive. Reference no. KOU 1.087.
6. Both Pangalos (1878–1952) and Othonaios (1879–1970) had distinguished careers in the military and fought in the Balkan Wars and the First World War. They both participated in the Asia Minor Campaign until 1920 when they were cashiered by the monarchists. One of the older classmates of Andrew in these photographs is Basil Kourousopoulos (1878–1929), who entered the Military Academy in 1895 and graduated in 1899. In 1922, Kourousopoulos served in Asia Minor as commander of 12th Division which a year earlier had been under the command of Andrew. In 1922 Kourousopoulos was a member of the Revolutionary Committee that sent Andrew to a court martial.
7. Danglis, pp. 198–232.

8. *Akropolis*, 15 May 1901.

9. That Andrew's examination lasted two days, see *Skrip*, 14, 15 and 17 May 1901.

10. *Akropolis*, 15 May 1901

11. Danglis, pp. 230–232.

12. For example, Boothroyd, p. 70.

13. *Skrip*, 17 May 1901.

14. *Skrip*, 22 May 1901.

15. http://www.royalchronicles.gr/merlinandboehringerphotos/.

16. Menelaos Metaxas would fight in the Balkan Wars of 1912–1913 and retire from the Army as a colonel in 1921. As a monarchist, he would not participate in the First World War and would accompany Andrew into his first exile from 1917 to 1920 and manage the Prince's property in Greece during Andrew's thirteen-year second exile from 1922 to 1935. Menelaos was a cousin of Ioannis Metaxas who was also a professional soldier. Ioannis played an important role in Greek politics until his death in 1941 as prime minister and then dictator of Greece. Contrary to his illustrious cousin, Menelaos kept a low public profile and avoided publicity. His only involvement in politics occurred shortly before his death in 1938 when he was the vice president of the National Conservative Organization. At that time Ioannis Metaxas as Greek dictator had outlawed all political parties but allowed organizations like that of his cousin Menelaos that supported his regime.

17. Parker, p. 13.

18. More than sixty years later Alice would describe to her grandchild Charles, the Prince of Wales, that when she first saw Andrew he looked to her like 'a Greek god'. Vickers, p. 52.

19. *Asty*, 25 December, 1903.

20. www.royalchronicles.gr/andrewandalicewedding/.

21. ΕΛΙΑ 04.16.3.038.

22. *Asty*, 25 December 1903.

23. Vickers, p. 66.

24. Vickers, p. 65.

25. ΕΛΙΑ 04.16.3.046, with the title , 'Ο Πρίγκηπας Ανδρέας με τον πίλον του Δ. Βουδούρη, 24 Απριλίου 1904'.

26. Vickers, 70. Palaiologou, 101–102. Ellen offended George V when in 1934 during the wedding of her daughter Marina to the Duke of Kent, she demanded that on the invitations she should bear the title 'Royal Highness'. It should be noted that at the time Ellen no longer had any royal title, as Greece was a republic. She wasn't even a Russian grand duchess as the Tsar had been toppled in 1917.

27. Louros, p. 181. Quoted by Palaiologou, p. 113.

28. For the top secret reports of the Austrian ambassador of 1910, see article by P.N. Enepikidis, *To Bima*, 20 November 1960. Among these is a letter by the Austrian ambassador to his Foreign Minister dated 12 February 1910 where he records that Sophia hated Greece, the Greeks but above all Alice. See also, article by G. Roussos, *To Bima*, 29 July 1961, where Alice is described as the princess who the Greeks liked the most.

29. Ziazias, pp. 15–16.

30. Vickers, p. 72

31. Karampatsos, p. 258. It is highly likely that this was the first time a car was driven to Thebes.

32. Ibid.

33. *Neon Asty*, 29 April 1905. The article, after mentioning that Andrew drove the British officers to Eleusis, goes on to say that 'Prince Battenberg and his wife Princess Victoria took their usual afternoon stroll at Zappeion [Athens]'. Alice's parents were at the time in Athens but the newspaper article does not mention them in the party that Andrew

accompanied on the excursion to Eleusis. However, it is possible that they were in the second car.

34. Vickers, p. 65

35. Many British newspapers recorded the fact that Tsar Nicholas II had given Alice a Wolseley, a car manufactured in Birmingham, as a wedding gift and as the best advertisement for the recently established British automobile industry.

36. Danglis, p. 238. Karampatsos, p. 258.

37. One of the seven cars was owned by Prince Nicholas, which the newspapers in 1904 recorded as the fastest car in Greece at the time. Therefore out of the seven cars in Greece at the time, four were owned by the royal family!

38. One year earlier, in 1906, during the so-called mid-Olympic Games held in Athens, there was a plan to stage the first motor race in Greece on this road (Karampatsos, p. 262). Andrew was one of the supporters of this plan but the authorities forbade it as too dangerous for the public.

39. Some modern Greek writers claim that Andrew had been buying cars from Simopoulos since 1900, but this is not borne out by contemporary sources.

40. *Akropolis*, 5 March 1907. After vividly describing the accident, the article ends with the comment: 'We only have seven cars and there are victims. Imagine if their number goes up to 70 what will happen!'

41. Karampatsos, pp. 265–266. The official investigation claimed that Euphrosyne was not married to Vamvakas the 'poor shoemaker', who was supposed to be her husband. Her actual surname was Kalogeras and the children she accompanied were those of Vamvakas by another woman. Vamvakas himself did not make a particularly big issue out of the accident, and very likely received payments by the wealthy people involved, something hinted at in the press.

42. For example, *Athinai*, 11 March 1907.

43. This is true also for Simopoulos, and it is ironic that in 1924 he was one of the founding members of the Greek Automobile and Touring Club (ELPA) which to this day places great emphasis on road safety. Even Menelaos Metaxas, a passenger in Andrew's car in the 1907 accident, developed a passion for fast cars. In 1917, a few days before Andrew was exiled from Greece for the first time, Metaxas sold off Andrew's cars and gave him the proceeds. This transaction may have given Metaxas the idea of starting his own car sale business. After retiring as an army officer in 1920, he became a major importer of German cars in Greece.

44. *Neon Asty*, 29 March 1907.

45. Quoted from Karampatsos, p. 264.

46. According to Karampatsos, p. 270, 'the royal automobile had crashed into Fafoutis' cart'. The passenger in the cart, Kyriazis, testified at Fafoutis' trial that even though the car was speeding towards the cart after Fafoutis waved to its driver, it stopped 25 metres behind them. However, Fafoutis' horse panicked and toppled the cart, causing the accident. Kyriazis' testimony is not reliable as she was a peasant woman from Kalamos and the main witness in a trial involving the King and his son. It is highly unlikely that she would have assigned any blame to them for the accident. Karampatsos' version of the story is reasonable.

47. *Empros*, 21 December 1910.

48. *Birmingham Gazette*, 18 August 1926.

49. *Sheffield Independent*, 17 April 1930.

50. Psaltiras.

51. *Akropolis*, 19 August 1909. When Constantine called the regiment to find out how many men were there, its commander replied: 'You won't believe how many I have! How many? Just me, and without my horse!'

52. Enepikidis, *To Bima*, 20 November 1960. It is interesting that in 1921 while Alice was pregnant with Philip, she harboured hopes that her baby – if it was a boy – could one day become king of Greece, as Andrew was no longer acceptable. Alice wrote to her brother, Louis Mountbatten: 'If the child will be a boy, he will be sixth in succession to the Greek throne. As things are today, with Alex dead, Tino threatened by Venizelos, and George and Andrew unacceptable, my son if God wills could become one day the King, if Monarchy prevails'. Boothroyd, p. 82.

53. Vickers, p. 84

Chapter 4: Troubles in Paradise: Balkan and World War

1. See the discussion by Vickers, pp. 93–104, about Alice as organizer of military hospitals and a nurse during the First Balkan War.

2. In Vickers, pp. 93–104. The most impressive of Alice's letters to her mother is dated 2 November 1912, where she recalls a scene at a field hospital following the arrival of wounded soldiers from Kailar, where the Greeks had won a battle: 'Our last afternoon at Kozani was spent in assisting at the amputation of a leg. I had to give chloroform at a certain moment and prevent the patient from biting his tongue and also to hand over cotton wool, basins, etc. Once I got over my feeling of disgust, it was very interesting.... [A]fter all was over, the leg was forgotten on the floor and I suddenly saw it there afterwards and pointed it out to Mademoiselle A[r]gyropoulo, saying that somebody ought to take it away. She promptly picked it up herself, wrapped it up in some stuff, put it under her arm and marched out of the hospital to find a place to bury it in. But she never noticed that she left the bloody end uncovered, and as she is as deaf as I, although I shouted after her, she went on unconcerned, and everybody she passed nearly retched with disgust—and, of course, I ended by laughing, when the comic part of the thing struck me.' The next day, Alice's mother's lady-in-waiting, Nona Kerr, arrived to see Alice. Nona wrote to Alice's mother, telling her how Alice seemed. '[It] would make you proud to hear the way everyone speaks of Princess Alice. Sophie Baltazzi, Doctor Sava, *everyone*. She has done wonders.' She also noted that Alice was 'very thin…At present she simply can't stop doing things. Prince Andrew wants to send her back to Athens to the babies [their three daughters] soon, but I don't think he will succeed just yet'.

3. See for example, *Makedonia*, 15 August 1930 .

4. For details about Alice's initiative and the creation of her fund, see Skiadas 1.

5. *Estia*, 9 October 1912.

6. Πολεμικόν εμβατήριον. Έκδοσις της εφημερίδος «Εστία». (Εις ενίσχυσιν του ωραίου έργου, το οποίον ανέλαβεν η Α. Β. Υ. η πριγκήπισσα Αλίκη υπέρ των εφέδρων). Τυπ. "Εστία" Κ. Μαϊσνερ και Ν. Καραγδούρη.

7. Vickers, pp. 93–104.

8. To understand today the impact that Alice's appeal had at the time, we may compare it to the appeal made by Captain Tom Moore during the coronavirus pandemic of 2020.

9. Vickers, p. 102.

10. Kastrinakis, www.royalchronicles.gr/george-a/.

11. Cited in Sabatakaki, p. 75. The officer was future dictator Ioannis Metaxas.

12. Const. I, pp. 33–4.

13. Petropulos, in Couloumbis *et al*, p. 40.

14. *The Tatler*, 12 January 1916.

15. *Lancashire Evening Post*, 3 January 1916.

16. Mackenzie, p. 48.

17. *Sheffield Daily Telegraph*, 11 July 1916. *Daily Record*, 27 July 1916.

18. Telegram n. 798, 26 June 1916. Published in *Eleftheria*, 22 March 1962.

19. See the *Dundee Courier*, 29 September 1916, which records that Menelaos Metaxas told Reuters that Prince Andrew received in London a cable from King Constantine urging him to go immediately to Paris and await there his directions.

20. *The Truth*, 11 October 1916.

21. *The Times*, 28 September 1916: 'Prince Andrew of Greece, the youngest brother of King Constantine, came recently to London. It is understood that his instructions, which were of precise nature, were to justify the action of King Constantine to the eyes of the British Government and the British Royal Family. There is no reason to believe that he found favour in the eyes of responsible members of the Government or its representatives.'

22. Mackenzie, p. 54.

23. Ibid, p. 56.

24. Ibid, pp. 67–68.

25. Eade, p. 23. According to Parker, p. 18, the nursery where Alice's daughters were playing at the time had a window shattered by bullets fired by soldiers of the Allies.

26. *The Times*, 31 January 1917.

27. Polykratis, p. 49.

28. https://storiacontroversa.blogspot.com/2012/03/h.html

29. *Eleftheria*, 22 March 1962.

30. *Sheffield Daily Telegraph*, 19 July 1917.

31. Quoted in Gould-Lee, p. 47

32. Andrew, pp. 15–16.

33. The first Greek royal to clash with Venizelos even before he became prime minister of Greece had been Prince George in Crete. In 1906, while Gorge was High Commissioner of Crete as an autonomous territory, Venizelos had led the revolt of Therissos against him and forced him to leave Crete. It is worthy of note that in later years Prince George kept a low profile vis-à-vis Venizelos, in contrast to Andrew.

34. Palaiologou, p. 103. Nicholas was passionate about fine art and was himself a competent painter; Christopher had a variety of interests including the study of the supernatural.

35. Andrew, pp. 15–16.

36. Vickers, p. 125.

37. See *Skrip*, 21 September 1920. Andrew had previously given a copy of his report to the Italian prime minister, Giovanni Giolitti, in Rome.

38. *The Scotsman*, 10 May 1920: 'The question was discussed at a council chaired by Prince Andrew. In another of Captain Papparigopoulo's letters it is recommended that the present regime in Greece be overthrown.'

39. Greek Literary and Historical Archive (Ελληνικό Λογοτεχνικό και Ιστορικό Αρχείο). Eleftherios Venizelos Archives, File 12–14.

40. See *Estia*, 13 September 1920, which published an interview by Andrew who refutes the charges that he had organized the attempt against the life of Venizelos with other monarchist conspirators. Andrew claims that for him the only way to solve political problems is through elections and not the gun.

41. *Skrip*, 25 September 1920. *Patris*, 26 September 1920.

42. Const I, p. 41

43. Ibid.

44. *Patris*, 25 October 1920.

45. *Nottingham Journal*, 19 November 1920.

46. First reported in *Eleftheros Typos*, 25 September 1920, where the sum is 500,000 francs. Nancy was quite rich and could afford such munificence. Two years later, as we will see, she gave a cheque for 500,000 dollars to the Greek Red Cross for the refugees of the 1922 Asia Minor Disaster.

Chapter 5: Andrew in Danger: Asia Minor and Court Martial

1. Details of their return are recorded in Maria's unpublished autobiography, see www.royalchronicles.gr/princessmariagreece/

2. *The Times*, 24 November 1920. According to Christopher, p. 152, the people were so happy to see Andrew and Christopher that they caried them on their shoulders from Phaleron – where they had disembarked from *Ierax* – to Athens (a distance of 15 miles) and forced Andrew to address them from the balcony of the palace.

3. See for example, *Liverpool Echo*, 4 April 1921; *Aberdeen Press and Journal*, 5 April 1921; *Western Daily Press*, 5 April 1921; and *Daily Herald*, 6 April 1921. Andrew's wife's parents in England learned from the newspapers about Andrew's supposed death on the battlefield in Asia Minor. According to a letter Victoria sent to Alice, this did not upset them as they knew that Andrew was in Athens at the time and that this news was a fake, but they were certain that it brought grief to his foreign friends who did not know this. See Vickers, p. 153.

4. Andrew, p. 8. Interestingly enough, Andrew makes no mention of the fake report about him in Asia Minor in April 1921.

5. Andrew, pp. 7–8.

6. Kinross, p. 303.

7. Quoted in Polykratis, p. 50.

8. Const, I, p. 489.

9. Kinross, p. 302.

10. *Kathimerini*, 31 May 1921.

11. Andrew, pp. 57–58.

12. Andrew, p. 39.

13. In later years Andrew was accused of giving orders to his 12th Division to burn down the shacks of Turkish peasants who were suspected of giving assistance to Kemal's forces. For this reason some of his men nicknamed him 'shackburner'. Much of this was used in Kemal's propaganda against the Greek Army (see Kostopoulos, pp. 121–122). Andrew, writing in 1928, was aware of these accusations. He claimed (pp. 32–33) that atrocities against Ottoman villagers were occasionally committed by some of the undisciplined elements in his division and that he personally was careful to treat the Ottomans with respect as he did not encounter any resistance from the non combatant population.

14. Andrew, p. 92. Katsis, p. 263.

15. See *Lancashire Evening Post* and *Pall Mall Gazette*, 27 July 1921.

16. Andrew, p. 92.

17. Benaki Museum. Archive of Eleftherios Venizelos. File 4-047-3254.

18. Quoted in Kinross, p. 316.

19. Kinross, p. 319.

20. Kinross, pp. 320–1.

21. Andrew, p. 152, describes the seizure of Kale Grotto by II Corps on 17 August 1921 as 'a pyrrhic victory' because of the great losses his men had suffered.

22. Andrew, pp. 187–188.

23. Andrew, p. 124. Rizas, pp. 269, 274, 304. Greek General Staff, II, 1965, pp. 36–39. For an analytical and balanced discussion of Andrew's actions relating to Sakarya and how they were presented by later Greek authors. See Ioannis Filistor, https://www.istorikathemata.com/2014/01/blog-post.html (Part 1) and https://www.istorikathemata.com/2014/01/19-1922.html (Part 2).

24. This photograph is published in Eade, (no plate number)

25. Andrew, pp. 188–189. As we will see, at the court martial of Andrew a year later, Papoulas testified that Gaballias was responsible for Andrew 'misunderstanding' his order and

that was perhaps why he refused to execute it. Some later Greek writers have accepted Papoulas' claim and suggest that Gaballias was the culprit but Andrew makes it clear in his book that Gaballias was the scapegoat and that he (Andrew) was fully responsible for disobeying the order.

26. Alexandra, 1.
27. https://www.corfu-museum.gr/index.php/el/59-corfu-notes/381-24-1921.
28. *Esperini*, 22 October 1921.
29. Andrew's letter to Metaxas is dated 19 December 1921. See Metaxas, pp. 757–760.
30. Andrew, p. 238, claims that he requested to be transferred to Epirus after he asked for authority to arrest Colonel Plastiras and Papoulas refused. This seems unlikely, and appears to be an excuse, as Andrew was still commander of II Corps and thus could have ordered the arrest of Plastiras any time as his superior officer.
31. See telegram to Venizelos on 5 April 1922 from the MPs of his Liberal Party at Athens entitled 'The Mission of Prince Andrew at Ioannina', where Andrew was supposedly sent by King Constantine to persecute the local Venizelists. Benaki Museum, Archive of Eleftherios Venizelos, File 316–59.
32. Kinross, pp. 359–60.
33. Alvanos *et al*, pp. 39–43
34. Eade, p. 33.
35. Parker, p. 27.
36. Eade, p. 33.
37. *Eleftheros Logos*, 8 October 1922.
38. In Sabatakaki, p. 39.
39. Some Greek newspapers on 15 October 1922 reported that Andrew lived in relative comfort at his eldest brother George's lavish mansion off Syntagma Square (now the Egyptian embassy), but that was not correct.
40. *Eleftheros Logos*, 8 October 1922: 'After his request to the Revolutionary Committee, Prince Christopher has been given permission to return to Greece to settle his family affairs, after which he will depart immediately'. In fact, Christopher returned to Greece to retrieve his personal items and also the jewels, stocks, cash and cat of Princess Ellen, wife of his brother Prince Nicholas. According to Christopher, Ellen's cat gave him considerable trouble while sailing away from Greece.
41. Gould-Lee, pp. 271–272.
42. As reported in the Greek press.
43. That Pangalos met Andrew before his trial and told him his life was in danger is mentioned for the first time in the *Daily Express*, 29 December 1922, without, however, quoting the actual exchange. This was first recorded in 1926 by Prince Nicholas in his memoirs, and the source would have been Andrew himself. It also appears in Prince Christopher's memoirs.
44. Papastathopoulos.
45. Ibid. The relevant decree authorizing Plastiras to deal with this matter came into effect on 14 November 1922.
46. On 27 October 1922, Plastiras in a press interview made it clear there would be no mercy on the part of the Revolutionary Committee for all those responsible for the Asia Minor defeat. See *Eleftheros Logos*, 31 October 1922: 'For those who misunderstood the mercy of the Revolution. Statement by Mr Plastiras'.
47. Photographs taken by Petros Poulidis now in the ERT Archive, with code nos: 0000005395, 0000005398, 0000005388, 0000005389, 0000005390, 0000005392 and 0000016305.
48. Andrew, p. 6, mentions that only three of the many witnesses he had requested to testify at his trial were allowed by the court. In fact officially there was only one witness for the

defence, and it appears that Andrew and the prosecution had requested in common at least two witnesses. These were probably Papoulas and Trivilas.

49. Karvounis knew Andrew before 1921 as both were freemasons; Andrew had been a founding member of the 'Hesiodos Stoa' of the Athens Masons (see Iatrides, p. 138). In later life, Karvounis became a communist and during the German Occupation joined the left-wing guerrilla organization of ELAS. He even wrote the anthem of ELAS, which remains Greece's best-known Resistance anthem. (See Papapolyviou.)

50. After the Second World War, Sarigiannis' daughter married a British Army officer and went to live in Britain.

51. In testimony printed in the newspapers, Papoulas, though agreeing that Andrew's decision not to follow his order was illegal, blamed Andrew's chief of staff, Gabalias, for the disobedience and that was the reason why he replaced him. Trilivas and Skylakakis, division commanders of II Corps, clearly stated that Andrew did not contravene the order he had received from Papoulas.

52. Papapolyviou,

53. Andrew, p. 7.

54. According to Andrew, p. 186, Sarigiannis' accusation was groundless as the decision to halt the push to Ankara had been taken on 20 August, a week before Andrew's supposed insubordination. Andrew answered Sarigiannis in his later book about the Battle of Sakarya, claiming that Sarigiannis was much to blame for the stalemate that ensued, as he had been the chief planner of the push. Andrew also accused him of indecision and lacking morale (Andrew, pp. 74, 158).

55. *New York Times*, 3 December 1922. Also in Eade, p. 37.

56. *Belfast News-Letter*, 4 December 1922, with the impressions of a reporter at the trial: 'When all the evidence had been taken, Prince Andrew read out his own defence. This statement had obviously been prepared for him'.

57. See for example the headline in the *Western Daily Press*, Bristol, 4 December 1922: 'ONLY A FIGUREHEAD. STRANGE PLEA IN PRINCE ANDREW'S DEFENCE'.

58. It is characteristic that in the press release by the Revolutionary Committee, Sarigiannis' testimony was emphasized, whereas that of the others was lumped together. According to Andrew, p. 223, on 6 September 1921, Karvounis, who visited him at Eskişehir having come from Brusa where the Greek General Staff was located, informed him that Sarigiannis was telling everyone that Andrew was to blame for the failure of the Greek push to Ankara. Thus Sarigiannis was well known to have been Andrew's main accuser many months before.

59. These details have been pieced together from reports in Greek newspapers, *Eleftheros Typos, Skrip of 20 November 1922*, and *Ethnos, Makedonia* of 19 November 1922

60. Ibid.

61. 'Trial of Prince Andrew, begun this morning, is concluded. Verdict according to your recommendation…'. Benaki Museum, Archive of Eleftherios Venizelos, File 032–56.

62. Both observations are by Papastathopoulos, who also records that according to article 7 of the 1911 Greek Constitution that was still current in 1922, and Article 1 of the then penal code, it was forbidden to pass a sentence that had not been specified for a particular crime nor recorded in a previous law.

63. Hellenic Literary and Historic Archive of the National Bank of Greece Cultural Foundation, Metaxas Sub-file 1.3.

64. If this was his intention, it was unsuccessful, as Andrew was found unanimously guilty as charged.

65. Andrew, p. 6–7.

66. Papoulas was asked directly by one of the judges if he believed that if Andrew had not been a prince he would not have disobeyed his orders, and Papoulas replied in the affirmative.
67. *Esperini*, 20 November 1922.
68. *Ethnos*, 20 November 1922.
69. Quoted in Gould-Lee, p. 271.
70. Nicholas, p. 3.
71. *Daily Express*, 29 December 1922.
72. Benaki Museum, Archive of Eleftherios Venizelos, File 042–48. Venizelos tells George to emulate his grandfather's example who fifteen years earlier had been forced to accept the military coup of 1909 and did not abdicate as he had threatened to do. That in the long run proved beneficial for the Greek royal family by strengthening it.
73. *Esperini*, 19 October 1922, reporting on the meeting between King George and Lt. Col. Fessopoulos, one of the senior judges at Andrew's forthcoming trial.
74. *Athenaika Nea*, 12 July 1935 .
75. *Minutes of the Meetings of the Fourth Greek Constitutional Convention in Athens*, Vol. I, Athens: National Printing House, p. 315.
76. In the telegram that Rentis sent to Venizelos with news of the verdict (see above) he added that there was incriminating evidence against Papoulas on his conduct in Asia Minor and it would be impossible not to send him before a court martial after Andrew. However, he could then be amnestied. In fact Andrew's court martial was the last such procedure.
77. Benaki Museum, Archive of Eleftherios Venizelos, File 042–48.
78. Parker, p. 28.
79. *Belfast Telegraph*, 29 December 1922: 'THE GREEK EXECUTIONS. PEACE SAVED PRINCE'S LIFE. NAVAL OFFICER AS ENVOY'.
80. *Sheffield Daily Telegraph*, 31 July 1930; 'the announcement in 1922 that Prince Andrew of Greece, a nephew of Queen Alexandria, had been court martialled and condemned to be shot for alleged disobedience...'
81. Vickers, p. 170. Boothroyd, p. 74, is one of the British authors who claims that Andrew was saved by the intervention of George V. However, the only piece of evidence he produces is a quote in a telegram from the Foreign Office to the British Legation in Athens in November 1922 stating that 'the King is most anxious concerning Prince Andrew. Please report on his Royal Highness's present position, and continue to keep us informed by telegraph of any developments'.
82. Vickers, pp. 168–171, gives in detail the actions of Talbot. At the end he acknowledges quoting Princess Margarita, that Talbot was sent by Venizelos. In fact, it was the decision of the Revolutionary Committee to spare Andrew thanks to George II and Venizelos. Talbot would have had some influence over Plastiras and Pangalos precisely because he was close to Venizelos. Boothroyd, p. 63, quotes two telegrams sent from the British Legation in Athens to the Foreign Office concerning the mission of Talbot to save Andrew. The first one dated 28 November 1922, three days before the trial, simply states that only Talbot had any chance of saving Andrew. The second telegram was sent on 30 November and states that during the previous evening, Talbot had met Pangalos and Plastiras who promised him that Andrew would not be executed and after his trial he would leave Greece in the charge of Talbot and on board a British warship.
83. *Pall Mall Gazette*, 7 December 1922. *Hull Daily Mail*, 7 December 1922. *Derby Daily Telegraph*, 6 December 1922.
84. *Yorkshire Post* and *Leeds Intelligencer*, 7 December 1922.

85. The headlines of British newspapers are characteristic: *Pall Mall Gazette*, 7 December 1922: 'PRINCE ANDREW'S ESCAPE. THANKS TO ENGLAND AND THE POPE. WELL TREATED. WHY H.M.S. CALYPSO WAS SENT'; *Portsmouth Evening News*, 7 December 1922: 'PRINCE ANDREW OF GREECE. ALIVE OWING TO ENGLAND AND THE POPE.' Paris, Thursday. 'If I am still alive it is thanks to the energetic attitude of England and the Pope," said Prince Andrew of Greece yesterday, at Rome, to the special correspondent...'; *Birmingham Daily Gazette*, 8 December 1922: 'GREEK PRINCE'S LIFE ONLY SAVED BY OUTSIDE INTERVENTION'; *Aberdeen Press and Journal*, 8 December 1922: 'LURED TO ATHENS. PRINCE ANDREW SAVED BY BRITISH INTERVENTION'.

86. For example, Parker, p. 28: '...he was thrown in a cell...'

87. *The Scotsman*, 9 December 1922.

88. *Dundee Courier*, 13 December 1922: 'PRINCE ANDREW'S NEW HOME. Prince Andrew of Greece has not been long finding a residence in London, for his wife and Queen Olga'. *Blyth News*, 14 December 1922: 'Prince Andrew's New Home. Prince Andrew of Greece has not been long in finding a residence in London...for the time being at any rate... to stay at Spencer House. St. James' Place, Piccadilly. Part of the residence'.

89. Credit: Topical Press Agency/Stringer Editorial #:3423517 Collection: Hulton Royals Collection. Date created: 1 December 1922. Source: Hulton Royals Collection, Object Name: 97s/51/10588/22. Published in the *Birmingham Daily Gazette*, 28 December 1922: 'The first photograph, taken on their arrival in England, of Prince Andrew of Greece, who was banished by the Revolutionary government, with Princess Andrew and their two daughters, Princess Theodora and Princess Margaret'.

90. Bertin, p. 282.

91. According to Nicholas, all members of the Greek royal family exiled after 1922 were stripped of their Greek nationality.

92. *Western Daily Press*, 1 January 1923: 'SAVED PRINCE ANDREW. Among the most interesting names in the New Year's Honours List is that of Commander Gerald T. Talbot, who saved Prince Andrew of Greece. He becomes Knight Commander the Royal Victorian Order. He is a writer of distinction, and has had a wide experience'. *Belfast News-Letter*, 1 January 1923: 'MAN WHO SAVED PRINCE ANDREW OF GREECE. The Daily Express says that among the most interesting names in the New Year's honour list is Gerald F. Talbot, who saved Prince Andrew of Greece. He becomes Knight Commander the Royal Victorian Order'. *Daily Herald*, 2 January 1923: 'The man who saved Prince Andrew Greece has been knighted. Why? Oh, Henry, how can you ask? It is not to question the saviour but the saved'. *Ballymena Weekly Telegraph*, 6 January 1923: 'Ill-fated ex-Minister was delayed – the representations of Commander Talbot would in all probability have saved their lives. Prince Andrew had now been under arrest in two rooms of a private house for five weeks. He was allowed no visitors for the first fortnight. So strict...'

93. *Pall Mall Gazette*, 5 January 1923: 'Truth About Prince Andrew. The Greek Prince, Andrew, was, I am able to state with authority, never in the slightest danger of being executed: General Plastiras.' *Belfast Telegraph*, 29 December 1922: 'THE GREEK EXECUTIONS -- PEACE SAVED PRINCE'S LIFE. NAVAL OFFICER AS ENVOY: The Revolutionary Committee then debated the issues of life and death. Princess Andrew boarded the steamer at Corfu. Her husband, Prince Andrew, had then been in custody some weeks. Neither the princess nor Commander Talbot knew of...'.

94. *Newcastle Daily Chronicle*, 30 December 1922.

95. *Nottingham Evening Post*, 12 January 1923: 'Prince Andrew of Greece left for New York on board the *Olympic...*'. *Sheffield Daily Telegraph*, 13 January 1923: 'WHY THE GREEK ARMY FAILED. EXILED PRINCE ON HIS ESCAPE. The exiled Prince Andrew of Greece, who has arrived at New York aboard the *Olympic*, cheerfully gave details of his narrow escape from death...'. *Nottingham Evening Post*, 19 January 1923: 'EXILED PRINCE'S ESCAPE. The exiled Prince Andrew of Greece, who arrived in New York yesterday, declared that he owed his life entirely to the intervention of King George, King Alfonso, and the Pope.'

96. *The Tatler*, 7 March 1923: 'TAKING NO RISKS. Andrew, accompanied by Princess Alice, sailed on the *Aquitania* to-day, and the Prince said he was not going to return to his native land, adding, "I am not going back to get strung up"'. *Birmingham Daily Gazette*, 23 March 1923.

97. See telegram with reference to article in the *Daily Express* about Prince Andrew. Benaki Museum, Archive of Eleftherios Venizelos, File 034–115.

98. Benaki Museum, Archive of Eleftherios Venizelos, File 034–29.

Chapter 6: A Family in Pieces

1. Const. I, p. 77.
2. Gould-Lee, p. 273.
3. Woodhouse, p. 211
4. Const. I, p. 62.
5. Andrew, p. 6.
6. *Makedonia*, 18 February 1925.
7. See, for example, *The Standard Union*, 7 May 1929.
8. *Eleftheron Bıma*, 13 May 1953. In 1970 Basil Boothroyd interviewed Philip's two surviving sisters, Margarita and Sophie about his childhood. The sisters are quoted as saying that Philip was very pugnacious and the other children were scared of him. At the time they thought that their mother was spoiling him as he was the youngest and the only boy, but that was not the case; it was because of this misunderstanding that the sisters were strict and disagreeable with young Philip. Boothroyd, p. 109.
9. Even though the Greek republic intended to confiscate Mon Repos there was a long lawsuit over its ownership which Andrew eventually won ten years later in 1934.
10. See, for example, *Western Mail*, 11 December 1924: 'LIABILITIES OVER £14,000: NO ASSETS. The public examination was held at the London Bankruptcy Court on Wednesday afternoon of Prince Andrew of Greece, who failed last July with liabilities over £14,000 and no assets whatever.' *Belfast News-Letter*, 11 December 1924: 'PRINCE ANDREW OF GREECE. Bankrupt Through a London Enterprise. The public examination was held at the London Bankruptcy Court yesterday afternoon of Prince Andrew Greece, who has fallen a victim of some misrepresentation ... failed last July, with liabilities...'.
11. *Birmingham Daily Gazette*, 13 January 1926: 'There is reason to suppose that behind the Dictatorship lies a design for the restoration of the monarchy in Greece, and Prince Andrew of Greece, King Constantine's brother, who is married to an English Princess, the daughter of the late Marquis of Milford...'. *Westminster Gazette*, 14 January 1926: 'About the situation in Greece, there would exist a hidden design for the restoration of the monarchy in Greece and Prince Andrew is mentioned as candidate for the throne.'
12. *Eleftheron Bima*, 13 June 1926.
13. Vickers, pp. 181–4.

14. For contacts with Merkouris and Ypsilantis see Vickers, p. 183. Andrew knew Ypsilanti well as he had been Master of the Horse of the Greek royal family in 1914–17. A summary of Andrew's letter to Efstratiadis is recorded in a note dated 3 July 1927 in the Benaki Museum, Eleftherios Venizelos Archives, File 418–090.

15. *Eleftheron Bima*, 8 November 1927.

16. See the Greek royalist newspaper in the USA, *Atlantis*, 9 November 1927, which comments that it was only natural for Tsaldaris to meet George and Andrew.

17. 'A ROYAL SHOPKEEPER: Princess Andrew of Greece in the shop which she has just opened in Paris, where she sells silks, perfumes, and many of the products of Greece. Prince Andrew is a son [sic] of the late King Constantine of Greece. In these days of kings without kingdoms many of the Royal families of Europe are forced into unexpected occupations, and it is seldom that they fail to make good'. According to Vickers, p. 178, the name of the shop was 'Hellas' and all its proceeds went for the refugees in Greece.

18. In an interview which Prince Peter, son of Prince George, gave to *Life International* in 1952, he recalled that his aunt Alice ran a shop in Paris but this had more to do with keeping in contact with friends in Greece; there people provided her with their products to sell and also kept her and Andrew up to date with developments in the country. According to Hough, p. 351, the shop did quite well as the customers were happy to be served by a princess.

19. The idea of Andrew writing a book as a way of exonerating himself of the accusation relating to the battle of Sakarya seems to have come to him shortly after his 1922 court martial and conviction. In an interview he gave to the New York Times on 22 December 1922 he claimed that he had 'ample documentary material for an appeal, and when the right time arrives I hope to publish the facts. Then the people of my country can judge for themselves whether I was rightly convicted…' Quoted in Eade, p. 40.

20. See note before last about details of 22 December 1922 interview to the New York Times.

21. Andrew, pp. 94–96: Officers of II Corps at each others throats; pp. 10–11: 12th Division was ill-prepared and poorly supplied because officers jealous of him wanted him to fail; pp. 11–12: Officers were conspiring against him.

22. Andrew, pp. 145–233.

23. *Illustrated London News*, 15 September 1928: 'Princesses on holiday at the seaside at Mamaia, on the shores of the Black Sea. Princess Margaret and Theodora are daughters of Prince Andrew of Greece, and Prince Michael, who was born at the Castle of Sinaia on October 25, 1921… [and] Philip, born in 1921'.

24. *Patterson Evening News*, 13 September 1928.

25. For Philip teaching American slang to Michael, see the *Sacramento Bee*, 17 January 1929. For Michael teaching Philip how to swim, see the *Patterson Evening News*, 13 September 1928.

26. *Baltimore Sun*, 10 June 1930.

27. According to Vickers, p. 199, Alice translated Andrew's book over a four-month period, working three hours each day during the winter of 1928–1929.

28. Andrew, pp. 234–242.

29. *Ethnos*, 8 July 1930.

30. Quoted in Vickers, p. 260.

31. Pipinelis, p. 81.

32. Ibid, p. 82.

33. Vickers, p. 199, mentions that the translation exhausted Alice and also that her long-time friend and lady in waiting, Virginia Simopoulos, thought that this work may have strained her.

34. *To Bima*, 23 May 1953.
35. Louros, p. 145.
36. Vickers, p. 195.
37. Ibid.
38. Rocco, p. 2.
39. Ibid.
40. Ibid. Quoted in Eade, p. 67.
41. Ibid.
42. Parker, p. 38.
43. Eade, pp. 70–71.
44. Ibid, p. 72. Philip recorded his view about his schooling at Cheam School in the preface of a history of the school published in 1974.
45. Parker, p. 38.
46. Mrs Violet Taylor had worked alongside her husband at Cheam School ever since they acquired the school in 1921. When Philip was punished for the first time with the cane by the Reverend Taylor, he asked Mrs Taylor if she liked her husband. Mrs Taylor replied by asking Philip if he liked him, to which Philip simply answered, 'No, I do not.' Eade, p. 71.
47. The letter is dated 26 March 1947 when Philip was sub-lieutenant in the Royal Navy and an instructor at the Petty Officers' School in Corsham, Wiltshire. We would like to thank the anonymous collector who owns the letter for giving us permission to include it in our book.
48. Parker, p. 38.
49. Pipinelis, p. 81.
50. Gould-Lee, p. 58.
51. Const. I, pp. 63–4.

Chapter 7: What To Do With Young Philip?

1. On the Nazi associations of Philip's brothers-in-law, see Petropulos, pp. 1–4, 91, 103, 116.
2. As we will see, these German connections, in fact, were to cause Philip some trouble after the war. Marr, p. 92.
3. Eade, p. 88.
4. Marr, p. 92.
5. Eade, p. 94.
6. *Portsmouth Evening News*, 16 December 1935.
7. *Aberdeen Press and Journal*, 23 October 1935.
8. *Dundee Evening Telegraph*, 14 December 1935.
9. *Des Moines Tribune*, 1 January 1936: 'Philip of Greece in Coastal Patrol'.
10. *The Scotsman*, 6 August 1937.
11. According to Eade, p. 99, in 1938 at Gordonstoun School there was 'a seamanship guild which took the place of an officers' training corps' and Lewty recorded Philip as one of its most efficient members.
12. Vickers, pp. 258–9. Eade, p. 104. However, in an interview that Philip gave Boothroyd sometime before 1970, he quotes him as saying that he was not particularly influenced by his schooling at Gordonstoun to seek a career in the navy, or by the fact that his Mountbatten uncles had served in the Royal Navy, though he admitted that Lord Louis Mountbatten may have persuaded him towards that direction. Boothroyd, p. 150.
13. *Aberdeen Press and Journal*, 15 February 1939.
14. *Dundee Courier*, 22 October 1934.

15. *Aberdeen Press and Journal*, 17 July 1937, where Philip is mentioned as opening batsman.
16. *Aberdeen Press and Journal*, 14 November 1938.
17. See, for example, reports in the *Aberdeen Press and Journal* of 18, 21, 28 July, 12 and 14 November 1938. Also 23 January 1939.
18. *Aberdeen Press and Journal*, 21 July 1938.
19. *The Scotsman*, 11 June 1935.
20. *Manchester Guardian*, 31 October 1940. It is worth noting that during midday breaks at Gordonstoun pupils trained at running, jumping and javelin throwing (see Eade, p. 96). This means that Philip was already highly trained in the athletic events he participated in.
21. *Aberdeen Press and Journal*, 2 August 1935.
22. *Dundee Courier*, 1 August 1935. *Aberdeen Press and Journal*, 2 August 1935.
23. *Portsmouth Evening News*, 31 July 1935.
24. *Macbeth*, Wikipedia.
25. Getty images collection. The photos show Philip on his own, with another member of the cast or three others. All photos have been taken at the same time. However, there is one photograph showing all four boys which was taken on a different occasion as can be seen by the fact that the costumes they are wearing have slight differences to those in the other photographs. (PA Images Collection: PA Images Date created: 8 August 1933, PA Images Object name: 1024235. Also PA Images / Alamy Stock Photo Image ID: G44RJM. Photographer: PA. Date taken: 8 August 1933. Location: Moray, Scotland). According to the record for this photograph, it is dated August 8, 1933 and shows 'the twelve-year-old Philip of Greece (second from left) taking part in an historical pageant at Gordonstoun School, Moray, Scotland'. This reference is obviously wrong, since Gordonstoun School did not exist in 1933. The right year should be 1935. If however the date of 8 August is correct, then it is likely that this is a photo of the cast of *Macbeth* rehearsing for another production of this play after the initial one on 1 August 1935.
26. *Aberdeen Press and Journal*, 31 July 1935.
27. *Central Somerset Gazette*, 23 August 1935.
28. *Aberdeen Press and Journal*, 28 July 1936. There is a reasonable explanation why this particular Gordonstoun play was kept out of the press and is almost unknown today, in contrast to that of *Macbeth* of the previous year. According to Boothroyd, p. 130, a few days before the performance of *Hamlet* by Gordonstoun School, Hahn found out that the pupil who was to play the lead role had gone out with a typist in Edinburgh during a school break. Hahn considered this a serious moral lapse on the part of the pupil and that it disqualified him from being in the play. Another boy who was Guardian, and who Hahn considered as morally impeccable, was hastily summoned to play the part of Hamlet. Unfortunately, he had very little time to study the role and may not have had an acting talent. The play turned out to be a disaster and an embarrassment for all who took part in it. Hahn may have tried to save his school's reputation, by making sure that local newspapers avoided any mention of this fiasco.
29. *Dundee Evening Telegraph*, 17 December 1935.
30. According to Eade, p. 99: 'Hahn maintained that the provision of public service to the local district was vital for the spiritual health of "his community of adolescent males"'.
31. *The Sketch*, 21 December 1938, in a section entitled 'The Literary Lounger'.
32. See for example, *The Age*, 23 December 1938; *Decatur Herald*, 24 December 1938; *La Grande Evening Observer*, 28 December 1938.
33. *Birmingham Daily Post*, 20 May 1940. *The Scotsman*, 20 May 1940.
34. For Gordonstoun, see Eade, p. 95. For travelling under the name 'Mr Philips', see the *Aberdeen Press and Journal*, 3 December 1934: 'Prince Philip travelled from Elgin incognito as Mr Philips, a sleeping berth being reserved for him'.

Chapter 8: Lucky Royals, Unlucky Andrew

1. Woodhouse, p. 223.
2. Vickers, p. 261, quotes a report by the then British Ambassador in Athens to the Foreign Ministry which includes parts of the editorial of *Eleyheron Bima* accusing Andrew of interfering in Greek politics. However, reactions to Andrew's letter by the republicans were much wider and more poignant than what the ambassador implies in his report.
3. *Eleftheron Bima*, 17 August 1932.
4. For Menealos Metaxas' business ventures, see *Eleutheron Bima*, 5 December 1928 (advertisement as car salesman) and 1 January 1932 (advertisement for camera sales) and *Bradini*, 3 March 1932 (advertisement of M. Metaxas' company with reference to it as supplying instrument to the Greek Air Force).
5. *Athenaika Nea*, 10 and 11 December 1932.
6. *Athenaika Nea*, 30 June 1933.
7. British publications record that Andrew gave the interview in early January 1935. The misunderstanding is due to the fact that *Laikos Agon* was a weekly newspaper and bore the last day of its circulation on each issue. *Eleftheron Bima* of 30 December 1934 records that the edition of *Laikos Agon* with Andrew's interview had circulated the previous day (29 December).
8. See for example, titles like: 'We won't get rid of the Raspoutin of Chalepa (the nickname *Laikos Agon* had given Venizelos as Chalepa in Crete was his place of birth) without blood-shed!'; 'The only solution is to hang him outside his mansion'; 'Allow us to put the noose around his neck'; 'The bloodthirsty hoodlum trembles as the time approaches when he will be cut in pieces'; 'It is only by blood-shed that we will root out the cannibal of Chalepa'; 'Our civilization is stigmatized because Venizelos is still alive'; 'He won't be exterminated only if he stepped on the neck until his dead'. One front page title even asks Venizelos 'Won't you give up quietly to Satan your dark soul you bloodthirsty wretched tyrant!'
9. Vickers, p. 263, make the point that Andrew's interview to *Laikos Agon* was a serious error on his part, without however going into detail about why this was so.
10. The telegram is quoted by Eade, p. 104.
11. Published in the communist newspaper *Tharros*, 23 August 1935.
12. *Athenaika Nea*, 18 August 1935.
13. Sabatakaki, p. 45
14. Gould-Lee, p. 59
15. Kalogrias, in *Istoria*, 19 December.
16. For details of this meeting, see *Laikos Aigon*, 30 October 1935.
17. Vickers, p. 265. Eade, p. 105
18. *Eleftheron Bima*, 29 October 1935.
19. Vickers, pp. 263–4. These details are recorded in a letter that Victoria sent to Dickie Mountbatten on 4 November 1935.
20. See for example, *Eleftheron Bima*, 30 November 1935, where the announcement of the postponement of Andrew's arrival to Greece is placed next to an article calling upon the King to stop having anything to do with the fanatic monarchists who were sabotaging his policy of uniting all Greeks under his rule.
21. *Belfast Telegraph*, 07 February 1936: 'This announcement was sent to Prince Andrew by his nephew King George of Greece. I understand that Prince Andrew, whose home is at Monte Carlo, does not intend to go to Greece'.
22. See for example, *Eleftheron Bima*, 20 May 1936.
23. *Ellinikon Mellon*, 20 May 1936.

24. *Ellinikon Mellon*, 22 May 1936.
25. For Hatzisarantos' letter to Andrew and the Prince's reply, see the article in the local newspaper of Chalkidiki *Foni tis Halkidikis* (Voice of Chalkidiki), 'Prince Andrew and (his) letter to the President of the Constitutional Youth', 30 May 1936.
26. For Hatzisarantos' exile by Metaxas, see his official biography on the site of Panathinaikos, one of Greece's most popular football teams, of which Hatzisarantos was chairman after the war and until 1967. https://paopedia.gr/%CE%BE%CE%B5%CE%BD%CE %BF%CF%86%CF%8E%CE%BD-%CF%87%CE%B1%CF%84%CE%B6%C E%B7%CF%83%CE%B1%CF%81%CE%AC%CE%BD%CF%84%CE%BF% CF%82/. In 1941, soon after the German occupation of Greece, Hatzisarantos was the founder of one of the first resistance groups in Athens.
27. 1936 was not a good a year to be a Greek politician; except Prime-Minster Demertzis, almost all other major politicians died in that year, including Eleftherios Venizelos, Panagis Tsaldaris, Alexandros Zaimis (the last president of the republic), Georgios Kondylis, Alexandros Papanastasiou (first Prime-Minister of the republic) and others! Even though all these politicians officially died of natural causes, conspiracy theorists in Greece believe that they were gotten rid of, opening the way for Ioannis Metaxas to become first prime minister and then dictator of Greece. However no evidence was ever produced showing that any of the above deaths was the result of foul play.
28. Vickers, p. 262.
29. See *Kathimerini*, 30 October 1936.
30. See *Kathimerini*, 22 March 1938.
31. *Eleftheron Bima*, 3 April 1937.
32. Vickers, pp. 266–7.
33. *Eleftheron Bima*, 20 May 1937.
34. The deed for the sale was made by the Athens notary, P. Kavvadias and has a record number, N. 11909/5-6-1937.
35. *Athenaika Nea*, 9 October 1937.
36. *Athenaika Nea*, 26 October 1937.
37. *Eleftheron Bima*, 12 February 1938. *Northern Whig*, 14 February 1938.
38. *Athenaika Nea*, 21 March 1938.
39. *Eleftheron Bima*, 21 August 1938.
40. *Athenaika Nea*, 24 October 1938.
41. *Ellinikon Mellon*, 20 April 1939.
42. *Athenaka Nea*, 27 April 1939.
43. *Eleftheron Bima*, 4 May 1939.
44. *Eleftheron Bima*,29 October 1939.
45. *Eleftheron Bima*, 9 November 1939.
46. *Eleftheron Bhma*, 23 January 1940.
47. According Boothroyd, p. 111, the sale of Mon Repos gave Andrew a tax free annuity of about 400,000 drachmas. Though this was a good sum of money at the time, it was not enough to finance his lavish life style. When Andrew died in 1944 it was revealed that he was heavily in debt, see Eade, p. 177.
48. Parker, p. 37.
49. For Andrew at the Casinos of Monte Carlo, see *Birmingham Daily Gazette*, 17 February 1936. *Tatler* and *The Era* of 04 March 1936, reported that Andrew was the guest of honour in a spectacular dinner attended by 300 people with many dignitaries in one of the casinos: 'Mrs. Stanley Smith, a well-known patron of the gaming tables, gave a party for the occasion, her guest of honour being Prince Andrew of Greece'. There were frequent reports in newspapers about the rich and famous with whom Andrew associated: *The Bystander*, 11 March 1936: 'Sun Migrants in Cannes and Monte Carlo

Midday Meeting Round a Cannes Table. The two in front are Miss Margot Hambling and Prince Andrew of Greece. Sitting at the back are Mr. Gilbert Beale, whose yacht is in Cannes harbour and Mr. David Townsend who is staying'.

The Era, 29 April 1936: 'Pierre of Montenegro, the Countess de la Salle, the Maharajah and the Maharanee of Holkar. the Maharajah of Kapurthala, Prince Andrew of Greece, Maurice Chevalier, Prince Cheriff-Moulay, Marquis Ricci, and the Archduke Francis-Joseph of Austria. Jean Rai... *The Era*, 10 February 1937: accompanied by his granddaughter, Princess Antoinette, now in residence in the Principality, and another Royal visitor, Prince Andrew of Greece, is making Monte Carlo his headquarters'.

The Era, 8 December 1937: 'The Riviera--Where There Is No Winter... aquarium, of retired literary gents Maugham and Michael, of social royalties the Grand Duke Boris, the superbly tailored Prince Andrew of Greece, of elder hostesses like Mrs. Vigo Hansen, and younger bloods like Lord Queensberry. You never know who will turn up'.

The Tatler, 10 August 1938: 'EDEN ROC AGAIN AND MONTE CARLO... MARJORIE LADY WARWICK AND THE HON. AMBROSE GREVILLE AT MONTE CARLO, ACTOR-DANCER WALTER CRISHAM AND MRS. DICKIE GORDON, H.R.H. PRINCE ANDREW OF GREECE, MME. DE LA BIGNE AND MR. GILBERT BEALE LESLIE HENSON WITH MRS. JOHN D. CRIMMINS'

The Sketch, 17 August 1938: 'RIVIERA ROUNDABOUT: A LETTER TO MISS SKETCH... There are more yachtsmen than last year. Mr. Gilbert Beale is cruising in Suzannah Jane, with Prince Andrew of Greece as guest'.

Yorkshire Post and Leeds Intelligencer, 16 September 1938: 'In the general company were the Grand Duke Dmitri of Russia, Prince Andrew of Greece, the Marquis de Pollgnac, Mr and Mrs Herman Rogers, M Maurice Chevalier and the Woolf Barnatos'.

The Tatler, 26 October 1938: 'Mr. Gilbert Beale whose yacht *Susannah Jane* has been, and still is, one of the chief attractions at Cannes, Prince Andrew of Greece having been one of the hospitable owner's guests this year. He is talking to pretty Mrs. Scott-Callingham'

Daily Mirror, 4 January 1939: 'huge crowds which included some of the most distinguished names in international society. Among hosts this year was Prince Andrew of Greece, and among those he has been entertaining have been Princess Aspasia of Greece and her daughter. Princess Alexandra'

The Tatler, 4 January 1939: 'Mrs. Florence Heaton and daughter Ninette get a welcome from the Henry Martineaus and a spruce Prince Andrew of Greece, monocle and all, gets a warm how-do from delighted intimates, while film star Jack Oakie...'

The Sphere, 7 January 1939: 'WINTER SPORT ON EUROPE'S ROOF: A Party of Skiers from Wengen and Scheidegg Making an Excursion to the Jungfraujoch... riders have been looking forward to the opportunity of setting up record times. Among the noted visitors to St. Moritz are Prince Andrew, Princess Aspasia, and Princess Alexandra, members of the Greek Royal Family'

The Sketch, 2 August 1939: 'the opening gala of the Summer Sporting Club at Monte Carlo was attended by 550 dinner guests. Prince Andrew of Greece, who has lived in Monaco for years, entertained Prince Francis Josef, who has been settled in the south of France'

Chatham News, 1 September 1939: 'Among the visitors who have attended the galas are the Duke and Duchess of Windsor, Prince Andrew of Greece, Prince and Princess Dmitri of Russia, Lord Patrick Crichton-Stuart and Lady Crichton-Stuart, Thelma Viscountess'

Belfast Telegraph, 4 April 1941: 'Prince Andrew of Greece lives aboard a brilliancy. The French casinos are deferred undated cheques signed by yacht which flies the Greek flag'

Chapter 9: Three Funerals, a Crown and a Boy

1. At the time, Hatzisarantos and the board of the Constitutional Youth who met Andrew in Athens told him that that was the number of signatures. See *Foni tis Halkidikis*, 30 May 1936.
2. *Bradini*, 18 November 1936.
3. Alexandra, pp. 52–53, not only noticed that her cousin had grown into a very handsome youth but also that the older generation of royals (of Andrew's generation) were impressed by this 'new up and coming member of the family'.
4. To this group will be added just one other person four years later: Prince Michael, son of Christopher, who was born in 1940 after the death of his father.
5. In fact, that is exactly what happened less than five years later in May 1941. However, this time it was not internal political strife that sent the Greek royals into exile but the occupation of Greece by the Axis powers during the Second World War.
6. Alexandra, p. 53.
7. For details of the radio coverage of the procession see *Bradini*, 18 November 1936, which also notes that the sound of the radio broadcasts was excellent and except the voices of the reporters the natural sound such as cannon fire and music in the procession could also be clearly heard.

Chapter 10: Whither 'Philippos'?

1. As we saw, in an interview many years later Philip said that his command of Greek was restricted to 'understanding a certain amount of it'. Alice in a letter she wrote to her brother, Dickie Mountbatten, on 14 September 1939 (see below) claimed that Philip, who at the time was in Greece living with her, was 'an utter stranger to the language and the people'. This meant that he had to be taught the language if he were to live in Greece and function as one the country's princes.
2. George had a long-time girlfriend, Joyce Britten-Jones, an English widow whom at one point he had contemplated marrying. Even if such a marriage had occurred and George had a son with Britten-Jones, he could not become king of Greece as the wedding would have been morganatic. In any case, George and Britten-Jones never married and their relationship did not bear offspring.
3. In fact, before his death in 1964, Paul had outlived all of his uncles. Prince George was the last surviving brother of Constantine. He died in 1957 at the ripe age of 88, when all the other brothers died in their 50s or 60s.
4. George's life-long lover was his uncle Prince Valdemar, younger brother of George I. The relationship was formed when George went to Copenhagen to study at the Naval Academy. Even when Prince George later married Marie Bonaparte he arranged that Valdemar accompanied them on their honeymoon and spent more time with him than he did with Marie. This situation caused Marie psychological problems that were treated by Freud. She also had a string of lovers, the most famous being the French prime minister, Aristide Briant.
5. Papamichail and Harkin, *Istoria*, July 19.
6. Ibid.
7. See the *Daily News* of 1 December 1935, the article by Princess Radziwill, 'Greek King's Dilemma: To Remarry his Queen or Breed a Successor': 'the way would be open for George to adopt 14 -year- old Prince Philip of Greece. Philip, a cousin of George, is the son of the late King Constantine's brother, Prince Andrew. His mother is a Princess of Battenburg and a cousin of King George V of England'.
8. *Athenaika Nea*, 20 November 1936.

9. Eade, p. 106.

10. Marr, p. 50

11. Hough, p. 357. Eade, p.106. As we saw, the three times Andrew was cashiered out of the Greek Army were 1909, 1917 and 1922.

12. It appears that Andrew had already made up his mind about Philip's future by early November 1935 when it became clear that George II would return back to his throne but without him at his side. Andrew told Victoria, his mother-in-law, that he wanted Philip after Gordonstoun to join the British Navy and get his training there as the Spanish Prince Juan had done. See Vickers, p. 259. Juan (Count of Barcelona and father of king Juan Carlos), after becoming a midshipman in the Royal Navy, returned to Spain. It would appear that at least to Victoria, Andrew was careful not to tell her yet that he wanted Philip to sever all ties with Greece.

13. *Athenaika Nea*, 28 November 1936.

14. *Athenaika Nea*, 12 December 1936.

15. See Alexandra, p. 54.

16. Ibid.

17. Eade, p. 119. Theodora does not say exactly when Philip told her about his decision. However, as she claims that it was sometime before Dickie Mountbatten noticed that Elizabeth was falling in love with Philip, it should be placed chronologically between 1936 and 1939.

18. Eade, p. 114.

19. This photograph in the Broadlands Archives was published by Eade (no plate number).

20. Though Andrew was at the time a general in the Greek army, at the funerals of Cecilia and her family he is wearing civilian clothes. While outside Greece he used to wear civilian clothes and exchanged them with his general's uniform whenever he was in the country.

21. *The Scotsman*, 29 December 1937.

22. Const. I, p. 69.

23. Eade, pp. 67, 110.

24. How this was possible is analysed by Vickers, pp. 274–5. It is interesting that Greek newspapers reported that Alice at the time was seriously ill and news of Cecilia's death would not be conveyed to her lest this made her condition worse. See *Athenaika Nea*, 17 November 1937.

25. Vickers, p. 274–5.

26. Vickers, p. 81: 'Alice took Ella's work at heart. She longed to undertake something similar in Greece, but it was to be many years before she could do so. She relished Ella's exploration of the spiritual, and the practical aspect of helping the less fortunate. The visit seeded thoughts and ideas in her'.

27. Vickers, p. 282. It would appear that it was during this meeting that Alice found out that Andrew, who was living on board the yacht *Davida*, had taken a French mistress.

28. *Athenaika Nea*, 9 October 1938.

29. Vickers, p. 280, erroneously places her first visit to Greece one month later, in November 1938.

30. Vickers, p. 308.

31. This agrees well with evidence of letters Alice wrote from Athens to a German couple, the Markwitzes (whom she had befriended while in the clinic), wherein she records her frustration with the fact that she was expected to perform duties as a member of the royal family and that she found it difficult to get accustomed again to the court procedures. See Vickers, pp. 282–3.

32. Vickers, p. 281. Eade, pp. 123–124.

33. Vickers, pp. 285–6: 'Alice certainly felt that Philip belonged in Greece and should take his place as one of the few princes of that country'. Eade, p. 123, 'She wanted to enable her son to spend time there and get to know the people whose prince he was'.

34. *Newcastle Journal*, 17 April 1944: 'The Prince said; "I last saw my home in Athens in February, 1941"'.

35. Parker, p. 80, quoting from Kurt Hahn's assessment of Prince Philip for Reuters in 1947: 'the lure of early and undeserved importance was keenly felt' by Philip and that there was 'no doubt that for a short time he was tempted both by the hazards and comforts likely to come to a Prince of Greece in residence at Athens'.

36. *Eleftheron Bima*, 20 March 1939.

37. *Eleftheron Bima* 13 April 1939.

38. *Londonderry Sentinel*, 24 December 1938.

39. See for example, *Ellinikon Mellon*, 15 April 1939

40. See for example, *Ellinikon Mellon*, 25 April 1939

41. Eade, p. 119.

42. Vickers, p. 433.

43. Weber, p. 65

44. Parker, p. 77.

45. *Birmingham Daily Post*, 3 May 1939.

46. According to *Eleftheron Bima* of 8 May 1939, Alice arrived at Tel Aviv on 2 May and would spend the next two weeks at Jerusalem as a guest of the Greek Patriarch.

47. Vickers, p. 284.

48. *Eleftheron Bima*, 19 August 1939. *Eleftheron Bima*, 20 August 1939.

49. *Eleftheron Bima*, 30 August 1939.

50. He was a grandson of Carl Merlin who almost half a century before had photographed Prince Andrew at the Greek Military Academy with his fellow students. Nicky Merlin was killed in action when the British submarine HMS *Perseus*, which he was on board as Greek liaison officer, was sunk by an Italian mine in the Ionian Sea in December 1941. The sinking of *Perseus* provided the unique case during WWII of a crew member escaping from the hatch and using the Davis Submerged Escape Apparatus while the sunk submarine was on the seabed. This was Stoker John Capes, and his remarkable escape was questioned for many years. However, the recent discovery of the *Perseus* almost intact on the seabed with the hatch through which Capes had escaped wide open shattered any doubts about his story.

51. Alice in a letter to Dickie Mountbatten from Athens, 12 March 1939. See Vickers, p. 283.

52. Vickers, p. 285 and Eade, p. 130, quoting a letter Victoria wrote to Dickie Mountbatten about Philip on 26 September 1939.

53. Vickers, p. 285.

54. Ibid.

55. Victoria, Philip's grandmother, records in the above letter that he was surprised that he returned to England. This means that Philip expected that he would be living in Greece and continue his naval training there.

56. For details of Elizabeth meeting Philip at Dartmouth in July 1939 and her reaction to him, see Eade, pp. 125–126.

57. Sir Henry Channon in his diary entry for 21 January 1941 recorded that while he was in Athens he saw Philip at a cocktail party and that his aunt Princess Nicholas (Ellen) mentioned to him that Philip would one day marry Princess Elizabeth and that was the reason why he was serving in the British Navy. See Boothroyd, p. 12.

58. Eade, pp. 129–130.

59. Carr, p. 128, quoting Prince Peter's war diary.

Chapter 11: A Prince in Love and War

1. Alexandra, pp. 60–63.
2. The best account on Cobina's meeting with Philip in Venice and their relationship is by Kelley, pp. 48–51.
3. *San Francisco Examiner*, 24 September 1939.
4. Kelley, p. 51.
5. Eade, p. 121, quoting a reference to an interview of Cobina published in the June 1973 edition of *Town and Country* where she revealed many details about her relationship with Philip.
6. *San Francisco Examiner*, 28 December 1940.
7. Kelley, ibid.
8. *El Paso Times*, 21 July 1939: 'Romance with Grecian Prince denied by Chicago Socialite'.
9. *Daily News*, 16 January 1940.
10. According to Kelley, p. 51, Cobina senior, who wanted Philip to marry her daughter, continued to correspond with him well after Cobina junior had made it clear that she was not in love with him.
11. *San Francisco Examiner*, 28 December 1940.
12. See, Eade, p. 121, and Kelley, pp. 48–51, who have collected information about the relationship of Philip and Cobina Wright Jr from interviews given by the latter and also friends of Cobina and Philip many years after the end of their affair.
13. The photograph was taken some time between May, when Philip entered Dartmouth, and August 1939, when he left for Greece.
14. For Sir Robert Peel, Sixth Baronet, see the entry in the internet site of his family: https://thepeelsociety.btck.co.uk/PeelHistory/SirRobert6.
15. *Daily Telegraph*, 7 April 1940.
16. *The Inverell Times*, 8 April 1940.
17. *The Australian Women's Weekly*, 20 April 1940.
18. *Daily Telegraph*, 7 December 1945.
19. Const. I, p. 72.
20. Mackenzie, p. 122.
21. This article also appeared in the 31 October 1940 edition of the *Yorkshire Evening Post*.
22. It is true that Philip was on active service at the time, but not in a war zone.
23. This was the Spanish Prince Juan who, as we saw, Andrew mentioned to Victoria as an example of a foreigner who served in the Royal Navy, an example which he wanted Philip to follow.
24. Reported in many British newspapers, see for example, *The Liverpool Evening Express*, 20 December 1940. At the time, Philip was serving on the HMS *Shropshire* having been transferred from the HMS *Kent* in October 1940 when the latter began operating close to a warzone. Parker, p. 79.
25. Vickers, p. 290.
26. See, for example, *Belfast News-Letter*, 3 April 1941.
27. Alexandra, pp. 68–69. Soon after Philip left Greece, he wrote in his Midshipman's Journal that: 'While in Greece I had ample opportunity for studying the campaign in Albania. Unfortunately I was unable to visit the front, and watch the fighting on the spot....Considering the unequal balance of numbers and materials, the reason for the success of the Greeks is their magnificent morale, and the Italien's [*sic*] lack of it...'. See Boothroyd, p. 90. This entry suggests that Philip in Athens may have been involved in contacts between British and Greek military staff and had access to classified information about developments on the Greek-Italian front
28. Eade, p. 135.

29. Eade, p. 135, erroneously mentions that at the time Philip also attended the funeral of his uncle, Prince Christopher, that was also held in Athens. But Christopher's funeral was on 25 January 1940 – not 1941 – and Philip did not attend it as he was serving on board the HMS *Ramillies* in the Indian Ocean at the time.

30. *Eleftheron Bima*, 1 February 1941.

31. For the history of Alice's villa at Neon Herakleion, see Megkos. http://www. royalchronicles.gr/princess-alice-villa-in-athens-greece/.

32. This was the first and only time Elizabeth visited Greece, her husband's birthplace.

33. *Northern Whig*, 3 April 1941.

34. Alexandra, p. 70.

35. Const. I, pp. 75–6.

36. Const. I, pp. 78–84. The letter, in Constantine's private archive, was publicized in 2015.

37. Gould-Lee, pp. 88–9.

38. Gould-Lee, pp. 90–1.

39. As told by Prince Peter to Gould-Lee; Gould-Lee, pp. 96–104. The same in Beevor, pp. 168–170 and Eade, p. 139. However, according to Boothroyd, pp. 98–101, Philip far from escorting his royal cousin to safety in Egypt was involved at the time in heavy action in the waters north of Crete. The *Valiant* along with other British warships came under attack by the Luftwaffe. Philip witnessed the sinking of *Greyhound*, and also strikes against other British warships, some of which sunk a few hours later – *Gloucester* and *Fiji*. HMS *Kelly*, under the command of his uncle Dickie Mountbatten, was also sunk by German bombers. Philip's own ship was hit by two bombs, but managed to sail back to Alexandria; an eight foot hole on the ship's starboard lay undetected for some days until Philip happened to see and report it to his commander.

40. Const. I, p. 98.

41. Gould-Lee, p. 105.

42. See for example, *Eleftheron Bima*, 25 April 1941.

43. Vickers, p. 296.

44. Besides a journalist, Eric Baume was also a novelist and radio presenter. During the 1950s he was one of the first to host a TV talk show in Australia and had a career in television until his death in 1967.

45. *The Truth*, 21 June 1942.

46. Not the infamous 'mountza' gesture; this is offensive but not terrifying to any Greek. There are a few rude Greek gestures all linked to sex – similar to the middle finger of the Anglo Saxons – which would offend a particularly religious Greek but it is not clear to which one Philip is referring to.

47. HMS *Ramillies*; because of the ongoing war for security reasons the name of the battleship could not be mentioned in the interview.

48. Marr, p. 96.

49. Jaffa, pp. 193–197. Olga Franklin was also impressed by Philip. In a letter she wrote to a friend she described her first meeting with Philip: 'I struggle to my feet. I get dizzy looking at him. His beauty is so dazzling. People don't look like this, surely, in real life? For once I'm at a loss for words, just when I need them most [....] This Prince Philip is stunning, with hair like gold coin only paler, a sort of ash-gold, eyes of deep blue almost violet in the electric light of the Jesmond Hotel lounge, tall, fine-featured, really a shockingly beautiful figure in naval uniform. It takes what feels like minutes getting my breath back. I think it's the surprise. Mr Wilson (Franklin's editor) said a Greek Prince and I thought, well a darkie perhaps, with a nose arched like his own and perhaps a Cypriot curl to the hair. I manage to stutter out my set speech...'. Ibid. p. 195

50. *Newcastle Journal and North Mail*, 17 April 1944.

51. *Daily Advertiser*, 12 June 1945.
52. Kelley, p. 50. Philip's words were: 'I am just a discredited Balkan prince of no particular merit or distinction'.
53. The last sentence is wrong as the Battle of Matapan predates that of Crete by two months.
54. Boothroyd, p. 107.
55. In the case of EDES, the word 'Republican' was included in its title and its opposition to the monarchy was recorded in the manifesto of its organization. Interestingly enough, EAM in its beginning avoided any mention against the monarchy, calling all Greeks to join it and fight the occupation forces. As a result, in its early days many supporters of the monarchy had joined EAM, including high-ranking officers who before the war had been ADCs to George II.
56. Plastiras succeeded Papandreou as prime minister on 3 January 1945 while the civil war was still raging in Athens. He was prime minister when the 'Agreement of Varkiza' was signed a month later. To show how close the Venizelists came to the monarchists-conservatives, we may point out that one of the ministers in Plastiras' government had been the judge at the court martial for those responsible for the 1935 Venizelist Coup. Plastiras was condemned to death *in absentia* by this court martial. In other words, Plastiras had in his cabinet the very man who had condemned him to death, exactly one decade earlier!
57. According to eyewitnesses, Churchill did not realize that he had been fired upon. It is also certain that the sniper had no idea whom he almost killed on Christmas 1944 as he was positioned hundreds of metres away and simply took a lucky shot against the embassy! At the time, Churchill's visit to Athens was still kept secret.
58. Palaiologou, p. 124.
59. *Trinity Mirror*, 30 June 1946: 'Now the Monarchist government....passed a Bill deciding that, even if King George is defeated, it will not be the end of the monarchy. Rumoured alternative candidates are Prince Philip of Greece and Prince Edward, the boy Duke of Kent'.
60. Parker, pp. 101–102.

Chapter 12: The Elizabethan Solution

1. The 'Christmas Pantomime Show' was held by Princesses Elizabeth and Margaret each year between 1941–1944 at Windsor Castle. Together with the two princesses, local children also took part in the play. For these shows see, https://www.rct.uk/collection/themes/exhibitions/an-exhibition-of-photographs-to-celebrate-the-80th-birthday-of-hm-t-10. For details of the 1943 show, see the *Sunday Post*, 19 December 1943.
2. Parker, p. 89.
3. The recording was released by Decca Records as catalogue number 18557. It was a popular song which stayed seven weeks on the *Billboard* magazine charts between July and September 1943 and peaked at number seven. See Whitburn, *Top Pop Records 1940–1955*, Record Research. The song was also recorded by Eddie Cantor and Ina Ray Hutton, popular singers at the time.
4. Marr, pp. 104–105.
5. Ibid, p. 165.
6. *Daily Telegraph*, 9 September 2019.

Chapter 13: Meanwhile, Back at the Ranch

1. Couloumbis *et al*, p. 115.
2. Leontaritis in RD, pp. 108–9.
3. Sabatakaki, pp. 62–3.

4. Quoted in Sabatakaki, p. 6.
5. Woodhouse, p. 294.

Chapter 14: What If...?
1. *Ethnos*, 6 March 1963. Parker, 3.
2. For details of the church of Saints Philip and Elizabeth and the visit of the Royals, see Skiadas2.
3. See for example, *Daily Mail*, 23 May 1956.

Appendix I: Alice – Away From The Spotlight
1. Vickers, p. 293.
2. Dickie was alarmed when Alice informed him that she was distributing to the children the foodstuff he had sent her; he feared that his sister would be famished and he was right.
3. Vickers, p. 293.
4. *Daily Herald*, 16 April 1945.
5. Vickers, p. 299–300.
6. See Antonopoulos.
7. Parker, p. 83.
8. https://www.yadvashem.org/righteous/stories/princess-alice.html.
9. This applies even today where most references in Greece about Princess Alice state that after the Second World War she became a nun.
10. The deposit for the purchase of the flat was paid by Philip, see Vickers, p. 332. 1n 1950 the flat passed under Philip's name. Philip sold the flat in 1963.
11. *Ta Nea*, 15 November 1951.
12. *To Bima*, 13 May 1953.
13. *To Bima*, 7 November 1952 and 17 November 1954.
14. *To Bima*, 15 November 1955.
15. In Vickers, p. 354.
16. Prince Peter, once in the line of succession to the Greek throne, also considered that Frederica damaged the monarchy with her behaviour and was chiefly responsible for its downfall. After the death of Paul in 1964, some Greek personalities suggested that he should become king instead of Constantine but nothing came out of this initiative.
17. See Megkos about this sign and his observation that in it a photograph supposedly of Alice is in fact Sophia, her youngest daughter.
18. On 10 February 2010 a standard donated by her grandchild, Charles, Prince of Wales, was placed on top of the Greek flag. https://www.synod.com/synod/eng2018/20180305_enremprincessalicebattenberg.html.

Bibliography

BOOKS

Alexandra, Queen of Yugoslavia, *Prince Philip: A Family Portrait* (London: Hodder and Stoughton, 1959)

Andrew, 1928: (*Ανδρέου Βασιλόπαιδος*), *Dorylaion-Sakarya 1921 (Δορύλαιον-Σαγκάριος 1921)* , (Paris: Agon, 1928)

Andrew, 1930: Andrew Prince of Greece, *Towards Disaster: The Greek Army in Asia Minor in 1921*, (London: John Murray 1930)

Anon., *Minutes of the Meetings of the Fourth Greek Constitutional Convention in Athens*, Vol. I. (Athens: National Printing House, 1924)

Beevor A, *Crete: The Battle and the Resistance* (London: John Murray Press, 2005)

Bertin, C, *Marie Bonaparte* (Thonon-les-Bains: Perrin, 1999) (Greek edition, Athens: Potamos, 2008)

Boothroyd, B., *Philip: An Informal Biography* (London: Longman, 1971)

Carr, J., *The Defence and Fall of Greece 1940–41* (Barnsley: Pen & Sword, 2013, 2020)

Christopher, Prince of Greece, *Memoirs of H.R.H. Prince Christopher of Greece* (London: The Right Book Club, 1938)

Constantine II of the Hellenes, untitled (3 vols.), (Athens: Lambrakis Press, 2015)

Couloumbis, T.A., J.A. Petropulos and H.J. Psomiades, *Foreign Interference in Greek Politics* (New York: Pella, 1976)

Danglis, P., (Δαγκλής Π.), *Memories, documents and correspondence (Αναμνήσεις, Έγγραφα, Αλληλογραφία)* (Athens: [privately published], 1965)

Eade, P., *Young Prince Philip. His Turbulent Early Life* (London: Harper Press, 2012)

Gould Lee, Air Vice-Marshal A.S., *The Royal House of Greece* (London: Ward Lock & Co, 1948)

Hellenic General Staff (Γενικό Επιτελείο Στρατού), *The Operations to Ankara (Οι Επιχειρήσεις προς Άγκυραν)* Vol. II, (Athens, 1965)

Hough, R., *Louis and Victoria* (2 vols.) (London: Hutchinson, 1974)

Jaffa R. (ed.), *A Letter from Oggi. The letters of Olga Franklin* (Kibworth: Book Guild Ltd, 2015)

Kambanis A., I.Polykratis, C. Petritis, P. Pipinelis, G. Leontaritis, and G. Koukounas, *The Royal Dynasty* (Athens: Metron, 2007)

Katsis, K. (Κάτσης Α.), *The Asia Minor Campaign and Catastrophe (Η Μικρασιατική Εκστρατεία και Καταστροφή)* (Athens: Empeiria, 2008)

Kelley K., *The Royals* (Warner Book, 1997)

Kostopoulos, T. (Κωστόπουλος Τ.), *War and Ethnic Cleansing. The forgotten side of a ten-year national drive (1912–1922) (Πόλεμος και εθνοκάθαρση. Η ξεχασμένη πλευρά μιας δεκαετούς εθνικής εξόρμησης (1912–1922)* (Athens: Bibliorama, 2007)

Louros, K.N. (Λούρος Κ.Ν.), *Past Years (Περασμένα Χρόνια)*, (Athens: [privately published], 1958)

Mackenzie, Compton, *Greece in My Life* (London: Chatto & Windus, 1960)

Marr, A., *The Diamond Queen: Elizabeth II and her People* (London: Macmillan, 2011)

Metaxas I. (Μεταξάς Ι.), *His Personal Diary (Το προσωπικό του ημερολόγιο)*, Vol. III2 (1921–1932), Ed. P. Sifnaios, (Athens: Gobostis 1960)

Nicholas, Prince of Greece, *My Fifty Years* (London Hutchinson & Co, 1926)

Palaiologou, A. (Παλαιολόγου Α.), *The Princesses of Greece (Πριγκίπισσες της Ελλάδος)* (Athens: Ferenike, 2007)

Parker, J., *Prince Philip: His Secret Life* (London: Sidgwick & Jackson, 1990)

Peter, Prince of Greece, *War Diaries 1940–1941 (Ημερολόγια Πολέμου 1940–1941)*, Vol I (Athens: Goulandri-Horn Foundation, 1997)

Petropulos, J., *Royals and the Reich* (Oxford: Oxford University Press, 2006)

Rizas, S. (Ρίζάς Σ.), *The end of the Great Idea. Venizelos, Antivenizelism and Asia Minor (Το τέλος της Μεγάλης Ιδέας, Ο Βενιζέλος, ο Αντιβενιζελισμός και η Μικρά Ασία)* (Athens: Kastaniotis, 2018)

Sabatakaki, M., *The Monarchy in Greece: A Controversial Institution* (Athens: Periskopio, 2008)

Taylor, A.J.P., *The Struggle for Mastery in Europe, 1848–1918* (Oxford: Oxford University Press, 1954)

Tsichlis, B. (Τσίχλης Β.), *The Coup of Goudi and Eleftherios Venizelos (Το κίνημα του Γουδή και ο Ελευθέριος Βενιζέλος)* (Athens: Polytropon, 2007)

Vickers, H., *Alice, Princess Andrew of Greece* (London: Hamish Hamilton, 2000)

Weber P., *La via di Lisbona: In fuga dal nazismo nella città sospesa* (Torino: EDT, 2017)

Whitburn, J., *Top Pop Records 1940–1955* (Record Research, 1973)

Woodhouse, C.M., *The Story of Modern Greece* (London: Faber and Faber, 1968)

Xanthakis, A. (Ξανθάκης Α.), *A History of Greek Photography 1839–1970 (Ιστορία της Ελληνικής Φωτογραφίας 1839/1970)* (Athens: Papyrus, 2008)

Ziazias, G. (Ζιαζιάς Γ.), *Searching for lost Larisa. 50 years of memories and recollections (1900–1950) (Αναζητώντας τη χαμένη Λάρισα. 50 χρόνια μνήμες και αναπολήσεις (1900–1950), Vol. II (Larisa, 2000)*

ARTICLES

Baume, E., 'Baume's Overseas Budget. Cabled from London yesterday', *The Truth*, 21 June 1942

Enepikidis P.N. (Ενεπικίδης Π.Ν.) 'The Secret Archives of Vienna' ('Τα μυστικά αρχεία της Βιέννης'), *To Bima*, 20 November 1960

Franklin, O., 'Greek Prince says he likes the North', *Newcastle Journal and North Mail*, 17 April 1944

Furness, H., ' "This will be such a shock": Moment Prince Philip learned his wife had become Queen revealed', *Daily Telegraph*, 9 September 2019

Iatrides, H (Ιατρίδης Χ.), 'History of Tectonism. Prince Andrew of the Greeks' ('Ιστορία του Τεκτονισμού. Ο Πρίγκιψ Ανδρέας των Ελλήνων'), *Tektoniko Deltio Pythagoras*, 102/2012, p. 138

Kalogrias, V. 'The Greek Royal House from Between the Wars to the Occupation and Civil War', *Istoria* magazine (Athens), December 2019

Karampatsos, C., 'Efrosini Crossing Syngrou Avenue: Automobile Accidents and the Introduction of the Automobile in Greece (1900–11)', pp. 255–280, *History of Technology*, Inkster, I. (ed.), *Special Issue: History of Technology in Greece from the Nineteenth to the Twenty-First Century*, Arapostathis, S. and Tympas, A. (eds.), (Bloomsbury Academic, Vol 33, 2017)

Lyons, L., 'Our New York Column', *Minneapolis Star*, 29 July 1939

Maury, P. 'Metropolitan Smart Set', *San Francisco Examiner*, 28 December 1940

Papamichail, E.M. and Harkin, M., 'The Enigmatic Prince Peter', *Istoria* magazine (Athens), July 2019

Petrie, U., 'A glamour bride's mother: Now it's my turn for love', *Tampa Bay Times*, 7 December 1941

Ploumidis, S. 'Antidote to Anarchy: Government and Ideological Parameters of the Greek Kingdom', *Istoria* magazine (Athens), December 2019

Radziwill, Princess, 'Greek King's Dilemma: To Remarry his Queen or Breed a Successor', *Daily News*, 1 December 1935

Randolph, N., 'U.S. Lad Beats Prince to Cobina Jr.'s. Heart', *Daily News*, 16 January 1940

Rocco, F., 'A Strange Life: Profile of Prince Philip', *Independent on Sunday*, 13 December 1992

INTERNET

Kastrinakis, George A: www.royalchronicles.gr/george-a/

https://storiacontroversa.blogspot.com/2012/03/h.html

www.royalchronicles.gr/princessmariagreece/

www.royalchronicles.gr/merlinandboehringerphotos/

www.royalchronicles.gr/andrewandalicewedding/

(Megkos: Μέγκος Α.) http://www.royalchronicles.gr/princess-alice-villa-in-athens-greece/

(Skiadas1: Σκιαδάς Ε.) https://www.taAthenaika.gr/i-fanella-tou-stratiotou/#_ftn1

(Skiadas2: Σκιαδάς Ε.) https://www.taathinaika.gr/i-agnosti-istoria-tou-naou-agion-elisavet-kai-filippou-sti-nikaia/

(Pallis: Πάλλης Γ.) https://amarysia.gr/arthra-sxolia-main/69025-ενθουσιώδης-υποδοχή-στον-βασιλιά-τη

(Filistor 1 : Φιλιστώρ Ι.) https://www.istorikathemata.com/2014/01/blog-post.html

(Filistor 2 : Φιλιστώρ Ι.) https://www.istorikathemata.com/2014/01/19-1922.html

(Papapolyviou: Παπαπολυβίου) https://papapolyviou.com/2013/05/26/nikos-karvounis-ioannis-tsangarides/

(Papastathopoulos: Παπασταθόπουλος Θ.Χ.) votanosdegrecia.blogspot.com/2016/06/blog-post_75.html

https://www.corfu-museum.gr/index.php/el/59-corfu-notes/381-24-1921

https://thepeelsociety.btck.co.uk/PeelHistory/SirRobert6

https://www.yadvashem.org/righteous/stories/princess-alice.html

https://www.synod.com/synod/eng2018/20180305_enremprincessalicebattenberg.html

(Karampatsos: Καραμπάτσος Η.Ε.). http://www.chandrinou-politistikos-syllogos.gr/prin-akrivos-83-chronia-prokirixi-iper-tis-laikis-dimokratias-sti-messinia-stis-23-avgoustou-1935/

https://paopedia.gr/%CE%BE%CE%B5%CE%BD%CE%BF%CF%86%CF%8E%CE%BD-%CF%87%CE%B1%CF%84%CE%B6%CE%B7%CF%83%CE%B1%CF%81%CE%AC%CE%BD%CF%84%CE%BF%CF%82/

https://www.rct.uk/collection/themes/exhibitions/an-exhibition-of-photographs-to-celebrate-the-80th-birthday-of-hm-t-10

(Antonopoulos: Αντωνόπουλος) https://www.lifo.gr/articles/archaeology_articles/212989/i-athina-sta-xronia-tis-katoxis-mia-tetraetia-protofanon-kakoyxion-alla-kai-agonistikis-eksarsis

Index